MY SOUL CRIED OUT...
BUT
I COULD NOT WEEP

Elisabeth Holyday

authorHOUSE®

AuthorHouse™
1663 Liberty Drive
Bloomington, IN 47403
www.authorhouse.com
Phone: 1-800-839-8640

First published by AuthorHouse 12/06/2011

ISBN: 978-1-4567-4041-2 (ebk)
ISBN: 978-1-4567-4039-9 (hc)
ISBN: 978-1-4567-4040-5 (sc)

Library of Congress Control Number: 2011903222

Printed in the United States of America

PROLOGUE

When I was a little girl I was always eager to go to church. I loved the way being in church made me feel. It's like I was being trained for a higher calling. Whether I was assisting with Sunday school classes, filling in at the Basic School, or directing a play for a Concert Recital, I was always involved in something at church. However, my dreams of becoming a Gospel Singer got shattered beneath a weight of pain, and shame. But I have come to realize that dreams don't die, they strangle.

I have been blessed with three children and like all families' lives, ours is not perfect. Its flaws are now in print for others to read and learn from. Bad things happen to good people and sometimes those things change the direction of one's destiny. But interwoven between all the tragedies of my life I have had some fun and laughter; and a few lucky breaks. And the bond I shared with my adoring mother leaves me with a lifetime of wonderful memories.

I still believe in dreams. I still believe that somehow something good is going to happen to me. I still believe that I have within me the power to do and accomplish great things—I still believe. I still believe that God has the power to take my wishes, my hopes, my dreams, my desires, my disappointments and all of my shortcomings and make something beautiful of them; I still believe. And I feel so much lighter now that I have penned my story that I believe my best half is in front of me. Yes, I believe.

Elisabeth Holyday

Dedicated to the memory of my mother,
Whose love and compassion has guided me
And on whose prayers I stood
when all hell was breaking loose.

MY SOUL CRIED OUT . . .
BUT
I COULD NOT WEEP

ELISABETH HOLYDAY.

To My Brothers & My Sisters

———————————————

You have been a tower of strength for me through some extremely dark times. And even now there are moments when I can feel your desire to cushion me from more pain and I really appreciate your concern. I know that you are all very private, and some of you might be very disappointed in me for rehashing this, so I want to apologise to you for any pain or embarrassment that I may cause, that was not my intention. My only desire is to give myself a chance to get from under this weight that has crippled me; begin to live, and give my children an explanation of why things are the way they are.

As you can see it has taken me practically a lifetime to do this; that should tell you that it was very difficult for me. I am aware that most nieces and nephews will be learning things now that they never knew, and for that reason you would prefer that I left things under the rug; but I hope you will stop and think for a moment of my grandchildren and the burden my children would have trying to explain what they themselves never knew and fully understood. It is for them that I have penned the story. And even though several years have passed, it is still much easier for me to write than to talk.

We are a family of faith who have seen and lived through more than our share; we will get through this, and who knows what good God might use this tragedy to accomplish. Your continued support is crucial and I look forward to it.

Elisabeth.

To My Grandchildren

I love you all. Read with an open mind. Seek parental guide if you must, and remember I am always a phone call away. Bad things happen to good people, mistakes are inevitable. This is the story of my life, but I would like to think that it doesn't define me. Some things happened when I was still a child before your parents were born, or when they were merely toddlers, so don't expect them to have to all the answers. Like you, they will be learning a lot now for the first time.

As you'll see I've been through a lot of tribulations but I survive, now I am sharing them with you. I need to, because if it's so painfully difficult for me to write, I can't imagine what it would be like for your parents in the future, to try to explain what they themselves never knew or fully understood.

As you grow older you will come to understand the many challenges life brings. I didn't ask for the life I was given, I only got the strength to see me through. My prayer for you is that you will never see yourselves as victims because you are not. Undefeated and proud you must stand. You are a promise, a part of the mystery of God. Love and care for each other and endeavour to always be at peace with each other. None of you are better than the other. You are the children of two brothers and a sister that sprung from my womb. Nothing would destroy me faster than to know that you don't care about each other. And embrace the opportunity you've been given forged by my audacity to pack a suitcase and moved to Canada with $60. Make the most of it, the DNA for greatness is in you.

Grandma.

ONE

I have existed. I have not lived. The skeletons in my closet have bound me with a weight that has had me trapped for decades. Even though I feel the call for a higher purpose, I am in a struggle. Each time I try to move forward they stand before me like a huge monster. And so, from a High School Student and Sunday School Teaching Assistant, who was practically in church from dusk to dawn, with aspirations of becoming a Gospel Singer and a Spiritual Healer; to a mother of three by age 18; including being raped and left with a child from the assault; a murder charge 6 months after giving birth and so much more; they created a lifetime of havoc for me that changed the direction of my life and left me stagnant. However, nothing prepared me for the hell I faced for 7 years and beyond when I tried to put the past behind me and gave my heart and my hand in marriage to someone I thought would shelter me under his wings. It is the chronicling of spousal abuse that will cause one's hair to stand still. And with so much shame and so much hidden; so many questions to answer and so much to explain; they shattered my dreams and left me frozen in silence.

For a long time I have struggled with the nightmare of sharing my story, but I didn't have the strength to go there and my pride restrained me from baring my soul to the world. But there is always a battle going on inside of me between who I am; why I'm here; and what became of the child in me who wanted to be a Gospel Singer and even boasted of becoming the Champion of the family and ridding it of poverty. It seemed the many challenges I faced, especially during my teenage years, knocked me off my feet, changed the direction of God's plan for my life and left me adrift. But I have always felt that there is an assignment awaiting my signature. I'm not sure what it is, but I realize now, that if I am to walk my predestined path, or, have the second half of my life better than the first half and begin to live instead of feeling that I'm just existing; then I owe it to myself to begin within, by cleaning out the junk so I can be free. My children need to hear from me too, they've been waiting all their lives. Later in the story you will learn about the article in a Memoir on Silence; the statement made during a Presidential State of the Union Address; the comment from my daughter; and the revelation from a childhood friend that broke the camel's back and spurred me to pick up a pen and share my story.

I was born in Jamaica during a turbulent storm that whipped the island following one of the deadliest hurricanes of that decade. My mother was the only parent I ever knew. My father died from pneumonia when I was nine months old and the only memory I have of a father-figure was a grand-fatherly gentleman affectionately called Preacher Man, who regularly came to play with me. Mother told me that he was my father's best friend and that he practically saved my life during the storm by running with me to a stronger family home while sheets of zinc from the roofs of houses all around were sailing through the air. I don't think Preacher Man lived in the neighbourhood, but from what I can recall, he visited regularly and I still have the memory of him crouching down before me trying to make sense of my small talks with a big broad smile and two dimples on his cheeks. TV Preacher James Robinson bears such a strong resemblance of him that I consider him the reincarnated version of Preacher Man.

I loved my childhood days up to age 15; I was very happy and I was loved. I had fallen at 14 but I picked up myself, dusted off and was convinced that there was no mountain too high that I couldn't climb. Before my world as I knew it crashed and left me at the edge of a cliff, I loved to give jokes and people always told me I was jovial like my dad. My mother was the light of my life, I adored her and I loved school, but I loved church even more. Like my mother, Church was my life; I soaked up everything like a sponge. From the moment I heard my mother said, "Elisabeth, see if you can find a bottle," I got excited because that meant we were going to church. I would take the bottle to the Shopkeeper for a Penny. Half-a-Penny would get us two ice mint sweets on our way to church to freshen our breath and the other half Penny would go in the collection plate. I always felt sad for my mother giving half Penny for offering. I just felt like we were the poorest of the poorest. At times in Church I wondered what we were going to have for dinner when we got home. On the contrary, one large kitchen on the church premises was shared by all who lived on the compound and every Sunday, before Sunday school began, I could expect to be called for a sumptuous dinner of rice with kidney beans, brown-stew fish or chicken, a slice of yellow yam and a glass of carrot juice. I never understood how they could afford those big rich dinners, seeing that the women were housewives, the men barely got by, the Pastor only owned a small cane field which was seasonal and only spare change was placed in the offering plate. But regardless, I lived and breathe Church, nothing could stop me. I got the idea though, that if ever I had my own church, one tenth of the offering collected each week would return to the Church's poor. No one should leave church after placing the "widow's mite" in the collection plate and wonder what they will have for dinner that night.

Apart from Gospel Singing, I cannot think of a single thing more precious than the times I spent soaking up any and everything religious like a sponge. When the moon wasn't shining, mother and I would make our own bottle torch by pouring kerosene oil in a bottle, then making a long cork of reeled newspaper. The Wednesday Night Prayer Meetings seemed like months away from Sunday night service. I was always early just so I could watch Mother Maggie in her mint white dress setting the table with white tablecloth, glimmering white candles, fresh flowers and water, looking every bit the same today as when I watch mass on TV. And she always hummed the same hymn, *I Have a Friend, a Precious Friend, Oh How He Loves Me.* I studiously watched her almost with a sense that someday I'd be doing the same thing.

Church on Sundays for me was from dawn to dusk: first there was Worship Service which started between 11:30 am and 12:30 that lasted about 3 hours; Sunday school at 5pm; and the 7pm Night Service which ended about 10pm. It was a long day but I had to get the whole works, because even though they held Healing Service on Mondays, by the time I got off from school it was almost over; so I had to scoop up everything on Sundays to last me until Prayer Meeting on Wednesday Night. I can still hear Captain announcing to the congregation at the end of Prayer Meeting to make sure I was safely taken home whenever my mother didn't return for the Night Service.

Open Air Meeting was another passion. Sometimes it was as close as a 10 minute walk, and I would purposely sit in the front row, hoping the Preacher would call me to do the Scripture Reading. The first time my mother took me to one, it was conducted by the only remaining cousin from the McCoo's side of the family who shared the same faith as my mother. He held the meeting at the biggest crossroads in the district where three grocery shops formed a triangle, and he used the steps of one of the storefront for his platform. That cousin was the most eloquent Preacher that I had ever heard as a child. I remember thinking that he was too intelligent to be a preacher because the pastor at our church didn't have a rich vocabulary like he did. And as young as I was, I have never forgotten the chorus that was sung at that Meeting, *"Ye Men of Galilee Why Stand Ye Gazing."* It sort of made me feel sad, like I was just gazing when God had work for me to do. And when I think about it now, it makes me wonder if there had been a call on my life long before I had the sense to recognize it.

Looking at my mother's appearance attending church, no one would have guessed it was the same dress and tie-head that she wore all the time for every occasion: Prayer Meetings; Concerts; Fasting; Funeral; Convention; you name it; everything. It was as though she lived by Ecclesiastes Chapter 9:8, always in full white with a laced embroidered handkerchief in her breast pocket and her Hymn Book and Bible in her hand, or as she liked to call them, *"Chart & Compass."* On one occasion, a brother in church said to me, "Elisabeth, if you can't afford to go somewhere don't go." He might as well have been talking to the dead. My dress was clean but a bit tight, that was no reason whatsoever to stop from Church. Anyone who knew me; knew that as long as I wasn't naked I was going to church; it didn't matter if it was worn, patched or tight. And in spite of the poverty that ravished our family, my mother's relationship with God was the bedrock of our family. The church was our anchor. We had no Sunday matinee or TV, not even a radio but there was always something happening at church; whether it was a Candlelight Service, Convention or Concert, something was always happening. To be in the audience at a Concert and listen to my mother recite a Poem, was as though she was guided by the Poet himself, flawlessly gliding from line to line with amazing grace and eloquence. Even though I recited, it was Mother who got the encores, especially when she did renditions of *My Lord and I, & The Oration.* Our passion for church coupled with the loving bond we shared glued us together. It is on that foundation that I have managed to stand, even now.

My earliest memories of home, was a one bedroom bamboo house with a hall. It was one of three homes in the yard forming a triangle with my mother's at the top, and Brothers Phil and Victor on either side at the lower ends. The root and the branches of a huge Nesberry tree in front of the house served as veranda for family gatherings. My mother's pride and joy was her heart shaped pink and white June Rose Garden perched on a slope to the right side of the tree root which she diligently attended to daily.

My mother, my sister, my little brother and I all shared the same bed which was created by setting pieces of board on wooden posts. The only disadvantage was that if a piece of the board shifted, one of us could fall off the bed, and the wood at times gathered little insects which stung like mosquitoes. Our mattress was made with dried banana leaves from the trunk of the tree which we stuffed in a blue and white pyjama—stripe bag. Whenever it got too flat, mother would open the bag, washed it, and we'd stuff it again with freshly dried leaves and mother would sew up the end. Each time a new one was created it was crispy so my brother and I would play jumping jacks on it while singing, "We get new mattress, we get new mattress, we get new mattress." The boards tumbled off, but that was part of the fun, to reposition them and to keep jumping and chanting. Our makeshift mattress proved far more comfortable than the heavily coiled spring mattress introduced years later that bore into our bodies, and caused us to wake up in pain.

Alongside our bed was a huge mahogany chest mother inherited, which served both as an ironing board and clothes storage but there were those who thought it was a chest full of money that she inherited. I'll never forget the time when she sent me to get credit from her Shopkeeper niece how she frowned and asked me what happened to the chest-full-of-money mother inherited. It hurts to see how we were struggling and a niece could feel that way. Thankfully my mother never sent me to her again, she would always send me to the other Shopkeeper across from her niece's and said, "go to Sister Williams, her mother has a lot of children so she understands."

Our living hall furniture was very minimal, a small wooden table with two chairs, a hymn book, Bible, a kerosene lamp with the home-sweet-home lamp shade and a small glass cabinet. All my life growing up at home, that little table was where countless devotion took place every night. It was where mother sat and did all her mending, and it was there by her feet, at that little table, where I first learnt about the Creator of the Universe. Gracing the bamboo walls was a huge picture frame bearing the words of The Lord's Prayer that was intricately carved through a bed of pink and white rose that my father had brought home from Cuba. Inside the little glass cabinet were two treasured items, a blue and white ceramic bowl that weighed about fifteen pounds which my great grandmother bought for six pence, my father's drinking glass and some made in England china wares which she inherited from her ancestors.

We made our own doorway mats by gathering scraps of materials from dressmakers and used hair pins to hook them on to crocus bags. It took a lot of scraps, patience and time but the finished product with the richness of a variety of colors complemented the strawberry-dyed hardwood floors. We never had a refrigerator but we didn't miss one because mother inherited a huge Spanish jar made from clay which kept our drinking water just as cool and refreshing as any refrigerator. And we never had a clock or radio to tell the time of day, but mother could guess the time of day by the position of the sun on the ground or when aeroplanes passed over.

We had a variety of fruit trees including avocado and a variety of herbs to make tea, but we were usually short of sugar. I remember picking chocolate and pounding it, then forming them into little balls and leaving them to dry until we were ready to use them to make chocolate tea; and I have never forgotten the aroma of freshly picked coffee beans boiling from a distance. There was yam and banana that we could harvest but the crops were far between so we credited groceries from the Shopkeeper. And like sugar, we were always short of meat. In most instances we settled for a little coconut oil on our food.

There were two homes close to my mother's on nearby family land: one behind and the other to the far left. It was pathetic to listen to the the way that man to the far left used to beat his wife, sometimes just months after having a baby, for hours. It sounded as though everything in the little one bedroom shack was being destroyed. One day when she escaped and ran to get his mother, it was a complete waste of time. When she returned with his mother he began to beat her again. His mother walked away with her behind shooting up in the air and her chest bowing towards the ground with the long bad smelling tobacco pipe in her mouth. As a little girl I could only look on in horror helplessly but I have never forgotten what that woman said as she walked away: "me nuh mek nuh match and mi naw bruk nuh match" (I didn't make any match, and I won't break any match). That's why many, many years later when the couple's son faced the capital charge I paid for his defence. He was a product of his environment.

A cousin, who lived a little further away, closer to where Brother Phil kept his pig tied, could be heard reading his Bible all day every Sunday. He sounded more like a child learning to count. By midweek when he began to beat his common law wife, it sounded like everything in the little bamboo shack was tumbling over. Amazingly, these men were never stopped. No one intervened, ever.

Another cousin who lived on adjoining family property behind our house had strange behaviours, he always talked to himself. Wherever he went, whatever was discussed, we could count on hearing him grumbling to himself about it. I didn't understand it because he was a brilliant man with fine penmanship and a retiree of the Royal Air Force with a steady job at the Sugar Estate in the capacity of a scale clerk; but something was needling him. I remembered Brother Phil beckoning to him to untie the pig from the sun on his way home for lunch one day but he didn't.

We knew that cousin Roger love to talk himself, so later that evening Sister Love and I sat quietly inside by the bedroom window to hear the day's events from cousin Roger. We heard, "eh, eh, look at a thing like hog, look how it black, what if my friends came along and saw me loosing hog, what would they think of me?" Cousin Roger was brown skin. But the truth is, he loved his family and he was well liked. There was a sense that he was there to protect the family and preserve the land, but maybe there was a little dark side of him we didn't know about. Whatever it was, it really didn't bother us. We were just eager to get by that little board window at nights, pulled it in, wrapped the twine from the window around the nail on the inside to make sure the window was safely closed, and patiently wait for the day's events when Cousin Roger began to grumble to himself, so that we could have our daytime soap opera the following day. We didn't miss having a radio at all when Cousin Roger was alive. He was live entertainment. Bless his soul. We were poor, but we had one another, the church was our anchor and we learnt to find humour in everything.

T W O

For a while, I thought the extent of the family were Brothers Phil and Victor who lived in their little bamboo shacks below our house, and us three little ones living with mother; but as I grew older I learnt that I had five brothers and five Sisters (2 siblings had died). And there was a whole lot more to learn. My mother and I had much more in common. She was married when she was 16 years old and my life began to unravel when I was 16 years old.

My mother was from a family of farmers and fishermen who owned vast amount of land. The heart of the family's wealth rested solely with the maternal side. But in spite of the wealth that rested with them, following the death of her mother at a tender age, the aunt wasted no time getting rid of her; so except for a few good years in her early childhood, most of my mother's life was one of hardship and suffering for which I have not seen the likeness of since. It wasn't common in those days for teenagers of our culture to be married so early in life, the aunt simply handed her responsibility over to the first man that asked for her. I don't know how old she was at the time, but they were married when my mother was 16 years old, and in 22 years they had 11 children.

Being from a very large family of farmers and fishermen with vast amount of land, she had good support for many years during her marriage. She was never in need of anything. But with all the support that they gave her after she got married so young and began to have children at the speed

9

of lightening, if they had only invested that in her education, heaven knows what might have been. They were wealthy. They practically owned every acre in the community, and according Sister Louise they even leased a plot of land to the Bus Company for bus depot.

My mother's grammar and poetic writing style, her penmanship and mathematical aptitude, her skills with quotation marks, and her ability to always keep us ahead of the class with her attentive home schooling, spoke loud and clear that she was destined to be an educator. And that's why I wasn't surprised when the Principal of our Elementary School tried to retain her to teach the Beginner's classes. With a little helping hand to complete her education, my mother's life would have taken a far different turn, she was well on her way; and her family could more than afford it.

Whether her husband was encouraged to farm, or he became a part of the tradition, I don't know. But he bought property some distance away in another area and farmed a wide range of agricultural products including rice; a smart choice indeed considering the rate at which the family grew. One Sister recalled her Pappy's farming being of such magnitude, mother could afford to give away food to the community, and my sister told me she even took some to school for teachers and classmates. According to Sister Louise, she has not tasted any watermelon so big and sweet like that which her Pappy cultivated. One can only imagine how productive his farming was, for a couple with eleven children and one income to have had enough to give away without putting a crunch on the family budget. But all things must come to an end; and so the challenge of raising eleven children alone, brought my mother to her knees when her husband deserted her after keeping his promise to do so after the older folks began dying one by one. According to Sister Love, "you should have seen what he left his family for."

When he left their food supply was cut off. They were left with nothing and no income. My mother heard that he sold a piece of the farm land to pay for his mistress' ship fare to go to England. I guess he thought she would have sent for him, but apparently her eyes opened up after she got to England and realized he and his children were too much for her.

His losses meant more loss for his family too as he abandoned them, the farming and the land, and then disappeared sometime later. After a while the Government seized the land because my mother couldn't afford the additional taxes, she had her own taxes to pay on the five acres of land that her old people left her to live on and eleven mouths to feed.

Times got very tough. All my mother had was the property she lived on and her children. The few Dickenson siblings were very poor and the one aunt on the maternal side wasn't known for her generosity, she would rather take the children and use them to farm the land. Sister Love told me mother was so desperate one day that she sent her to beg Pappy for money. Pappy she said, tied Two Shillings and Six pence (that is 25¢) in a handkerchief on to her wrist and she ran with it to give mother. I didn't remember to ask her how many of them were home at the time with mother, but I wondered what he thought she needed; salt or matches. And my Mother told me that she was reduced to a single dress on her back which she washed at nights. I bore witness to that later too.

My mother said, tears came to her eyes when she heard the church bell ringing one Sunday and wanted to go to church and couldn't go. When she went and begged her husband for a dress, she said he told her, *"the next time I give you a dress two Sundays meet."* So help me God, if I were born at the time, he probably wouldn't have had any teeth left in his mouth. That wretch! Years later when I remarked that I wished her husband could see her closet now she had tears in her eyes. Because of that reaction it used to bother me if I had clothed her enough. Yes I sent money for her care and always took things to her from foreign, but did I clothe her enough? I just don't know, I just don't know.

There were so many times as a child when I sensed that even though she appeared calm on the surface she was shredded to bits by the horror of what she was living compared to the life she once knew. And it was often the old spiritual hymns she sang, that revealed her state of mind: *When things don't go to suit you, and the world's turned upside down; I must tell Jesus all of my sorrows, I cannot bear my burden alone; Let Jesus fix it for you, He knows just what to do; Nobody knows the sorrow I bear; Take the name of*

Jesus with you; and her all time favourite, *"Tell mother I'll be there in answer to prayer."* That one tormented me. I interpreted it to mean she was either crying out for her mother's help or, she was surrendering her will to go on. And without her, my little brother and I would probably have ended up with strangers. As young as I was, I developed an understanding of what she was experiencing by each hymn she sang. They taught me a lot, and they drew me close to her, but I don't think I realized the depth of all she bore until I began to pen this memoir. And my determination at all cost to protect her from further pain has probably silenced me for many years. If she was alive, there is no way under the sun I would have penned this memoir. I would not stand by and see her suffer one more ounce of pain. But I am glad that I always showed compassion, and my love for her was no secret. Now, her grandchildren can get a glimpse of the woman, her life and the price that was paid.

As the twelfth of thirteen children, I do not pretend to know it all. The older ones, especially the first two, they have a reservoir of information. They were extremely close to mother as well and I am sure she confided in them a lot, plus, they witnessed and experienced much more. However, for the little she confided in me and what I observed, it was brutal. That's why I never quite feel like I did enough for her; because enough was never enough to wipe away the hardship I witnessed. Throughout the pages of this volume, she will be mentioned periodically, not only because of the bond we shared, but primarily, because most of the challenges I faced happened when I was still a child living under her roof.

When my mother met my father she was not yet divorced from her husband, but he had deserted his family and she still had several mouths to feed. I remembered her showing me a newspaper clipping of the Notice of Separation. Two older children, a brother and a sister, were the only resources she had, but my sister had started her own family and later migrated to England leaving 5 children behind. Brother Phil had no desire to leave his mother.

I was nine months old my mother said, when my father complained that he wasn't feeling well. After having his usual mug of coffee and his

Cuban cigar, he rested on his back and asked his friend, Mr Skytoe, to pass the baby to him. Mother said, he then lifted me three times towards heaven and said, "God bless you, God bless you, God bless you," and handed me over to her. She instinctively knew he was feeling worse than he pretended to be, so she called a friend and they hurried off with him on the horse drawn buggy five miles away to the doctor. He was still sitting up in the chair after the doctor attended to him when he took his last breath. He died from pneumonia, she was told. At the time my mother was expecting her thirteenth child. There were no Social Services to help her; no food stamps; no welfare cheque; no dollar store; no thrift shops, and the only job she ever held was mother/housewife. It's no wonder she said that in one of her darkest moments following the death of my father, she found herself sitting under a tree and heard what sounded like voices talking and the sounds of children playing; she must have been on the verge of a mental breakdown. He was her sole provider, the love of her life; she was 3 weeks pregnant, and had several mouths to feed, including me, the 9-month-old-baby.

One brother who is said to be the most brilliant among siblings referred to him as the wind beneath his wings. He said my father would spend his last farthing to make sure he was never wanting for anything in High school. His world crumbled when my father died. Sister Lyn lovingly remembered how they got a lot of food to eat when he was alive; Sister Ilene remembered his handsome Asian looks; Sister Love remembered him being more of Asian nationality too, and to his buddies and the community, he was affectionately called Wong, or the Banjo man. Mother told me that he lived in Cuba before she met him. After a live performance entertaining friends on Friday evenings with his Banjo, he went home with his Cuban cigars and a small bottle of rum tucked in his back pockets. He slept with me face down on his chest, she said and he chose to name me after his sister Elisabeth. And given the attention my mother showed to the spot where my dad was laid to rest, I could tell there was deep affection, in fact I believe she was loving my father through me; very special and my godmother later confided the same belief to me. That's why some siblings believed I was her favourite. I soaked up everything about my father like sponge and I still keep two CD's of Singer Andy Williams close by because his eyes reminds me of my father's passport photo.

Things got pretty bad for my mother and my siblings following the death of my father. The family was shattered. In order to survive, some of my siblings were sent to live with relatives but I would have been too young to realize, that's why for a while it appeared to me that the extent of the family were the two brothers living close by, and the three of us who lived at home with our mother. And up until my mid twenties when I met my oldest sister, Louise, the only thing I knew of her was that she was in England and she sent money to Mother to help with us and a parcel for us every Christmas. Luckily she got away and was able to sponsor Brothers Victor and Edmund later, but she had left behind five children to sponsor, plus they had four more born in England. It couldn't have been easy for a young couple to have all that responsibility, and to care for our mother and her three little ones. That's why the family was scattered, mother could not cope. Times were tough.

Brother Phil, the oldest sibling, who lived nearby was warm and caring. He was never far away and he seemed to have spent his whole life taking care of mother and helping with us. Brother Victor was very tender with us but Lord he had a temper. I strongly believe that by his father abandoning the family; my dad's death; and then the family being scattered all over the place, largely contributed to his anger because he was very tender with my little brother and I. I recalled a girlfriend living with him for just one day. And maybe that was 24 hours too much. What Miss Biggy did I don't know, but something went wrong when she was ironing because I saw my brother grabbed the iron from her and went towards her face like he was about to brand her. I was shocked. I still have the memory of Miss Biggie leaving that same evening with her little coal stove on her head going up the hill. That's why it didn't surprise me to learn from Sister Louise later that it was mother who suggested she sponsored him first to England instead of a sister who felt she was denied an opportunity. I have to agree with my mother, she didn't want Brother Victor getting into trouble. I loved him and will always remember him as the gentle giant who was overly protective of us. And that is why on the morning of his departure when he sneaked away while I was asleep, I knew it was because he didn't have the courage to tell me he couldn't give me his "wrist watch" that I had asked him for.

Sometime after Brother Victor left for England I began to wonder why Brother Phil didn't go to England too even though he had applied for his passport. Then all of a sudden one day I came home from school for lunch, he asked me to wait for a letter to mail to Sister Louise. It required more than Job's patience to wait on my brother for a letter. If it took him thirty minutes to write a letter, it took sixty to address it; and if there was a "t" to be crossed or an "i" to dot; add another half an hour. Months later things slowed down, the letters became fewer and farther between. Finally I worked up the courage to ask him what happened. With his head hung low and swung to one side pensively, he said, "Sister, you know I can't leave my mother." "What if I went to England and they recruited me for war, I would never see my mother again?" "Furthermore, who would help mother with all of you little ones, who would protect my mother?" "Who would care for the land?" "Who would pick a breadfruit for her?" I was speechless. The depths of his love for his mother echoed in every question. I didn't have the answer. I simply stood in awe of that great icon.

It was very common to lie in bed at nights and hear Mother and him under the Nesberry tree talking. They consulted with each other about everything. As mother always said, "Like it or not, Phil's decision is final." Greater love hath no one than those two for each other, and deservedly so. He stood by Mother's side through thick and thin, always making sure we were provided for and taken care of. He did get married, and even now, some fifty years later, I still remember the times after his marriage, when he would climb a bread fruit tree and just sat there for hours savouring a piece of his wedding cake.

There was a time when it seemed that he would have a second marriage, but his home was burglarized and several things were stolen, or so he claimed. The Sunday morning following the reported break-in, all his church brethren came along singing:

Never be downhearted, no, no, no.
Never be downhearted, no, no, no.
Sorrow will go and sorrow will come,
Take it to Jesus wherever you go,
Never be downhearted, no, no, no."

A few days later all the missing items were found in an alley behind my brother's house when my mother and I were cleaning off my father's grave. We suspected that my brother could not afford wedding expenses and with all of the exciting plans underway by his young bride-to-be, he staged the robbery. I remembered feeling so very sorry for him. He just could not afford it. I was a child, but I saw how he gave all he had to mother to help take care of us. He had two sons, but we were all treated alike. One pot served for everyone. I have never forgotten the Christmas season when my brother brought home his pay and spread it all out on the dirt in the kitchen while he and mother penciled out the various expenses to be covered. My God, I thought to myself my brother Phil doesn't have a life. He was still a man at home with his mother. The only thing she didn't do for him was his laundry. And I noticed that he never had a partner for long, may be because he was always so wrapped up with mother's responsibilities, that they never stayed long. I took his meals to him at the Sugar Estate which was mainly rice and sardines, and he always had enough to share with a co-worker and leftovers for me. Not once had he ever returned a lunch pail without a little something left in it for me. Juice was mainly lemonade, or sugar and water if we had no lime. Sunday was the day for carrot juice. Each time I looked into his eyes they were always red; it was like looking into the window of a soul hanging on by grace. And I'm sure his little five feet frame didn't carry more than 105 pounds.

Children adored him, and they always expected something from him. One evening on his way home from work, a bunch of kids swarmed him for the one mint ball sweetie in his hand. My brother took a hammer and splintered the mint ball and every child got a piece. That single act of thoughtfulness and generosity has been one of life's greatest lessons to me; we always have enough to share. He was a rare and precious gem. God knew what He was doing when He chose to bless my mother with such a precious son. It's as though he was ordained to take care of his mother and his siblings.

The servings on our plates dwindled considerably after Brother Victor left for England. The family's farmer was gone. Brother Phil could climb and pick fruits, chopped a piece of cane or dug a piece of yam, but in my opinion he wasn't a "grounds man" like Brother Victor, he just didn't have the strength.

On one occasion when mother prepared the little she gathered from the land for dinner, it was just enough to fit on a saucer, so she placed the saucer on the floor before the three of us; my sister, my brother and I. I've never forgotten how I looked up at her and said, "Mother, eat some." But she meekly said, "no, oono gwan" (go ahead). I remembered the three of us dipping our fingers on to the saucer cautiously, making sure each other got a little bit, while Mother sat beside us on the chair with her head bowed towards the garment she was mending, making every effort to keep the one-eye-looking-glass on her nostrils. I always remember looking up at her each time I lifted my hand to my mouth. She went to bed without dinner that night. And there were countless more like that, but that particular night and the sight of her mending our clothes while we ate, has never left my rear view mirror. And that's why later in life Claude Monet's Painting, *Madam Monet and Child in a Garden,* came to bear such significance to me, it's a picture of the night mother mended our clothes while all three of us sat on the floor at her feet and ate from the little saucer. As small as I was then, I recalled thinking that day that I was going to do all I can for my mother when I got older to make sure she never went to bed without dinner. I was going to be the Champion of the family with the big house for the entire family.

THREE

I first met Sister Lyn when she returned home to occupy the little bamboo flat vacated by Brother Victor when he left for England. Sister Lyn said she was sent away to live with a Preacher Lady after my father died because mother didn't have it to buy food to feed everyone.

There was never a dull moment with Sister Lyn around. She always had something for us to laugh about. She even entertained us with her stutter. And according to her, food was never a problem when she went to live with the Preacher Lady. As soon as the cupboards were running low, Miss Lyneth would "tune-up" her goat skin drum and they would conduct Roadside Prayer Meeting then use the proceeds from the offering plate to purchase groceries. I never grew tired of hearing that story, it's as though I was always hearing it for the first time. The way I saw it that poor lady didn't rob a soul, she simply did what she had to do, to keep food on the table, and that was "to sell the name of Jesus."

I always remember Sister Lyn for her light heartedness and her generosity. Each evening when she made dinner, she always gave one of us a plate. But it went in a circle because she couldn't afford to give all three of us every evening. I couldn't wait for my turn, especially if it was red-peas-soup. I really missed that when she moved away later. And apart from my mother, no one else combed my hair the way I liked it, like Sister Lyn, especially when she combed it in what she called "the cup and saucer hair style." But there was a very special assignment that she had for me every morning on my way to school, that always had me cracking up. It seemed like another lady was after her boyfriend, so every morning when I was leaving for school, she would tell me the worst things to tell Dorothy. And on my way home in the evenings, Dorothy would be on the lookout for me, ready with her share for me to take to my sister. I enjoyed my job very much, because what they were fussing over didn't seem worth it to me. And I was right, because in the end none of them won. My sister was left with two children, and I'm not sure how many Dorothy was left with, but I doubt any of them got a penny to purchase a tin of baby food.

Another Sister, Ilene, recalled that when she was about six years old, my mother said to her, *"Ilene, I have nothing to give you to eat, so I'm taking you to my aunt."* But knowing my mother, she agonized over it many sleepless nights before reaching that decision. In fact I vividly remembered my mother sharing with me how she had to make that painful decision after the death of my father when two sisters drowning in perspiration, pitifully looked up at her and said, *"mi hungry."* I am sure that Sister Ilene was one of them. My mother had nothing. She told me it was a tablespoon of sugar from her good friend Maas Joe to sweeten a big mug of mint tea that probably saved their lives. She was the third child to be sent to Auntie Maggie and the fifth that Mother sought help with. Of the two brothers that were sent before her, Brothers Edmund and Daniel, by the time I learnt of that, one was in England and the other had left for the city.

Sister Ilene told me that she ate well at her Aunt Maggie. There was no shortage of food. Auntie Maggie grew her own rice, made her own cornmeal and honey, she even owned a big concrete house with a grocery shop and a brick oven which she rented to Bakers for weddings; but she worked twice as hard. Even from the tender age of 6, Sister Ilene said every morning at 4 a.m., she tagged along behind the older ones with her little crocus bag picking up coconuts on the farm and by the time she got back home she would rather be going back to sleep than to get ready for school.

I remember accompanying my mother down to Aunt Maggie to use the oven to bake buns to feed us, and to sell door to door Sunday mornings.

Mother always gave Sister Ilene a bun, and my sister always served me a big bowl of home-made honey sweetened cornmeal porridge, but I don't ever recall seeing a smile on my sister's face. When I look back now, I cannot imagine how agonizing it must have been for her, to see her mother and her sister coming to use the oven and then leaving her; regardless. My God! I remembered seeing another girl about the same age as Sister Ilene at Aunt Maggie too, but at the time I didn't know who she was. Many years later, Sister Ilene told me that the little girl was given to Auntie Maggie at the market because her mother was too poor to take care of her.

Ironically, years later when Sister Ilene came home and had a baby, mother was still struggling. Even when she got married I wasn't able to attend; but just to get a glimpse of her in her wedding gown, I pretended to be asleep all day, then in the evening I ran as fast as I could bare feet and in my "yard clothes" straight to the church. My Sister and her husband were just leaving the church so I took a quick peep and ran back home. On the way home, the kids teased me for going to my sister's wedding without shoes and wearing my "yard clothes." I tried to convince them that I had forgotten about the wedding and fell asleep, but they all knew that it was "hogwash." We all lived in the same community. The only time they ever saw me in shoes, was when I went to church, but it was all I could think of saying just to get the chance to see my sister in her wedding gown. This is one sister whose life story I'd love to read. Even with 6 children, there is some remnant of pain I'm sure, but she keeps the door closed.

Another Sister, Bev, was sent to live with a wealthy Catholic grand-aunt after the auntie had a dream from her brother, (Mother's father) that Mother needed help. Even though the family had a maid, they wanted Sister Louise, the oldest and strongest looking daughter, but Sister Bev said mother insisted on keeping Sister Louise; so they settled for her. She was only seven years old. Many years later, Sister Bev told me that she was glad mother stood her grounds and didn't give them Sister Louise, because chances are if they had taken Sister Louise, she probably would not have met her husband and gone to England and we would have drowned in poverty.

Not so long ago, Sister Bev confided in me that our aunt's daughter didn't like the Dickenson's, her maternal side of the family, because they were too poor. She said food was not a problem, but she worked like a child slave from seven. Went to bed tired, woke up tired, rarely went to school, and when she did make the 3-mile journey, she was ridiculed by her teacher and classmates for her poor attendance. That explained a lot, because she always look like a lost soul to me; is not very trusting, and always sat and stare at me. I never knew why, but I believe now, that it was the trauma of what she experienced after being rooted up from her home, and the thought that I got the chance to grow up happily with mother. In one instance after she arrived in America I wanted to take her shopping at a very big Mall, but she refused to go with me. Later that night when I got home, she telephoned to ask me if I wanted to take her some place she didn't know so she could get lost. At the time she was about 65 years old; but what disturbs now when I think of it, is the fact that even today, that street from the house to the school is still very lonely, so it must have been frightening for a seven year old to be doing a 6-mile round-trip on a lonely street like that some 67 years ago, my God! Her fear of not wanting to go to a place she didn't know had deep roots. And it took me almost a lifetime to learn that.

Sister Love is my closest sister because of our age difference, and we were two of the last 3 children that mother held onto. Even though she was a few years older, folks used to say she was soft and quiet and I was bright so I felt the need to be protective of her as I was of my younger brother. And that's exactly how I feel even today about her, a tendency to want to shield her. When we were little, if she had a toothache and sat up all night crying, I sat up and cried with her all night too. If she was sad, I was sad too. And that's why I love Shorthand, because she was extremely good at Pitman's Shorthand and I was fascinated by the speed at which she did it so I learnt it too.

I have no memory of this, but Sister Love told me that she too had a stint of briefly living with Aunt Beloved, a tall, big bone, strong looking woman with white hair peeping out from underneath her "tie head" (head scarf). She looked like the last of mother's old people but extreme poverty was written all over her, especially her teeth. Sister Love said that she didn't stay with Aunt Beloved for long, because mother had a dream from her ancestors shortly after she took her to the auntie, telling her that they wanted their gold ring back. Mother was sure that they were referring to her because she had light complexion and red hair so she went and got her.

For my mother to have considered Aunt Beloved a worthy Guardian was a testament to how desperate she was, because that very poor aunt, apart from having a good heart, had nothing. The very floors in her dry weather house needed twice the amount of hardwood to cover the empty spaces; luckily we wouldn't have far to fall. But even as a child I sensed that Aunt Beloved had a special place in her heart for Cousin Lenny's children. Wherever she met us, she always reached for the handkerchief in her bosom and diligently untied it to give us a couple pennies from the few she had. Sister Love and I have never passed that auntie without getting a little change from her to buy our sweetie, even if it was a Penny. And she was always eager to take us home for a meal. If I have learnt anything from that precious soul, it is that we always have enough to share in spite of poverty; even if it's "the widow's mite." I really loved that auntie.

My little brother was the youngest. To this day I am still protective of him and I love and treat his children as my own. A part of me feels like there was something I got that he never did. Maybe because I had the opportunity of being held by my father for nine months and he wasn't; plus in a household of four he was the youngest, and the only male. And he was always so sickly, which I am sure was due to lack of proper nutrition. In fact even today he is still very delicate. I cannot think of anything harder on a child than to feel deprived, but I knew my mother didn't have it to help us as she would have liked to so she sought help in whatever ways she could just so we could survive. If the circumstances were different, he would probably have been a Historian. His ability to read and retain in my opinion makes him a walking encyclopaedia like Brother Daniel.

"I marvel at how times have changed. For the most part, the three of us little ones growing up with mother had experienced so much, yet, despite the hardship she held onto us. We were like peas in a pod. Today we have all

grown, gone in different directions with families of our own making, but I can never reckon with the fact that we three would ever be separated. It is sad that we're not closer. I miss the way we were; just the three of us with our mother under the same roof, sharing the same bed. We should have a bond so close that not even our children came between. Now our children have established families of their own and we still don't seem to have time for each other. I still hold dearly to the bonds we shared but I long for the warmth that comes from being together, even occasionally. The little skirmishes we have sometimes happen because we don't spend time together anymore, so hopefully by me working the muscles a little bit now, the blood will begin to flow again."

Long before I met Brother Daniel I loved him and was anxious to meet him because of the bond mother said he and my dad shared. He wanted to be rich and to make the family comfortable; that was my brother's ambition. And my father would spend his last farthing on his education, but when dad died and they were scattered all over with different family members, his world crumbled. For all the years I lived at home, mother mailed letters to him without ever getting a reply, yet she never stopped praying for him. It was as though he vanished after the death of my father. As mother said, "Dad was the wind beneath his wings."

The more I understood the relationship between my brother and my father, the less judgemental it made me, but I never understood how my mother kept giving me letters every week to mail to a person who never replied. From the time I started going to the Post Office when I was a little girl in school up until I left home at 18, mother gave me a letter to mail to him every week. Only a mother could do that. As a mother now, I can only imagine what she went through. What a lesson! I love my brother. There is goodness in him. It just happened that he lost his way when my father died and the family scattered. I value his friendship and I've learnt a lot from him. He is a walking encyclopaedia of Shakespeare's writings. He once said to me, "letters are the thoughts of a person, they should be respected, should never be discarded." It was a painful reminder of some earlier letters from my mother that were never saved. What a loss!

We weren't the only ones that paid a heavy price for poverty, the dog did too. She was a healthy little mongrel that my mother's friend gave to her. My mother loved having a little dog around but we never had it to feed dogs, because we never had much ourselves, so Tricksy ate whatever was left around the kitchen at nights, and then we cursed her that she was thief. Eventually, she became withdrawn, and when we called her she cowardly approached us, didn't even have the strength to bark at nights. When she gave birth to five adorable brown puppies, I recalled taking a little of the cow's milk that Sister Lyn sent me to buy for cornmeal porridge, to feed them under the cellar of our house but sadly, only one puppy survived. Tricksy was just skin and bones. Malnutrition was written all over her little body. At times there wasn't even a bone to feed her because we didn't have bones from meat ourselves, and whenever there was an occasional fishbone everything was sucked off.

Many, many, years later on Park Avenue in New York City, I saw a string of Golden Retrievers out for a stroll with their caretaker. It broke my heart. I can't say I felt guilty because we didn't have it to feed her, but to remember how her little body succumbed to the ravages of hunger was very sad. Now when I see how dogs are nurtured and cared for, I think of Tricksy and sometimes even reflect on the day when my husband, his best friend and I were travelling to the countryside and a dog was struck. Larry got so nervous, that my husband had to get in the driver's seat. He said that hitting a dog was no less than hitting a child. The very moment he said that I remembered Tricksy and I thought we didn't hit her, but she suffered a slow death from malnutrition and we wouldn't have done that to a child. It was a sick feeling in my stomach. The thought that we didn't have it ourselves was no consolation. It was still very unsettling. I have a special love for Golden Retrievers and can see myself owning one in my golden years, but I wonder if Tricksy has something to do with it.

FOUR

When we were little, every Monday morning, Mother left my brother and I with Cousin Brenda to find work at the Sugar Cane Plantation. I use to wonder if Mother would be paid the same day she worked because she never took lunch with her, and all she ever had before she left was a cup of mint tea with one cracker. And she must have trusted Cousin Brenda because she never had lunch to leave for us, but Cousin Brenda had a lot of children, and she treated us just like her own. We could always count on having a big bowl of cornmeal porridge for lunch, and a friend of my father's, Brother Gillie, always had some big red and white mint ball sweetie for us when he passed by.

My mother was never so lucky. Of all the women who lined up every Monday hoping to have their names called for a week's work throwing fertilizer on the cane field, my mother was never given a break to put a night's dinner on the table for us. I was so very sorry for her. Even now the memory of her returning home looking dejected and wearily pulling the slippers held by a single toe while trying to bury her pain in a song, is still hauntingly sad. I don't feel like I've made much progress since that imagery. She always had the same answer each time I asked her what happened: they told her, *she didn't need work, because she had children in England.* My God Almighty! It was the same blue frock she wore all the time with the little piece of slippers barely hanging on around the big toe and they had the gall to tell her that. Spitefully, my mother was always the only person to be turned away each week.

Once after she was turned away, whether there was nothing to make for dinner or what, I don't know; but with a hand on one side, she looked to the right and to the left and said sometimes she felt like packing her little box and just run away. My God have mercy! I felt so sorry for her that I can't recall if I said or did anything. For a woman of faith that was so uncharacteristic of her, that I made it a habit of walking up to meet her when she returned home to sort of cheer her up. She wasn't one to say much, but I could read her eyes and by prying a little and showing love and compassion, I reached into her soul and in the process I learnt a lot. Sometimes I wonder if those Sugar Plantation gods who denied her a job to get us something to eat knew she had little ones at home to feed. They couldn't have. And I'm glad I never knew them, I wouldn't want to live with such hatred; it would destroy me.

We never had much income except for Brother Phil's paycheque from the Sugar Estate on Fridays; Brothers Victor and Edmund periodically from England; and Mother could count on Sister Louise's every holiday plus a barrel with clothes at Christmas. My sister told me years later that a lot of times when she sent money to mother for us, the family fed on cornmeal porridge for weeks. Sister Love and I got some beautiful hand me downs from our nieces but we were always short on shoes and underwear. Thankfully, Mother could do a little sewing, so she collected the flour bags from the Shopkeeper, bleached out the marks with kerosene oil, and used them to make some very durable underwear for us with little drawstrings in the waist. Shoes didn't bother us, we were used to having our "10 commandments" (10 toes) on the ground with lots of coconut oil to make our feet shine. And we were so bright in school that I don't think anyone had time to notice that we were bare feet; but thankfully, we always had one pair for church and "special callings," even if we had to tip on our toes or carried it in our hands. My little brother wasn't so fortunate because Sister Louise had eight girls and one son. In fact, I don't recall him getting anything much from the barrel. As a little boy, he must have been so confused that I believed he hid his pain by being the best at what he did. If mother sent him to the shop, he would run so fast that he could be back before she finished telling him what she needed.

My mother never had a husband to help her, but she lived by prayer and fasting as though she was the only one God had to take care of, and it worked. One evening when there was nothing to cook she lit the firewood and placed the pot on it like she expected God to rain down manna from above. When I asked her why she put the pot on the fire and there was nothing to cook she said, "Go to the Post Office, you will get money, open the letter and ask the Post Mistress to change the money and get a string of fish from Miss Ethel on your way home!" I remembered staring at her as though she was talking nonsense, but she just smiled and said, "run-along, if you don't get money I'll put a stone in the pot." It was my first experience of faith in action from my very own mother. It made me realize later in life what the Holy One meant when He told the Centurion that, "He never found one with such great faith, not even in Israel." Matthew 8:5-10. Because of that experience, I've never forgotten the sender, Brother Victor. That's why years later when he severed communications after his wife took their only son home on a visit against his wishes and the baby died from heat exhaustion, I vowed to find him when I grew up. And I did.

In spite of hardship, mother always made sure we never had to beg or borrow soap, matches, and kerosene oil. Those were basic necessities. The soap enabled us to bathe and keep our clothes clean, matches to light the lamp or outdoor fire for cooking and chasing mosquitoes, and of course kerosene oil for the lamp which enabled us to get our homework done and to read the Bible at bedtime. Later when I attended High school and had the opportunity to wear shoes and socks, the "Home Sweet Home" lamp shade became the ideal place to dry my only pair of socks at nights.

Christmas, we never had toys but she shared the spirit of the season by getting each of us to tie a foot of socks on the bed posts. Just before shop closed on Christmas Eve, the both of us would sneak out, get a couple candies and place them in each foot of socks so we could all have presents on Christmas morning. It was always exciting to open our one foot of socks Christmas morning and get our big red and white mint ball sweetie. That was our Christmas gift. But I find it very sobering that despite unimaginable hardship, she was never tempted to sell even a chain of the five-acre property her ancestors left her. I have to assume that either she knew the value of land, which we are just realizing or, she was intent on preserving it so that we could always have a place call home even if the land never had a proper house on it.

As a child, there were times when it felt uncomfortable to be poor. My mother was a woman of class and good etiquette who had the potential to become whatever she chose to but out of sheer poverty, she was left to gather from nothing. No one I knew had the sort of penmanship my mother had except for an older aunt. It was the envy of many. Her mathematical skill was nothing short of genius. She added, subtracted, and multiplied faster than any calculator whether it be single or double figures. There wasn't a subject in school that she couldn't assist us with. She was the best at Spelling and Punctuation marks, and there was a sense of pride when she talked about a cousin she helped in school with his maths who became a prominent politician. She baked, she sewed and she could cook, but losing her mother so early in her childhood, then being tossed to a man by her aunt when he asked for her; marriage at 16, thirteen children in 25 years, then left alone to care for them; it successfully demolished her.

Her father had a sister who I occasionally spent holidays with. The auntie was a middle class educated Roman Catholic. The family owned a large two-storey Victorian home with a 12 seat dining table on the upper floor overlooking the ocean. Across the street from the house, a boardwalk jutted out into the ocean, and just a few blocks away was a wharf from where they exported banana. It was at this aunt's house that I was first introduced to the Catholic Faith. The difference between them and my mother was like night and day. They were filthy rich, and my mother was dirt poor. When I was asked to take the ham and the bacon from the refrigerator, I had no idea what they were talking about, didn't even know what they looked like. And it wasn't until I got older that I realized it was the very aunt's home where Sister Bev went to live at when she was seven years old and ended up working like a little maid . . .

Interestingly, I don't remember lifting a finger to do any work there and I loved spending time there because their big upstairs house by the main road overlooked the ocean and it made me feel rich. And I admired the way my grand-aunt would cross her legs on the veranda and read the newspaper while her maids did all the work. Another aunt who seemed just as wealthy was far more thoughtful. She always had a little something for me to take to my mother. She knew I wasn't just sent there to look for her, we were looking for help. I always look forward to visiting that auntie because no matter how small a package it may be, she always gave me something to give my mother along with a kerchief tied up with a little change.

When I look back now, I have to wonder how it is that none of my mother's two sisters and two brothers helped with us, especially the sisters who had no children. My Uncle Cecil who worked at the Sugar Estate was so mean I was never lucky enough to get even a sweetie from him. Uncle Charley—the Police Corporal who drove the Queen's Representative and lived on the compound never helped us. My adorable Aunt Edith who always had a cheerful smile and the only sibling I recall visiting my mother, never had much either. My other auntie, Aunt Sera who only lived a few miles away from us leaned towards the wealthier side of the family. Uncle Charley and Aunt Sera were close and they visited each other. At Aunt Sera I heard Uncle Charley name a lot but never heard any mention of my mother, Sister Lenny, Aunt Edith or Uncle Cecil. I have to believe they were too poor to be spoken of. I don't even recall seeing her come to visit us. I'm sure mother sent me there for holidays because I would get a proper meal but I didn't feel it was a child's atmosphere. It was nothing but a lifeless, well kept house with a couple living in the midst of a forest.

One weekend when Sister Bev visited, she told Mother that Uncle Charley and his family were coming to see us Sunday. I boasted on all my classmates that my rich uncle who drove the Queen's Representative was coming to visit us. My mother was so excited she borrowed chairs and extra utensils and made a big pot of rice with brown-stew snapper fish and a big kerosene pan of lemonade. I was sure the creditors would have to wait until money came from England.

When my uncle and his wife came, they didn't even have a glass of our lemonade, much less to taste my mother's finger licking brown-stew snapper fish. I don't even recall them taking a seat, and they didn't bring their children, which was a very big disappointment because Sister Bev hinted that the children were beautiful so we were really looking forward to meet them. I remembered looking at my uncle's brown skin wife with her hands crossed behind her back like she was afraid to touch us, and feeling very sad for my mother who was hoping to meet her nieces and nephews.

The tall, dark, handsome man, in what appeared to be a "two-in-one eye glass" probably thought he couldn't identify with us. I didn't know how else to put it. My God! How could he come to look for poor Sister Lenny and not even bring her a soda pop or a couple sweets for his little nieces and nephews, much more to leave without tasting her "cooking." No doubt mother thought she would get a little spare change from him to help cover the extra expenses she incurred that evening. After waiting all day and boasting to classmates how my mother's "well-to-do" brother and his family who lived only 55 miles away were coming to see us, that was the memory I was left with, while the little "well-to-do-sister" living less than half an hour ride from us often boasted of the many visits her brother and his family made to their home for weekend getaways.

Several years later when I visited my mother's burial spot and left without placing flowers because the tomb was freshly painted, my son Colin got a dream from her, *"Mom, Granny said to tell you even a stranger would pass by and put flowers."* Even the dead expect something when they're visited. It was a reminder of the Sunday my uncle and his wife visited and didn't even put a little mint-ball-sweetie in our hands or "wet" his sister's palm with a little spare change.

I am convinced that we survived the storms of life through prayer. Every need, every want; every circumstances we faced was turned over to God in prayer, and it was a global affair. Long before I knew what Lunatic Asylum was, I heard Mother praying for those inmates; those against the Prison Wall; those in the Hospital; those who had lost the love they had; and many, many, more. But in every single prayer, there was a statement that she made that really pierced me: *"Lord, every time I stretch my hand to pick a rose, thorns and thistles in the way.*" It tortured me. I can never reconcile with those words, and I don't want to ever imagine what she constantly wrestled with, it would strangle me. She had a lot of heartaches, but she never complained. She sang; read the Bible; fasted; and took everything to God in Prayer, or according to her, "*The Throne of Grace,*" so listening to her Prayers was like getting a peep into her soul. And whenever she prayed, as soon as I heard the words, "*When I was going up to the Mount of Olives, You went up with me, and now Lord I am coming down,*" I understood that it was time for me to get out of bed and kneel by the bedside with her to close with the Lord's Prayer. And if I pretended to be asleep she would tickle the bottom of my feet until I got up. It was never a moment I looked forward to, because I was usually half asleep, but those prayers were worth recording, they would be sure to make a Prayer Bible today.

For years Sister Louise and I use to wonder what mother meant when she referred to going up to the Mount of Olives in every prayer; until a couple years ago in a sermon from Bishop Jakes, I learnt that the Mount of Olives is a place acquainted with grief, that's why Jesus stopped there before the bastards got hold of Him because He knew that the same thing the Olive went through was the same thing He would face, so He stopped there for strength. My mother did the same each time she prayed. She stopped by the place that could relate to what she went through daily. And, in a miraculous way, I realize now, that I was being taught how to deal with the challenges of life and where to go for strength. It was a good thing she did.

I don't remember being strapped more than two times. The look in my mother's eyes would always communicate when I was stepping out of my boundaries. A severe punishment would have me standing in a corner with my right hand holding my left ear; my left foot bent at the knee with the left hand grasping the left ankle while balancing on the right foot. But there was one exception that taught me a lesson when I was about seven years old. When I was leaving my Godmother after holidaying with her to be home with mother and my siblings for Christmas, there was a two shillings and sixpence coin (25 cents coin) in the kitchen so I took it and bought a little baby doll for my Christmas. When my mother asked me where I got it, I told her Goddie gave it to me not even thinking that my mother would walk all the way from our house to tell Goddie thanks for giving me a doll. The Sunday morning as we were about to leave for Church, my mother took me by my hand in my church clothes and led me behind the kitchen. I don't remember how I got on the ground, but I remembered that ankle length black skirt that Sister Louise sent her from England all over my face and my little feet up in the air with my behind and the strap all for herself. I have to admit that for the first time and maybe the only time in my life, going to church that Sunday morning was not exciting. And I am sure that by choosing my favourite morning of the week she was making a statement, one I would never forget throughout my career in banking several years later in life.

The life she led, the examples she set, the love she gave me and the bond I shared with her, is the foundation on which I stand. And I could feel the love of my father through the warmth of his friends, especially my Godfather, and that was very gratifying. Even the tender care my mother exhibited to the very place he was laid to rest was a testament of the love they shared. I have thrived on that. I consider myself truly blessed to be the offspring of such an amazing couple. That's why it disturbed me at her passing when I heard someone referred to her as "hand bun." Whether it was an attempt to be condescending to her or what, I am not sure, but I was left with the impression that my mother's humble little livelihood to put food on her table, didn't quite measure up to "standard."

We need to remember that an honest day's labour to put bread on one's table, whatever the task may be, should not be looked down on. A lot of those who paved the way for us often did menial work so we could have a better life. Some picked cotton; some cleaned toilets; some caught crabs in swamps; some chopped cane in roasting temperatures. They all did what they could to survive, and today we owe our very existence to the sacrifices they made and the price they paid to make life a little more decent for us. My mother baking a few buns to sell doesn't earn anyone the right to refer to her as "hand bun." Even if all she could afford was flour, sugar, water and yeast, she deserves to be respectfully spoken of. Even in death.

Later in life when I faced my greatest battle, Sister Love said someone remarked to my mother, "Elisabeth was well made." It's because of the examples of Brother Phil and my mother. I learnt to love and feel the pain of others; I learnt to give sacrificially, I learnt the power of prayer and fasting, and I learnt to be strong in times of adversity. My strength, my courage and my determination though somewhat weakened from the struggles of life, are a result of my childhood environment. Nowhere else could have given me such rich heritage. I consider myself truly blessed to have had a brother so special and a mother so precious who, by their own example prepared me for the road I would walk alone.

FIVE

Long before I entered Miss Fanny's Basic School underneath the tamarind tree in her front yard, I knew my ABC's, most of my timetables, and I could count. The little school was spotlessly clean and Miss Fanny used two rows of bamboos as benches. I always remember her as the tall and slender fine teeth lady in "eyeglass" walking around with a little broom in her hand sweeping the dust away when the wind blew. I don't remember being there for long, and looking back, I wonder, what was the point of being sent to Basic school when so much tutoring was done at home. Whatever the chores were around the house, I was never far away with my little piece of chalk and slate to write on. Reading, arithmetic, spelling and penmanship was practiced in the home on a daily basis. In arithmetic I was challenged to do it mentally, which is coming up with the answer without working it out on pen and paper. Penmanship to me was like an artist at work. My fingers were guided to go up with a light stroke and down with a heavy one. Periodically, I would be sent for recess. Every moment with mother was an opportunity to learn something. The environment at home prepared us for that, that's why I have never been able to remember anything I learnt at Basic School; I had already been taught the basics at home.

My first three classes in Elementary School were called A, B, and C but they all seemed to join together and were taught by the same teacher, Miss Levitt, a Caucasian lady about 4½feet tall, who liked to wear a big broad belt. I skipped A and B classes and moved straight into C in a very short time. And the only thing I remembered about C class was a song Teacher taught us about a Pussycat which I was a bit uncomfortable with because I grew up in a culture that considered "pussycat" a bad word. So while Miss Levitt was straining her little voice at the top of the class to get the words of the song across to us, I was cautiously singing to avoid that bad word. But even with the most challenging group of kids that sounded more like bees in a closed drum, Miss Levitt remained cheerful, singing her way each day in our hearts and minds amidst steaming hot temperatures and a classroom without even a fan.

I loved my days in Elementary school. I was brilliant, and except for one occasion when the Principal told my form teacher to give first place to another student so that I could keep working harder, I was always first in my class. And I loved to play, couldn't wait for recess to play baseball.

Sister Love was still in Elementary School when I got there, may be not for long but I am sure she was, because I remember the time when school re-opened and we borrowed our shoes, wore it to school in the morning and then hid it under the Guinep tree when we went home for lunch, but Mother was always one step ahead; she knew we would hide them so the moment we got home she just smiled and asked us to bring them back before we had lunch. They were for church only. And I remember another time on our way home for lunch when we teased a lady that used to break stones by the wayside (Miss Mattie). We called her a nickname and we couldn't go back to school after lunch because she threatened us with a stone in one hand for our Mother and a hammer in the other for our Father. And I vividly remembered us coming home from end-of-term Prize Giving together with first prizes for our respective classes.

After Miss Levitt's, my next class was Miss Donmills 1st grade class, a teacher I remember who was cool with those who were bright but vicious with those who didn't learn fast enough for her. She would rather beat the child than spare the rod. God help those who weren't so smart. I never encountered another teacher who used the strap so much, and it always seemed geared towards the same students over and over again. The woman literally climbed on top of the desks in her calf-length flair skirt, crossing over each row from the front of the class as she headed to the back to rain down what seemed like her body weight into the strap on the backs of some wonderful boys who I thought were so afraid of her that they sat in the back. I often think of a young man in our class who had a very mean streak in him. I associated it with those unnecessary beatings and it seemed he never wanted to give her the pleasure of seeing him cry which seemed to have enraged her even more.

Another schoolmate I've never forgotten was a young man named Carol. He always had a big broad smile displaying those ivory teeth. A little shy, wasn't very brilliant, but he was a kind and gentle soul. Every Monday morning Carol wrapped a copper three pence (3¢) in a piece of brown paper and passed it to me via other students all the way from the back of the class to the front bench. For as long as I was in Elementary school, he was sure to channel that three pence brown coin to me every Monday and I never knew why until recently when I ran into him during a visit back home and decided to ask him. He shyly said, "It was love," with his usual broad smile. I guess he meant he loved me. It is sad that because he wasn't one of the brighter students he sat in the back. But it was almost understood that students who were a little slower in learning felt more comfortable away from the teacher. And it didn't seem to me they were well served either. They were victims of the teacher's leather strap; which was very sad for our young men of the future who got dressed up in their little khaki shirt and short pants only to be beaten up by their teacher. Carol might have been a slow learner, but he was a quiet, good mannered kid with a heart of gold, a contagious smile, and from a good decent family. With a little TLC from a supportive teacher, heaven knows what might have been. Sometimes all it takes to boost a child is a pat on the shoulders; it's like a bridge over troubled water.

Miss Donmills & all the Bullies, who think they have a right to throw their weight on the weak, should remember that children grow up, and children don't forget. Anyways, for the sake of those young men, I was delighted to learn recently that there is a hefty fine now for teachers using the strap.

For those of us who were fortunate enough to learn a little faster, our Elementary School days were one of fun and laughter, lots of baseball at lunch break, slip-in-the-middle on the way home from school and scooping up the first, second and third prizes at the end of term. Most of all, it was a place where bonds were formed that grew into lifetime friendships. The friendship between Jasmine and I is a testament to that fact, never one to spread my wings so we stuck together like peas in a pod. One shopkeeper, Miss Roberts, used to think we were sisters. The few friends I added later remain the same throughout the years and can still be counted between my fingers, but Jasmine was the one I aspired to be like. Her family had the luxury of living in a big concrete house with water in their yard so she never had to haul buckets of water on her head from a distance. I loved sleeping over at her house; we had a big bed for ourselves and she always gave me one of her "shortie pyjamas" to sleep in. In fact that's where I learnt that pyjamas were not for men only. Her dad lived in England but there was no time to feel poor around Jasmine, she was too likeable. We attended a Pentecostal church briefly but my memory is vague there, the most I remember of that church is Brother Phil on his knees saying "Thank You Jesus" over and over again as Mother Welgy, the Evangelist, tried to get my brother filled with the Holy Spirit. It didn't work, but he got what he went for, his wife.

Back in Elementary school when the yearly Spelling Bee Contest got introduced to our school, I was chosen to be the school's representative. Between home and school I was drilled for hours each day. I don't remember exactly how many schools competed but I was the 5th runner up. It was devastating. I knew Mrs. Hollinger would be very disappointed in me. My chaperone Teacher Miss Carnegie was proud of me but we both knew I would be in deep hot water when I got back to school. Nothing but the best was good enough for Lady Hollinger so I was really scared of going back to school after the contest, but since they didn't know the outcome yet, students and Teachers were on their feet when Miss Carnegie and I returned with my little prize in hand. As soon as the Headmistress learnt from her what my position was, she asked me to spell the word I failed on. When I did, she walked up to me with an expression of disgust on her face; looked me over from head to toe in my brand new fire red uniform, shoes, socks and all and said, "You dress too much." She was mad as hell. Failure was not an option for Mrs. Hollinger; moreover, it wasn't expected of me. Regardless of my 5th place position, the following day when the newspaper showed me among the finalists, the entire school hovered over the newspaper to get a glimpse of me and no one could rob me of the joy and pride I felt from seeing my name and photograph in the newspaper, not even Mrs. Hollinger. My mother was so proud she kept it under the mattress for decades until a hurricane destroyed it.

Mrs. Hollinger wasn't just the best Teacher ever, she really cared about her students and I always sensed that she had high expectations of me. When I failed, she failed too. It was an injury it seems that got to the very core of her soul because she gave her best to bring out the very best in me. My mother swept the school three mornings per week and many mornings when she returned home it was the generosity of Mrs. Hollinger that helped us to get a little breakfast to go to school if there weren't any fruits in season. Whether it was a little flour from the canteen or a little spare change, she always helped, and that's why when Jasmine and I skipped Sewing Class one Thursday afternoon because I found it boring, the Friday morning she made sure that as long as we were in school, we would never entertain that thought again. And we never did, because the wrath that came down from the strap in our palms that morning was a reminder that hell hath no fury like Teacher Hollinger when she gets mad.

There were other teachers who must be mentioned too: the unforgettable Miss Monsoon who was thorough and diligent. I don't think there was a student who didn't feel like Miss Monsoon was their second mother. No other teacher was as clear and articulate as her. She was the only one that rivalled Mrs. H. The gentle soft spoken Misses Longfrock and Pirate were like angels on my shoulders. And I enjoyed Miss Pirate's class a lot because she paid attention to penmanship, very much the same as my mother did. But it was my Godmother, the Pianist that caught my attention, always wanted to be close to her just to watch her fingers scrolled up and down the keyboard playing The Lord's My Shepherd at devotion every morning. I had my first and only piano lesson from her. Yet, it was Mrs. Hollinger, with those piercing eyes that had the power to pluck the best out of me. No other teacher I knew had the intensity to steer a child to see the potential that lies within, like Mrs. H. We were preparing for High School Common Entrance Examination when she walked into the classroom, row by row, bench by bench to see how we were doing, then she stood before me, eyes wide open and said, "Elisabeth Holyday, you must pass, I'm not begging you; you must pass, and remember 'I' before 'E' except after 'C,' you must pass." She actually made me believe I could do anything.

I remembered spending a summer with her and while we were standing by the veranda, she made a sobering remark that I have never forgotten as she watched the neighbour chopped a tree down at the front of the yard: *"The Time Will Come When One Will Need To Know Botany Before Taking The Life Of A Tree Because If He Knew The Value Of A Tree He Wouldn't Chop It Down."* I believe it was the summer of 1963, the year after Jamaica gained its Independence. These days when I listen to all the talks about the earth and saving the Planet, or preserving the Environment, I am reminded of Mrs. Hollinger's words nearly fifty years ago.

Anyone who has passed through Teacher Hollinger's hands and didn't grasp something for life wasn't paying attention. There was something about her that pen and paper cannot justify. One must have experienced it to appreciate it. And since I didn't stay long in High School, I have to give all the credit to my mother and my Elementary School teachers for their tutoring; it is through the training I got from them that I am able to pen my story and do my own editing, however, that was several years ago so it might not be flawless.

SIX

I almost scared the life out of Mrs. Hollinger when the results for the Common Entrance Examination for High School in the newspaper didn't show my name; then a couple days later we were notified by mail that I won half-scholarship. Only the names of students who won full scholarship appeared in the newspaper. When my mother took me to get the required Medical Certificate for school the doctor examined my teeth and recommended that a strong, healthy tooth be extracted simply because it looked slightly stained. In those days I never had the luxury of toothpaste and toothbrush, I used chew stick, so I had brilliant white teeth. It was sheer hell on the dentist getting that tooth out and contrary to what I thought then, forty-six years later, the tooth has not grown back.

When I was led to the examination room and instructed to change my clothes I didn't see the need for all that, if all I needed was a Medical Certificate for school, so I left both my undergarments on. When the doctor returned, he said, "Little girl, I asked you to take your clothes off" then he left again. When he came back, I was just the way he left me. "Little girl," he said, "The first thing you have to do when you go to school is to learn to obey." And having said that he walked away; frankly, I was just anxious to get to school to join Jasmine who won full scholarship and had left earlier to settle in since she was boarding on Campus. Thankfully, when I got dressed and walked out, my mother was patiently waiting on me with the certificate in her hand.

My first day in High school was the first time I wore shoes (and socks) to school, except for the time in Elementary school when my Sister and I hid our church shoes and wore it for half a day. My royal blue button front uniform donated by Teacher Hollinger was stiff and shine with every pleat in place; thanks to Sister Love, I wasn't good at ironing but she always made me look good. Brothers Edmund and Victor in England along with Sister Louise pooled together to pay my school fee.

When I got to school, I had a rousing reception from my friend Jasmine and some friends she met on campus in the dormitory. They were right there to meet me as I alighted from the coach. All the girls looked so very rich and strikingly beautiful of every race, it was almost intimidating. It was a new world for me. Some of them even had hair much longer than mine. From the reception I got, I could tell that Jasmine had announced my coming.

Looking at Jasmine and all those girls with such healthy looking glow, I thought to myself they must have been getting the best of the best to eat on campus. They seemed so mature and well spoken. There was nothing "country" about them so I even wondered if some were foreign students; on top of that Jasmine had the audacity to tell them that I would be boarding with her too at school and that both of us would have the same clothes, same shoes, same everything. Poor me; the one uniform on my back, wasn't even sure if my mother would have bus fare and lunch money for the next day, much more to even dream of boarding out at school. I almost felt foolish being around them. To have been from such humble beginnings and suddenly found myself among wealthy kids was so intimidating. I remember thinking that all of them boarding on campus were just a bunch of spoiled little brats who could just as easily get on a bus everyday like all the rest of us instead of looking like little school princesses. But at the time I think I was just jealous of them having more time with my best friend.

The school, I believe was run by the Quakers. It was breathtakingly beautiful and was perched on a hill overlooking the ocean across the street. A huge almond tree with the branches shaped like an umbrella made for a cozy bus shelter with the rich sound of rolling waves from the ocean.

There were several buildings on campus housing teachers; dormitories for male and female students and a multitude of classrooms. But the thing that impressed me most was the very large church on campus that could accommodate the entire school. Every morning before classes began we gathered for devotion. I loved it. After devotion one morning, I distinctly remember Mrs. Merchant addressing a group of us on the danger of wearing dry face powder. I wasn't sure if she was a teacher, acted as a Mediator between students and principal, or, if she was in charge of the Girls' Dormitory; but her face was extremely wrinkled and I don't think she was old but the wrinkles gave her a much older appearance, as a result I have never worn face powder, dry or wet.

Roughly 10 minutes walk away, was the school's Track and Field Grounds, the size of a huge golf course. It was common to find several classes conducting Physical Education there at the same time, and was known to have served as the hosting playground for numerous track and field sporting events for schools across the island. I loved my American Physical Education Teacher. She was the best at what she did. I can still hear her walking us through the movements; one, two, three and four and one, two, three and four. That's one teacher that I always remember with a smile. Track and Field was definitely not for me though, certainly not relay.

Except for Geometry and General Science which I had difficulty mastering, High School was fun. There was a sense of pride to be dressing up every day in uniform and shoes and socks going to High School, mixing with kids who I thought were of such wealthy background, that I almost felt like I was someone special to my little community. I didn't have an appreciation for Geography in school so I still don't know how to read a map but I found History very interesting, except the teacher moved too fast. I didn't feel like I had enough time to nail one period of events before he jumped to the next, but I found it interesting enough to still make me want to delve into it. And maybe that's why I love to read biographies. I loved Arithmetic, English, Spanish, and Drama. Mrs. Marlton was a delightful Spanish/Drama teacher, however, I disappointed her in my first semester when she cast me for a role in a play and I didn't show up. I simply could not afford to go; didn't have a proper dress. It was the first term and my mother had exhausted every resource to get me started. The play was cancelled and I don't think either Mrs. Marlton or the participating students ever forgave me.

Mrs Dickson, my American geometry teacher never looked happy. Maybe the heat was too much for her. From a distance, I could easily tell when she was approaching, the sound of that board slippers clapping on her heels was unmistakable and nothing she said or wrote on that blackboard made sense to me. It's like she was in a hurry to get it over with and moved on. She was never able to smile and always seemed mad with the world.

There was one teacher whose class I never wanted to miss even if it meant going to school without lunch or walking the 8 ½ miles; and that was Religious Knowledge with Reverend Black. He was also Pastor for the Baptist church in my community but I didn't attend his church because I found it lukewarm and boring. In class when he was teaching, that's where he really came alive and made a strong impression on me. He had my undivided attention from the moment he entered, to the end of the class. It wasn't a specific lesson that he taught that captured my imagination it was what he did at every single class that had a profound effect on me. He would be illustrating a story to us, and suddenly, in the midst of making a point, as if in a trance, he strolled a few steps from the class like his attention was drawn to something else, a force he couldn't resist. With his arms outstretched and his eyes lifted towards heaven he would say, "And I, if I be lifted up, will draw all men unto me . . . , and I, if I be lifted up, will draw all men unto me . . . , and I if I be lifted up, will draw all men unto me." At the time I had no idea he was quoting from the Scriptures. It was mesmerising. My eyes followed his every move as he strolled away from the class. I remembered feeling drawn to what he did, it's as though I was moving alongside him with outstretched arms too, pining to be lifted up.

There was something very divine about what he did and what he felt because I felt it too but I lacked the spiritual insight to put into words what

I felt, so my spirit wrestled with it and left me with a constant desire to be raised up for a higher purpose: what exactly, I didn't know at the time, but I felt it was something spiritual and I wanted it so I could draw all people to me. There were classmates who felt I was good at Mathematics, Spanish and Drama; some thought I'd become a Linguist, but it was Reverend Black's Religious Knowledge Classes that I always yearned for. It seemed my path had been chosen long before I recognized it.

One of the things that amazed me when I started High School was how some of the older people in my district were interested in knowing what I was studying. It was like facing a quiz every evening after school. I guess being the only little girl in the neighbourhood attending High School made them curious. When I mentioned that I was doing Spanish, some expected me to be able to speak to them fluently in Spanish, not just naming a few objects. I don't think they realized that learning was a process that didn't happen overnight, but their expectations of me was like a stamp of approval, that even though we were poor we had something that set us apart; thanks to my mother's commitment to our education long before we could even hold a piece of chalk and slate properly.

Before the semester was over, Jasmine landed a blow on me that changed my life forever, I believe. I am not one for many friends. The few I have, I hold on to for life like prized possessions and at the time she was all I had, and the person who I was aspiring to be like. When she disclosed to me that her father had filed for her and she would be leaving for England soon, my wings dropped. Already she was sent away to live on Campus, now he was about to divide us forever; leaving me abandoned. It all happened so fast, here today, gone tomorrow. It was difficult to deal with. She was my little role model. I wanted to be like her living in a big concrete house with water in my own yard, never having to go bare feet, never having to haul water in a bucket on my head from a distance. I thought for her to be enjoying all those privileges and to leave it all to go and live in England, it must be Paradise. Poverty began to breathe insecurity and lack of self confidence because she was the only friend that I had and she was all I was aspiring to be like.

For as long as I live, I will never forget the day she left. On the morning in question, I vividly remember her standing with me by the Post Office at the intersection where students from the area congregated to await the coach for school. Whether I didn't know how to deal with it, or it was just too painful for me, I don't know. But when the Coach arrived, I picked up my books and proceeded towards the Coach without saying goodbye to her. As I stepped away, in a very sombre tone she said, "Elisabeth, you mean you leaving and not telling me goodbye?" To this day, I don't recall what I did or said, but I distinctly remember getting on the Coach in a race for the back seat and from there I watched her standing by the Post Office alone, looking on, until the Coach rolled out of sight. I bawled all the way to school. That was not my best day in school. The wind beneath my wings had been taken away. With Sister Love being a couple years older and having friends of her own age, I felt lost. For a while I became uncharacteristically quiet, pretty much kept to myself, and I no longer felt a connection to Jas's friends on campus. It was just hi and bye.

I had Sister Love and my brother but with my sister being a little older she had her own friends, and they loved to meet and have what sounded like one story after another; plus Sister Love always like to get the latest news so any friend who could find the latest one to share with her was always welcome. Patricia and Gloria were never short on them. They made sure she was well supplied. At times I was jealous of them spending so much time with my sister especially when Jasmine left. Without television and radio, I guess them getting together created their own little soap opera, but it didn't prevent me from silently seething with rage to see them marching into my yard taking up so much time with my sister as if they were closer to her than me. I don't think I ever forgave them.

A couple months later I suffered another defeat when my Sister left to attend Tutorial College in the City. It was as though someone had whipped me with a broom and left me to sit in a corner by myself. For Jas to have left was bad, but to have the one sister I had known all my life, suddenly uprooted and sent off to College leaving my little brother and I with Mother, was devastating. So many evenings I anxiously waited for her to get home from Commercial School just so I could read to her and watch her transcribe it in Shorthand, or watch her hurrying home to get the 5pm news in Shorthand from Brother Phil's little Grundig Radio. At times she would bring home a taste of what she learnt to cook in Home Economics Class, all that was gone. On Sundays I used to stand beside her and watch her whenever she pressed my uniform and I use to love to sit before her on the floor and have the dandruff scratched from my scalp like she was doing it to last me a month, all that was gone too. There are some wounds that never get healed, and the worst are those that cannot be seen.

It was very easy for other classmates to sense that something was wrong. I didn't need to say a word because even my appearance changed. I wasn't good at ironing and no one gave me more pride in my uniform like Sister Love; the pleats stayed in place all week when she ironed.

It seemed that I was either very unlucky, attracted to bad luck, or it had a way of finding me. Just as I was trying to deal with the departure of Jasmine and Sister Love along came another dilemma. A bunch of sores broke out on my ankle and for almost a term I went to school with shoes and socks on one foot and sandals on the other. No matter what my mother used, the foot would not heal, which was very odd because my brother and I had what mother called fish flesh; which was a tendency to have a minor cut turned into big sore before it was healed; but she was always able to cure it with her remedy from the "Doctor Shop".

It was so humiliating to be wearing shoes and socks on one foot for so long and sandals on the other. And to make matters worse, a "so called hungry belly Rastafarian rat" had nothing better to do every evening than to await me and teased me all the way home. I despised him. And what hurts now, is that he is either dead, or he can't read, so he will never know the hell he put me through. That scavenger! Out of shame and frustration I walked down to my father's resting place one Sunday evening, brushed the leaves off his grave, stood on it and began to complain as though he was listening. The following week, all the sores dried up and I've not had another sore foot since.

There was another obstacle, the biggest one; and a constant battle: financial problems. It was a daily challenge. We were dirt poor. Our only resources came from Sister Louise in England who had nine children and two brothers who chipped in now and again. It always seemed like the day-to-day responsibility of running our home rested on Brother Phil who lived next door with his two sons. Of course Mother did a little baking as a supplement sometimes, but it was mostly when she got money from England. The proceeds from the Sunday morning door to door sale was barely enough to pay the Shopkeeper to allow credit for the next week, furthermore, we ate most of it and my Mamma always loved to give a little present whenever she baked. She delighted in that. The tougher times got, the more we borrowed, whether it was a spoon of sugar for a cup of tea, or, lunch money and bus fare for school. Sister Love hated it. It wasn't something Mother could get her to do so she always sent me, but even then Sister Love did not like it either. She always had a frown on her face especially when mother sent me to a certain gentleman, but mother was just doing her best to keep me in school.

Two classmates, Cynthia and Thelma, became my acquaintances after Jas left. I think my aptitude for Arithmetic, Drama and Spanish drew them to me. We all lived in separate neighbourhoods but we travelled to and from school together on the Coach. Cynthia would always find something to make me smile after Jas left because I talked about her so much, but all Thelma ever did was talked about her mother in England and how many parcels they got for the year. The little change purse she carried always, was like an advertisement to the school that she was rich and ready to spend. I never understood how they could afford to purchase lunch everyday instead of taking paper bag lunches and still be able to afford after school snack. Nevertheless, I looked forward to be the first in line to get on the Coach on Fridays, just so I could get to the back seat to sit and enjoy my jerk pork and hard dough bread.

I was barely making it to school, many times without lunch and a couple times without bus fare, but Brother Phil always had a water coconut ready when I got home. We could drink that and eat the meat inside the coconut which is very filling especially if a dash of sugar was added. My Mother was trying her very best with my Sister at college and me in High school. All the resources were stretched to the max. Every morning, I would go to Mass Joe, a good friend of my mother's about the same age. He was a very wise old man with an encyclopaedic knowledge of farmer's almanac. Mass Joe knew when it would rain, what month to plant whatever, and when the moon would full. I loved Mass Joe, he covered a lot of things we would need a radio announcer to tell us and we couldn't afford radio. *"Good morning Mass Joe, Mother said please if you can send a spoon of sugar."* Not once had Mass Joe turned me away empty handed. Even if he only had a tablespoon, he would send a half and leave a little knowing I'd be back the next morning for more. He was right. Next it was to the man my sister didn't like mother sending me to for bus fare or a ride to school. I was so used to him not answering me even though his car was in the garage, that at times I went and stood right by his bedroom window and shouted the message, *"Good morning Mr. Hannikim, my mother said please if you can lend her some change for my bus fare."* Practically every morning for as long as I was in High School, mother sent me to him for help but he never answered my calls. Sister Love hated it.

Two things mother could never get Sister Love to do, borrowing from people and crediting from Shopkeepers. She hated it. That sister was wise beyond her age. Each time she was around and heard mother sending me to borrow, she always frowned and said, "I don't know why Mother keep sending you to that man." On a couple of occasion when Mr. Hannikim would be passing by my school he'd send word to me the evening before, and on those occasion, I'd get a ride from him but that didn't mean I wouldn't return the following morning to get lunch money or bus fare if we didn't have it.

At times I didn't want to get up for school because I knew we had no money. I remember one morning when Mother woke me up, I said, "Mother, why you bother to wake me and we don't have any money?" It was my way of avoiding to bother that man who never once answered my calls for assistance. But my wonderful mother in a gentle way just said, "never mind, God will provide, try him again." She held a three-morning-a-week sweeping job at the Elementary School but it was short lived. I don't think she had the strength, and by the time she got paid it was barely enough to repay the Teachers.

Anything Brother Phil gave on Friday evening could easily be finished by Friday night. She did the best she could even if it meant sending me to borrow from the same people every morning. The people she chose to send me to borrow from were those she held in high regards. She stuck with those she knew and trusted even though it would prove later that one of those trust was misplaced. The same thing applied to Shopkeepers, even though her niece had a grocery store across the street, she insisted that I went to Mrs. Williams shop which was right across from her niece's because Mrs. Williams' mother had plenty children and she would understand. She was right. Not once did Mrs. Williams say no to mother, no matter how high her past due bill was; that's why it didn't surprise me many years later when Sister Ilene told me that only Mrs. Williams knew what they ate for dinner many evenings, and even years after she lived in America she was still sending her money from America to cover past due bills. My family was poor.

On a couple occasions when I never had bus fare for school, I pretended like I forgot it and went on the Coach but that could only be done a couple times before students realized what I was up to. Other times, I would wait at the intersection where Mr. Hannikim would travel if he was visiting his constituency and where I was sure my Geometry Teacher would pass by in her royal blue elephant looking Ford car. That car had to be about thirty years old at the time. No other car on the road sounded like it. Occasionally, Mr. Hannikim would pass by and I'd get a ride to school but I was never favoured with a ride to school from my Geometry Teacher. The woman never had a bone of compassion in her. It didn't matter how much or how many mornings I flagged her down, whenever she saw me, she quickly turned her head in the other direction. Her conscience must have been pricking at her one day in a class, she said. "Elisabeth, I can't give you a ride to school because other students will want the same too." My God Almighty! I was always alone at the intersection after the Coach passed by if I had no fare. I made it a point of standing there so I could be seen because she was one of the two people I knew who would have to pass by that way. I've never understood how on earth she had the nerve to pass me by. To this day, I still find her meanness to me very painful. I was just a little girl trying to hitch a ride to school. A little ride in her old ford hunch back motorcar that looked like an elephant on the street would not have scarred her one bit. There was no way under the sun that I could have had an understanding of, or, develop a likeness for Geometry after the way she treated me, too painful. Her lack of compassion blocked me from grasping anything she taught.

Brother Phil's friend Mass Lucas had a son-in-law living at home that worked at the same Sugar Estate where Brother Phil worked and at times when he got off work in the mornings, if he saw me walking, he would turn his Phillips Bicycle around and give me a ride to where I'd pick up the School Coach. It went on for a while because he liked me, and on a few occasion he gave me a red five shillings paper money. From there, one thing led to another.

There were those who felt Mother could do better but she gave away the little profit she got from the baking. I disagree. Totally! She did what she loved doing. She always had a present for someone. She thrived on that. She never had much, but whether it was the best fruit that was picked, or a bun with a little extra butter or little more trimmings, she was always giving from the little she had. I even remember being sent to haul water for Sister Ilene and a neighbour when they had their babies. Giving was a way of life for her. I don't even think she knew at the time that it's in giving, that we receive, but her investment has paid off big time. The mere fact we made it to a foreign country years later, with the opportunity to make it better for the next generation is living proof that from the little she gave sacrificially God used it to open the doors of heaven for us. That indeed is a blessing for which we can take no credit. Sister Louise's sacrificial giving to mother has blessed her beyond measure and mother's little giving opened up doors for us that we could never imagine.

When a letter came from my Sister's Guardian that she needed to see my mother, she took me along with her. I was excited at the opportunity to visit my sister and to know the big City. Our bus was scheduled to leave about 5 a.m., but without a clock or radio, we had to depend on the crowing of the Rooster at 3 a.m. It must have crowed at midnight because heaven knows we needed a mattress at the bus stop to complete our sleep. I was happy to see my sister but the first thing I noticed was how broad her waistline had gotten. It was easy for me to notice because I always wished I had a small waistline and broad hips like hers. They didn't let me hear their conversation but when we were about to leave I overheard my sister said to mother "I thought you were going to quarrel." It was at that point that I put two and two together. Sometime later after my sister returned home she spent practically a whole day walking around and crying. I followed my sister around crying with her all day too. I didn't know she was about to have a baby.

SEVEN

When a member from church told my mother she saw me getting a ride on a bicycle to the bus stop a couple mornings while in my school uniform, mother "put her foot down" firmly, but the Sister must have told mother months later because by the time she asked me, that was long over. I had cut him off abruptly and stopped taking the ride because a brother from out of town who came to live on Church premises with the Pastor had started coming to church, and from day one, we began "eyeing" each other. He was strikingly handsome, about 5 years older with sparkling white teeth and big bold eyes. Sparks flew from the first time we set eyes on each other but he was living on the church compound so we communicated with our eyes. I didn't quite understand why a young vibrant man of a different faith suddenly showed up living in the church yard with a bunch of older folks while his only job at the time was leading the Worship Service; teaching Sunday school and running a Basic School with a few toddlers whose parents couldn't even afford the 25¢ per week for tuition.

At times I would get to church early just to get a peep between the bamboos as he was walking up from his house into the church. Even though they were only a few steps, I always look forward to see him strolling in, always crisp and clean, with his bold black eyes complemented by what seemed like the same black and white pin striped shirt inside his tailor made gray suit. His black shoes glistened like a French diplomat I worked for years later in America.

Whenever I got to church after him, it was fun to watch him preaching, and then the moment I walked in and our eyes met, it was as though he lost his speech. When he became the Sunday School Teacher, every Test Paper he handed out, he was sure to pass a note to me underneath and I always had a long letter prepared way ahead ready to be turned in. He expected it so he knew how to carefully retrieve my papers. Anything to do with the Bible, I absorbed it like a sponge. I can still hear him telling me to put the answer in my own words. If I was asked to tell a story within a chapter or two, I would literally study and retain the chapters word for word like Fannie Crosby.

On one occasion when he went to Early Childhood Education Course, he asked me to fill in for him at the Basic School. I loved it. At Sunday school when the class became too much, he divided it and allowed me to do the younger ones while he did the older ones. I couldn't be happier. We were a team. We were in church together, the perfect place to form bonds for life. And in a mysterious way, it was there in his Sunday School Class where I learnt a Memory Verse that would prove to be a life saver a few years later: *"It is better for one to bear the yoke in his youthful days."*

Every Sunday after church there'd be a baseball game in the church yard until it was time for Sunday school. That was my favourite sport, folding my fist to punch the ball when it got to me and then running to the base. But it was music to my ears when the both of us were notified that dinner was served. I always wondered why they served us together in the Pastor's house where he stayed. Did they suspect something? Anyway, it was the closest we got to each other, having dinner together and playing with each other toes underneath the dining table.

When he began to meet me in the evenings when I got off the Coach from school, the eyes of the church, particularly the Pastor watched us like a hawk. He would meet me and we'd walk most of the way then he'd ride off on his bicycle as we were getting nearer to church. I guess for those who noticed that, their suspicions were fed, but it was all innocent because all we did was talk. We were going to be stars for the Lord. He would be Pastor and I would be the Pastor's wife playing the organ and be in charge of the Sunday school. He never gave me anything but that didn't matter to me, I just dreamed of the day when we'd be a family with our own church. Twenty four was my magic number, it was always my idea that by the time I turned 24, I would be married, have two children, a home and a career and be very active in the church while pursuing a profession in Gospel Singing. My mother adored him. I am not sure if she suspected something between us or what, but the best of everything she gave was sent or taken to him when she went to church. Whether it was the best fruit, or a freshly baked bun with extra trimmings or a little more butter; he got the best of the best.

He was brave enough one evening to walk me home. The moment we sat down, Pastor was right there to march him home. I don't think my mother was aware; she simply thought that her dear Pastor came to visit her, but up until his death, it was the only time he had ever been to our house and that was to march the young brother home. I don't know how he climbed the hill to get to our house with the huge stomach he had, and I never understood why he took such an interest in doing everything he could to keep us apart. He watched us like a hawk as though the brother was a prized possession. Interestingly, when another brother began dating a classmate from Sunday school he didn't bother them he simply married them off in a matter of weeks. The week following the wedding when the poor child returned to Sunday school she said, *"Elisabeth, I eat curry goat, I eat curry goat, I eat curry goat, I wish I could get married every week."* Poor child never had a clue of what marriage was all about all she could talk about was all the food that she got to eat. By divine intervention though, the marriage survived and the union produced a Minister of the Gospel who is still active in the Ministry. God always find a way to silence His critics by using simple things to confound them. Amazing!

Trouble was brewing in Paradise but I had no idea. My uniform began to feel a little tighter around the waist but I paid no attention. He never touched me; I had no reason to worry. That young man who used to give me the Five Shilling paper money sometimes and a ride to pick up the School Coach had molested me, but that was long ago so I saw no need to worry either, furthermore I didn't even know missing a period could mean pregnancy.

One Sunday morning before church I was out selling buns, so I stopped by the church yard to see if anyone needed to make a purchase. A church sister I was close to who stood up for my defence when members gossiped about us, called me inside her house. I climbed up the steps and over the baby rails running across the doorway anxious to hear what she had to say. She looked very puzzled, almost like she was questioning herself, and she kept staring at me. As soon as I got inside, she stuck a finger in the base of my neck as though she was taking my pulse and said, *"I dreamt a man last night, him must be your father, you look just like him; he said to ask you, when was the last time you menstruate?"* Up to now, I don't remember what my answer was, because at the time I don't think I understood what the implications were. If something was wrong with me I didn't know; I didn't recall missing a period, and even so, I didn't know that missing a period could mean being pregnant. I didn't say anything to my mother when I got home but I thought on what Sister Mac said to me a lot and I really began to notice that I didn't have a period anymore. As usual, my mother picked up on something but she thought it was a cold. Mother said cold can stop it. That was a relief. Later on, she said I probably I had worms so she gave me Worm Medicine and to use a pail when I wanted to go to the latrine so she could see if I passed any worms. I didn't. One day, she said to me, I have been spitting a lot. I had no idea what to make of that but she was a mother of thirteen (two died), she was way ahead in the game.

My mother took me to see that same doctor who I refused to strip for when I went to get that Medical Certificate for school. He confirmed that I was three months pregnant. All of hell broke loose and fell on my head! The five mile walk back home with my mother was the longest most shameful walk of my life. My mother in the one white dress that she wore to church every Sunday and for just about every other occasion almost looked like she was walking with a limp. It was my worst nightmare. Already we could hardly find what to eat. Whenever we were going to church, she always sent me to find a bottle to sell for a Penny so we could get an icy mint for half Penny to freshen our breath and the other half Penny for the collection plate; now this. I don't recall my mother saying two words on our way back home. I don't remember anything more about that day and there was no devotion the following morning that I can recall. I just remember waking up to the feeling of the big broad strap flogging me on both feet in bed, like the one Mrs. Hollinger used on Jas and I when we skipped sewing class. Yes I cried, but the tears were for my mother, not for me. I couldn't have been more embarrassed, and I vowed that day, no matter what, I was going to get back in school and I was going to make up for it so she could be proud of me.

Before long, students in school were becoming suspicious but I insisted on going to school. My belly was still tiny enough to fit into my buttoned front uniform so I continued school until the summer break. Incidentally, I finished out the semester the end of June and had the baby the first week in September. Amelia must have landed the news to Teacher Hollinger because she asked my mother if it was true. When I heard that Teacher knew about my pregnancy, I vowed to God that she would not see me for a long time. I didn't want to have the memory of that look lodged in my head.

Nothing was said to my friend at church, I was too frightened. I guess I thought it would all go away and he would never know. Even when he became suspicious, I still felt I could get away without saying anything to him for a little while longer, just so I could continue going to church. At Convention that year my dress was a bit tight because of my stomach and he must have been embarrassed because he turned his head and said, "Elisabeth, if you can't afford to go somewhere you shouldn't go." The truth is anything Church related consumed me; the drums electrified me, I have never had enough.

Whereas my School uniform helped to conceal my pregnancy, my dresses weren't very accommodating and rumours began to fly in church that I was pregnant with his child. Maybe I was in denial because I don't know how I continued going to Church and Sunday school despite rumours, but I did. Church was my life and my life was Church. *For as long as I live I will never forget that Sunday evening in class when he looked*

me coldly in my eyes and said, "what happen to you couldn't you wait on me?"
I was so ashamed. I remembered staring at him like a lost soul; so ashamed
I didn't have an answer. I was just as devastated and frightened as he was
but I guess he couldn't stand to look at me, so right after the question he
asked me to take my half of the class underneath a tree outside. The most
painful thing for me was the thought that he would dare to think that
I was cheating on him. I don't think I ever get over the thought of that.
But looking back now, I wondered how on earth I managed to continue
Sunday school classes, coming so close and looking in the face of the man
who was planning to be my future husband. It was cruel. I was so sorry for
both of us. I could no longer hold my head high when he entered church.
Our eyes were now avoiding each other while the rumours in the church
that it was his child intensified.

When the church was called upon to hold a Prayer Meeting at his
parents' house because stones were being thrown in the direction of the
house without any identifiable source; I remember thinking to myself that
God was showing his parents a sign for uprooting him from his church and
family; and shipping him off to live with a Pastor who was of a different
fate and the audacity to watch us like a hawk. I went to that meeting
with one intention, thinking in my childish mind that since everyone was
already running up their mouth that it was his child, his mother would
probably give the two of us a room for ourselves then I could just say it's his
child. I just could not see myself losing him. But I got the disappointment
of a lifetime when another woman showed up on the scene and they were
both given a room together. She was the mother of his child. It was my first
time learning of her, or a child. All I got was a kiss from him the following
morning. We never talked about it until many years later.

Even when my mother said the Church was planning to marry us, I
knew in my heart I could not lie about him and feel good about myself.
Many felt I was trying to protect him and even continued to feel so for many
years. I wish that were true, but it wasn't. To help ease my pain, I asked my
mother to write me the words of one of my favourite hymns, "Jesus Saviour
Pilot Me". She never did, my guess is that it became too much for her.

A couple months into my pregnancy my mother took me to see the doctor again. I was ashamed, but thankfully, there was a new doctor in town and everybody wanted to go to him after learning he was a native son who had studied in England and returned home to serve his people. The doctor was tall dark and strikingly handsome with bold piercing eyes that showed no emotion and serious as a Judge. Folks joked he was so expensive a simple "how do you do?" could cost a patient a fortune. He took one look at me with my little pumpkin shooting out, he didn't have to say a word, his eyes bore the question; "What the hell are you doing, shouldn't you be in school?" When he led me in the examination room, he did what seemed like a stool test but I wondered what that was all about. As far as I was concerned my mother could have done that at home, she always had a cure for everything. When hot water burned Sister Love, she didn't run with her to a doctor, she spread butter all over my sister and she was healed without the help of a doctor. When Faye pushed a grain of corn in her nostrils, she didn't run to the doctor with her, she simply got her martyr stick and grounded peppercorn with Faye standing over the martyr until she sneezed it out; plus, she was widely known for acting as a midwife for most of her grandchildren and several children in the neighbourhood, so I couldn't understand the need for going to see a doctor. But I think it was his eyes that scared the daylight out of me.

I don't remember if the doctor said anything to my mother but I left there feeling very ashamed. Here was a poor kid who was born in humble beginnings just like myself or worse, finished his schooling, went to Britain where he furthered his studies, became a doctor, returned home to his very own community to help his people and instead of me heading in the same direction, I was going to him with a pumpkin sticking out in a dress so tight around my stomach it should have been retired three months earlier. I was an embarrassment. At least that's how I felt. It was even worse when I think of how my mother must have been so ashamed to know her Church Sister had a little shop right below the doctor's office, exactly where we use to buy our icy mint sweetie to freshen our breath on our way to church. I am sure my mother felt very embarrassed.

Another very embarrassing moment came when a busy-body friend of my mother's heard I was "*in the family way*" and went out of her way to peep at me when I passed by: "eh, eh, but child you look like you *insprigment?*" It was the closest she could get to the word pregnant. Many years later when I shared the joke with Sister Louise in England, she told me the lady was illiterate, that mother use to do all her correspondences and they took turns delivering each other when they were having children. But my precious mother was so dignified, she never said I was pregnant; if any one enquired, she always said, "The devil got on my track." So typical of her, always shielding us, always making us look good no matter what the situation. Even when I had to go to sell the buns on Sundays, she knew how embarrassed I was so she took a piece of linen cloth and wrapped around my belly underneath my clothes in an effort to conceal the pregnancy.

Without the luxury of maternity clothes I wore my usual clothes, but as I grew bigger, I stopped going to Church and Sunday school. And I was ashamed to look in Hezekiah's eyes too. Surprisingly, he visited me regularly; at least three times a week and that fed everyone's suspicion even more. One evening, while we were sitting in the hall talking as we usually did; my mother left the outdoor kitchen and quietly crept under the cellar of the house to listen to us. She too must have had her suspicions. I made a sign to him by pointing my fingers down to the floor. He caught on and we stopped talking until she left. Looking back now, I'm sure that our silence fed her suspicion. And for a long time there were those in church who felt I tried to protect him because of the church, and I'm sure only the stark resemblance of the child to his biological father convinced them several years later. To have lied on him would have truly been a travesty of justice.

Being home was extremely boring. The only little pleasure we had as children growing up was church, Sunday school, and occasionally a game of baseball down at big yard on the weekend so when I became pregnant and all those things dropped, my little world got even smaller. I didn't want anyone to see me anyway so I used the time to challenge myself as though I was still in school by creating my own classes, even preparing exams for myself on everything except Geometry and General Science.

One evening I was sitting in the little booth across from the kitchen glued to the textbook trying to solve a mathematical problem. I noticed that my mother looked worried but I was afraid to ask because I always had a feeling she was worried about me. Eventually when I asked her, I learnt that she was in need of a pair of scissors and she didn't have the money to get one. Many times when mother needed something badly, by divine intervention a letter with money would arrive from England in the neck of time. The following day she paid up the Shopkeeper and eagerly left for the 7-mile round trip to the Community Haberdashery. I couldn't understand what the big deal was about getting a pair of scissors. I thought getting a pound of flour and ¼ pound of codfish, or a little rice and a string of fish so we could have our big dinner would be more important, but not this time. As usual, mother was always silent about her plans.

When she returned home, I was sitting in the bamboo booth with my textbooks doing Arithmetic. Like mother, I had an aptitude for figures. That very evening when she came back with the scissors, while she was in the kitchen preparing dinner, I noticed that she kept eyeing me. I was feeling a bit uncomfortable with what felt like sporadic abdominal cramps. Each time I twitched and grimaced, I would find mother's eyes glancing at me. I didn't think anything of the pain. As far as I was concerned, they were just abdominal cramps. Mother called to me, "Elisabeth, go and bathe". "I just bathe this morning ma'am," I replied. "Never mind, go and bathe again," she said. That's my mother: always one step ahead, she sensed something. I don't recall having dinner that evening. After my shower she insisted that I got into bed, but I was more interested in solving the arithmetic and fighting off the pain. Ironically, it was two days less than a year ago to the date that Sister Love gave birth to a glorious nephew, and just five days earlier Sister Lyn gave birth, but I had no idea what was going on or what was about to happen, not a clue. In the past when I asked Sister Lyn where babies came from she told me that the aeroplanes that passed by at 11am brought them. A couple years later when I met a female at an Institution with goggle like eyes I realized I was not the only one that was kept in the dark. The poor lady said she was told that babies came out of the mouth, so when she started feeling pain and she was alone she kept swinging her arms backwards while tilting forwards with her mouth wide open hoping to vomit out the baby, and so she ended up straining her eyes. My God, I have never seen another person with eyes like those in my life! I was glad I took the time to ask her rather than staring at her because I learnt something. Thank God for my mother.

Before I got into bed my dear mother handed me her one "special calling" nightgown that Sister Louise sent her from England and ask me to put it on. Luckily I didn't have to walk in it. While I was lying in bed my mother stood by the bedside and began to pray. And as she prayed, she anointed my stomach with olive oil. Her prayer was like a desperate cry for help. Afterwards, she clasped her hands around my right hand and told me to push when I felt the pain. In the meanwhile, my nephew went to call Nurse, the Community Midwife. God bless what sleep if any, Nurse got, because I can't recall a day when I was attending Elementary School that I didn't see nurse on her Philips bicycle decked out in full white from head to toe ringing her bicycle bell like an emergency vehicle. Any little sleep she got must have been daytime because for whatever the reason, most babies made their way out at nights. And what was even more interesting was how dramatically different the profession of Nurse and her husband were. While she was busy bringing the joyful sound of little angels into the world, her husband was busy building coffin to bury the dead.

By the time Nurse arrived, mother had already taken care of business. Baby was asleep. And I learnt why getting a pair of scissors was so important. My mother needed it to cut the navel string (umbilical cord). She stretched out her middle finger on her right hand, then using the thumb of the same hand, she swept the thumb up to touch the middle finger twice from where she originally placed the middle finger to establish the appropriate length at which I should make my knot and then cut, should I find myself in a situation where I needed to help myself or someone else. Without a knot before cutting she emphasized, it could be fatal. I always have a bottle of olive oil and a pair of scissors.

When it was time to register my son's birth, his father met me at the Post Office. I was so embarrassed when the Postal Clerk asked me my occupation. I had just turned 15, did not know what to say, so she wrote down home-duties. When the clerk turned the form around to us to get our signature, I signed first then to my surprise the father could neither spell nor sign his name. I was shocked. To have watched him attempt to spell his first name was pitiful. He kept repeating the first three letters like one who stuttered until the clerk got him to make an "x" and then signed for him. I knew his mother could not read but I had no idea he could not read either.

The next step after having the birth registered was to have the baby blessed at church, but I was ashamed to face the brethren especially Hezekiah, so Mother got him blessed for me. I don't know what mother was thinking, but she chose three Godparents from the church, a Godmother and two Godfathers: Hezekiah, the young Pastor who the church suspected was the father; the Pastor who watched us like a hawk; and a female choir director became his Godmother. The third Godfather was the pastor for another church. Excellent choices, Colin adores his Godparents. A few months later when she got home from Prayer Meeting, she landed me with the news I had long, long dreaded. The church she said had a Prayer Meeting for the brother. He was due to leave with a visiting pastor to one of the islands with destination USA in mind. My guess is they did it to silence the rumours in the church and the community. What surprised me though was how he visited almost every day throughout my pregnancy but never came to say goodbye. That was one blow I didn't expect, but bearing in mind all that was being said at church, he was probably afraid of coming by.

Many, many years later when my mother received a letter from him enquiring of my whereabouts, in a matter of weeks he visited me in Canada where I resided but trying to pick up the pieces after life's ups and downs had taken such a toll on the both of us didn't seem like the right thing and there were 9 children between the both of us. The same passion wasn't there and at the time I didn't feel like I qualified to be a Pastor's wife. From all that life had thrown at me, the sacredness of what was so pure, innocent and precious had been lost. I could not be the same, at least in my mind I didn't feel like I was the angelic little girl I used to be. This I do know, if I had to live my life all over again, I would pick up the pieces from those days in church before I got soiled; when I was wholesome, pure and clean.

At times when I look at Televangelist Couples, I can't help wondering what might have been. I feel like I have short changed myself and it really hurts. The Body of Christ has been robbed of what might have been one of the most dynamic duos in TV ministry which would have seen it roots in a little bamboo church in a remote, poverty stricken corner of the world. There are no words to describe that disappointment but I am thankful for my son. He's a part of God's plan for my life. I love him dearly. I hope that Hezekiah writes his memoir, I am sure he has a lot to say but knowing him it would have to be dug out from the cemetery. And I wouldn't be surprised if he crucifies me for penning my story or, doesn't speak to me anymore. All I can hope for is that he watched enough Oprah to learn that anything that happens to one happened to at least 10 more before.

EIGHT

Learning how to take care of my baby was embarrassing. But to have my mother who had been through so much, trying to teach me, her fourteen year old daughter, how to care of my baby was difficult for me. I couldn't even bathe him without him sliding out of my hands in the water. It was even more awkward to have my mother teaching me how to nurse the baby and how to take care of myself. I was so very sorry for all the shame I had brought, plus, I missed school, I missed church, I missed Sunday school, I missed Reverend Black's Religious Knowledge Classes, I missed everything.

By this time, mother was no longer cleaning the school so that was one less income. Brother Phil's little pay could hardly stretch to feed us. The baby needed food and clothes. His father never gave anything. I didn't think he had anything to give. He had not been actively working for a while and had just been sitting around like he was sick. I gathered he might have been depressed because I shunned him when Hezekiah came to live on church premises and nothing changed after I found out I was pregnant, except when I needed him to meet me at the Post Office to register the child. And after discovering that he could not read or write I did not expect anything much from him because I knew he would have a hard time getting a decent job. Sister Lyn's baby was just five days older, so it was rough on everyone financially, but since she always supplemented nursing with Lactogen Baby Food she got an extra one for my baby too. By genetics, my son was very skinny even as a baby, so when I noticed that

Sister Lyn gave her baby a spoon of dark liquid every morning, assuming that it was baby vitamin I asked my mother to get one for me when Sister Louise sent money from England to help him gain a little weight, not knowing, that it was a laxative until many years later. But the thing that concerns me still is that, even in his teens he suffered from a lot of broken acne like pimples all over his hands and feet and watching him scratch them as a baby was pitiful. It's like his body was being ravaged by plagues especially during mosquito season. I still wonder if the laxative I unwittingly administered to him everyday thinking it was a vitamin contributed to the sores on his body and was aggravated by mosquitoes. I just don't know. But if that's the case his body paid a hell of a price for being the product of a teenage mother.

After a few months at home I was becoming bored with the parenting business. I needed to go somewhere but I wasn't ready to face my church; too embarrassed so I decided to visit my teachers at my Elementary school, carefully avoiding Mrs. Hollinger. Miss Monsoon was excited to see him and being the mother like teacher she was, she had the most adorable little black and white outfit for him. It was a God-sent because for every occasion that I took him outside of the home he wore the same suit for about two years. And I successfully ended my visit without seeing Mrs. Hollinger. I knew the look I'd get from her would be worse than the one I got from Dr. Cunningham so I kept out of her way. I just didn't need to have that look planted in my memory; it would torture me.

About six months following the birth of my son, I returned to church. The hunger and the anxiety far outweighed any shame or guilt I had. Church was my life and I was literally perishing for it. It was the air that I breathe. Even if I could live without school, I couldn't survive without church. I soaked up everything in church like a sponge.

Being back in church meant I was on top of the world again; back in my element; church on Sundays, Prayer Meeting Wednesday Nights; and all day Healing Service on Mondays. Sister Love helped with babysitting when she could but she had a baby only a year earlier and Sister Lyn was busy with hers born just five days before Colin so for the most part Mother and I took turns. I stayed home when she needed to go, and vice versa. A bigger break came when Brandon, Brother Phil's son started helping out. He was always there when I needed him and I felt comfortable leaving Colin in his care. To this day there's an unbroken umbilical cord between those two cousins because of all the time they spent together just so I could get all the time I needed for church.

Once I started going back to church, I felt the urge to get back in my uniform and back in school. With the stigma of being a teenage mother, I couldn't be accepted back in the same High school so I applied to another geared toward Secondary school subjects which also included Secretarial subjects like Shorthand, Typing and Bookkeeping. My love for Shorthand was inspired by Sister Love and it has never left me. Having a desire to return to school was great, but I faced an uphill battle. The family had greatly increased now with no extra income. We all depended on the little Brother Phil made at the Sugar Estate and whatever Sister Louise sent Easter, summer, and Christmas. There were forms to be filled out with a Letter of Recommendation and School Fee attached. The Justice of the Peace filled out the necessary forms and dictated the Letter of Recommendation to me. In the body of the letter he said, "Said Elisabeth is fairly intelligent and always showed "*attendency*" towards her educational standard." For quite a while I retained those lines in my attempt to associate the power of big words with intelligence. It wasn't until a few years later that I realized it was "a tendency" and not "*attendency*."

Once all the documents were ready, I made up my mind to wear my old navy blue uniform from High School to my new school. I didn't expect to get school fee and money to buy uniform. Like my mother, I was prepared to receive a miracle but time was against me. Two weeks after classes began I was still waiting on the miracle when my Mother sent me to the Post Office with the usual instructions to open her letter and exchange the Sterling money. The evening in question, it was a letter from Brother Victor with £15. I gave mother £10 pounds and submitted £5 with my documents for school without saying a word to her. The Shopkeeper needed to be paid so we could continue to get credit and I was determined and eager to get out of the house and get back in school.

The baby was about nine months old when I returned to school wearing my old High School uniform instead of the required green skirt and white blouse. On the third day, I was reprimanded so I wore whatever I could find. Only after I started school did I tell my mother what I did. Of course, I expected a whipping like the one she gave me that Sunday morning, but this time I escaped it. I guessed it was because I was honest enough to explain to her instead of her finding out from Brother Victor; or maybe she realized it was a part of a desperate plan to get back in school.

I hadn't weaned my son when I returned to school so by the time I got home in the evenings, I felt as though I was carrying a basket of groceries in my bosom. Squeezing all the milk out of my breasts every evening was a painful task but I had to do that before nursing him. The scar of teenage pregnancy no longer determined who I was. I was on top of the world again back in my element, back in school and church and loving every minute of it. Some days were rough on me in school when he didn't sleep well the night before, but once I heard an older telling Sister Lyn that sometimes to get a few things done in the days she had to drunk the baby so that the baby could sleep. On a couple occasion I employed that method and it worked. By putting about ¼ teaspoon of rum in a tablespoon of water, the baby slept very well and I got my rest. I realize now that it was wrong to do that. I was feeding a baby with alcohol.

The second term things didn't look too good; too much struggle and half of the school fee was still outstanding from the previous semester. And it's even more frightening when you are trying to keep your head above the water and all that you can see around the neighbourhood is everyone having babies.

One night I was hauling water with my bare feet as usual when the same JP who gave me the Letter of Recommendation for school, spotted me and shouted, "Elisabeth, you're a big woman now, it's time you stop walking bare feet, the next time I go to Town I am going to buy you a crep." I was so embarrassed. Luckily it was night and no one was around. The next time I saw him I avoided him because I was ashamed of being seen still walking bare feet. He never did get me the crep for my feet as he had promised, but he introduced me to one of his employees at his office, Mr. Dawson . . . Occasionally, I would bump into Mr. Dawson and he was always curious to know if I was doing some studies. He impressed me as one who understood the importance of an education even though he may not have gotten very far himself. When I shared my dilemma with him that I had a baby, was back in school but couldn't make the second semester because there was money still owing from the first semester he promised to help. Within a few days I was back in school. Since my school was near his office, at times he gave me a ride home on his bike. Later it became more than just a kind friend, we got intimate. It was a secret I hid from my mother and the church but he was very keen about me getting my education so I felt I could get away with it without anyone knowing.

Since my life was revolved around church all day Sunday, Healing Service on Mondays and Wednesday night Prayer Meeting; school on Mondays felt like I was robbing myself of the thing I held dearest. The very way I rushed home from school on Mondays to reach Healing Service before it was ended, was the same way I hurried home on Wednesday evenings to feed the baby, get his laundry done, do my homework, then head out to Prayer Meeting. I always liked to be early to watch Mother Maggie set the table with a big white table cloth, freshly cut flowers, water and candles. I never wanted to miss that or her humming, *"I have a Friend a Precious Friend."*

On my way home from a Prayer Meeting one Wednesday right in front of that Doctor's office where mother took me earlier when I was pregnant, a car stopped beside us. I was in the company of about four to five senior members including the church's Mother, Mother Burkely. From what I can remember, the driver was one of a couple of people with a motorcar in the neighbourhood that was known to everyone. After all, he was the very person who signed my documents for me and gave me the Letter of Recommendation to return to school; the same person who a not so long ago introduced me to an employee in his office; the same person who gave me a ride occasionally when I was attending High school; the same person who my mother sent me to repeatedly to borrow money from for school; no stranger, well known to everyone, the most famous person in the community; the same one who recently promised to buy me a crep for my feet because he was tired of seeing me bare feet; the type mother regarded as "decent, intelligent, respectable people".

My mother wasn't at Prayer Meeting; she had stayed at home with my son so I could attend. None of the brethren I was travelling with that night were from my district. They would have to go a little out of their way to get me home which was never a problem. I guess Mother Burkely took everything into consideration when she gave the JP the okay to give me a ride home. A forty-five minute walk would now be a five minute ride and I would only need to walk about five to seven minutes from his house to mine. As I was getting in the car she said, "Tell Sister Chamberlin good night." "Yes ma'am," I said. And he drove off.

Within minutes after I got in the car, Mr. Hannikim made a right turn instead of a left. I said, "Mr Hannikim, where you going sir?" He said Alice (his wife) asked him to bring home some hog meat for the pigs so he was just going to pull a handful from the sidewalk. He drove for a couple of minutes then he made another sharp right turn. The car didn't feel like it was on asphalt. It felt like it was driven off the road through some shrubs and then stopped. It was pitch black. He got out and went around the back for what I thought was to get hog meat. A few minutes passed and then I felt a sudden grab of the car door. My arm was resting on the window. In quick succession after grabbing the door open, he grabbed on to my arm and began hauling me like a dog on a leash. I had no defence, no time to act or react. Fear gripped me. It was pitch black and I didn't know where I was. It was hell. I didn't scream out, I don't know why. I don't know what I thought. Maybe I was too frightened, I just don't know. I just remember the horror of being grabbed and drawn suddenly and trying to fight my way out of his grasp; but dear God in Heaven I was no match for that animal that walked and rocked from side to side. I tried so hard to fend him off but my little body didn't have the strength. My head felt like it was either close to the car or sliding back underneath the car, I don't know. I was pinned while I looked on in horror with no control over my lower body. As the beast ravaged me all I could do was, wiggle my head from to side and slapped my palms on the ground. It seemed the only thing I had control over were my eyes to see what he was doing to me. He must have had a back light or something in the car because even though it was pitch black, I could see what he was doing to me. It seemed the more I slapped my palms and tried to get some control of my lower half, the worse he got and the harder he pinned my feet. I never forget how I tried hard to shuffle my legs out of his grasp so his sperm wouldn't go directly in me but dear God Almighty I was pinned. I didn't have the strength. The man had no mercy. It was vicious. The pain was excruciating. When he had his orgasm, he deliberately rested himself in me for a while, and then he slightly pulled out what felt like a two litre bottle. Then still standing on his feet dipping slightly at his knees grasping both of my feet, he pointed his penis in me again, squeezed it with his fingers as though to make sure every last drop came out in me. I never forgot the sight of that. Never! Never! Never! And I'll never forget as long as I live. When he felt he had emptied the last drop in me, he pulled out, shook himself off and with a smirk on his face he said, "That's a boy!" and dropped my feet on the ground. That's what wakes me up at nights even now, more than forty years later. That's what makes the act unforgettable. That's what has imprisoned my mind all these years. The pain will go away, what he said and deliberately did to me will never! If I do not have a CD playing continuously at my bedside at nights you can rest assured that the rape will be the last thing on my mind at nights and the first thing when I am awake. It was as though the man was taking revenge, and no one in my family had ever hurt him or his family. The only thing we were guilty of was trying to get a little assistance from him with bus fare and lunch money so that I could go to school and not once had he ever answered my calls for help. There have been times when I wonder if he had surveyed the scene, realized my mother wasn't around that night and used the opportunity to make his move. I will never know. No one could touch him. He was a big shot.

If I had the slightest idea that the man was about to rape me, I could have gotten out of his car easily beforehand. The car had to go over a steep hill, which meant it would have to travel slower, possibly shifting gears, so I could have dashed out even if I suffered a broken leg. I would not have waited for him to get over the hill and made a turn, and even so when he made the turn, that thought never crossed my mind. I simply said, "Mr

Hannikim where you going sir?" and he said Alice asked him to get some pig feeding so he was going to get a couple handful. No reason to doubt him. On a few occasions I rode with him to school when he was visiting his Constituency and there was never a reason to remotely consider him hurting me; never. All those things made it so difficult to believe he was the same person. Imagine going through that horror and then having got to get up off the ground, pull up my underwear, and get back in the car with the beast in order to get home. It's hard to imagine anything worse than that. It was dark, no moonshine. I had no idea where I was.

Just as he was approaching his gate, he remarked that Miss Alice had given him a stout to drink earlier that evening, as though to absolve himself from his crime or to break the silence. God forbid! I got out from his car when he reached his gate without a word. Shocked, frightened, confused, discomfort; I scorned myself. I didn't tell my mother I was too ashamed and frightened, plus I was always protective of my mother too, not wanting her to suffer any more pain. The following morning before I left for school I remembered kneeling down on the ground with my head in the palms of my hand. As usual, mother was quick to notice everything. She sensed I wasn't well so she gave me an Indian root pill, one of her little home remedies. Whenever we were sick, it was a dose of castor oil, Indian root pill, baby herb, senna and salt or as in the case of the flu, juice extracted from a plant known as the tree of life mixed with honey and lime.

I never understood why I was so ashamed and I don't think I can explain how I really felt because I was too frightened and confused. The worst thing I could have done to myself was to attend school the following morning, but I desperately wanted to get away. Even the sight of my mother was frightening because I knew no matter what; I didn't want to put one more ounce of stress on her. But I think now that shame was killing me even more, which is not something I can explain. It was only a couple months earlier that he prepared a Letter of Recommendation for me so that I could return to school. In addition to his woman and children at home, he had a gorgeous girlfriend at least three years older attending the very school I was attending.

School was hell the day after. I felt as if I had committed a crime against his girlfriend. I was so scared to look at her in school. It was the worst thing I could have done to myself, returning to school the morning after. I remembered feeling very ashamed, anxious and defensive. It was as though the entire school knew I was raped and I was trying to prove them wrong. Did they notice how I walked, I wondered, was I smelling like him? It was hell. Looking back now, it wasn't school where I needed to be the morning after, I was frightened and ashamed and was just looking for a place to hide, to be alone, to get away out of my mother's sight; away from anyone close to me who may become suspicious and try to question me. If my mother had the slightest idea I was hurting, it would put stress on her. My mother had to be protected at all cost. She couldn't take any more. I had to get away; but it was only for a few hours.

The extreme I went to in order to protect my mother from further pain became my pain. From the day I heard her said that she felt like packing a little box and running away, I vowed to protect her at all cost. And remembering how she said that after the death of my father she heard what sounded like children playing and the voices of people talking only to realize she was sitting under a tree by herself; and to hear her in every prayer saying "Lord, every time I stretch my hand to pick a rose, thorns and thistles in the way" All those things left me feeling helpless and sad for my mother, the only thing I could do in my heart was to pledge to myself that she would never carry anymore.

I had to get away the morning after, I was so confused, but it was only for a few hours. It just didn't make sense that such a big man with a family living in the same community just minutes away from me who by his very position could get anyone he desired, would bother to destroy me; the little bare feet girl who he just promised weeks earlier to buy a crep for my feet because he was tired of seeing my ten toes on the ground. It just didn't make sense.

To see a family so devastatingly poor with a little girl potentially as their investment and to mentally destroy me the way he did that night wasn't just a blow to me but to my innocent mother who could hardly afford a second dress. It was not an accident or spur of the moment. It was a diabolical plot, premeditated and wilfully orchestrated, just waiting to be executed and he made his move on my way home from Prayer Meeting with church brethren when my mother was not around knowing full well that his employee, Mr. Dawson whom he had recently introduced me to, had just helped me back to school and was secretly involved with me. At times I even wonder if he had set me up with Dawson to rid me from bothering him; I just don't know. I just don't know.

We all grew up knowing about Psalm 91; of leaving the Bible open at Psalm 91 on the bed for protection so I have to admit I couldn't help questioning God, especially about the timing. "Raped after leaving a Prayer Meeting?" "Was He not supposed to have His angels all around me guiding me and protecting me in all my ways as He promised?" I'm still not sure I want to try to understand how God works where that is concerned; I might get confused and risk allowing my faith in Him to be shaken. To this day, I vividly recall Sister Love frowning at mother whenever she heard her sending me to borrow money from him and I used to think mother sent me because she knew my sister wouldn't go to get credit from the Shopkeepers or borrow money from people. My sister was older and wiser, she probably knew something of his character that I was too young to know and our mother was far too saintly to see evil in anyone. When I got older and realized the many children he had fathered with the various women, I wouldn't be surprised if my sister knew of someone whose life was ruined by the man but was helpless to do anything about. He was far too powerful. No one dared say anything.

For a little while I continued going to school but my mind was somewhere else. I couldn't focus, couldn't talk about it with anyone, too ashamed and frightened. My only prayer was that God would use His power to make sure I wasn't pregnant. That would be a nightmare. Falling asleep after the rape was almost impossible. It took a big effort. Most mornings, I got up more tired than when I went to bed! The weight tortured me. It was easier to stop going to school now than to be bothered with it. I was only making up numbers but I had to get away from my mother. The more I was around her, the more she was going to sense something and I couldn't talk about it. I had to protect her; or so I felt. The shame and the memory of what was done to me was enough to silence me for life, but I've always wanted to live for my mother. I don't think I worried so much about my son like I worried about my mother. She was older, very fragile and she liked to confide little things from her past with me so I always wanted to be there for her. But inside I was falling to pieces.

I wanted revenge desperately. The desire for revenge was empowering but at the same time it was like a painkiller. Instead of hauling water mainly in the early mornings as I had started doing after "the beast" embarrassed me about my bare feet, it was now mainly nights, depending on when water was available. I had no patience in leaving vengeance to God; I needed to get even instantly. It's like revenge would take all my pain away, that's how I felt. And the only thing I thought of at the time was to burn his house down flat while he slept so he could feel what I feel and roast. I lived for that moment. It was empowering.

Every attempt to flatten the dam house was blocked by his bunch of barking mongrels and I must have been so intent on flattening the house that it never occurred to me to poison them. And the more they stood in my way, the more determined I was, but the noise was too much. I was afraid of getting caught. Later I wondered why I didn't damage his car by just cutting up the wheels or do something. But at the time, that wasn't what I thought of. My sole determination was to flatten the house while he slept. Every trip to fetch water, I had my bottle torch ready to execute without the slightest thought about getting into trouble. All I hoped for was to find the dogs asleep so I could quickly set it on fire while he was asleep and leave the scene without anyone seeing me but it was not to be. I was desperate for something that would take away my pain, wipe away my shame, erase what I saw and blocked out what I was told and that's all I could think of doing. When I think of it even now, I wished to God he had stuffed my ears and covered my eyes so I wouldn't have to live with that memory. And on top of that he left me with a life sentence with no chance of parole. That's how I feel. But I am thankful now that God stepped in and blocked me from carrying out my plans, it would be far more devastating on me to live with the agony of his suffering and death.

I was too confused to remember if I had missed a period or not but within months I knew I was in trouble and I didn't know what to do. All along I kept hoping it wasn't for the beast, practically convincing myself that getting raped doesn't necessarily mean getting pregnant. I believed in my heart that I truly expected God to see the plight I was in and do something, make it the way I hoped it to be. Honest to God, I expected a divine intervention. After all I was returning home from Prayer Meeting. I had gone back to school, trying desperately to put the stigma of teenage pregnancy behind me. Mr Dawson was helping me and secretly dating me, but he was so obsessed with my education that he didn't want me to get pregnant. I just could not make sense of a person who would see me doing the best I could to keep my head above the water and then deliberately drowned me.

I made a decision to take matters into mine own hand. Older folks use to say if an expectant mother drank a certain mixture, the child could be aborted but I was afraid to try one of the ingredients so I excluded that one. The taste was awful; I couldn't finish all that I had mixed. For days I kept going to the latrine but the frightening part was, I was also doing a lot of vomiting and I began to wonder if I had hurt myself. I even became so weak and listless that at times I sat there for hours. My attempts failed and I was too scared and weak to try again because no matter what, I wanted to live for my mother.

I'm not God I had no way of knowing for sure if the child was for "the beast" or Mr. Dawson. I had doubts, but all I could do was hope and pray, except I couldn't pray. If I did, it was a silent one, no spoken words. After my home made abortion failed, I worked up the courage to tell Mr, Dawson that I was pregnant. He was leaning on his motor bike with a toothpick gliding between his teeth. He didn't disown it, but the comment he made just added more weight to the nightmare, "I feel like taking you away on my bike and kill you." His comments frightened me so much that I didn't say a word; I just stared at him like a lost sheep and stifled my feelings. I felt so lonely. I hardly saw him again till the child was born and he didn't know why. And he didn't learn that his boss raped me until nearly 40 years later when I decided to pen my story. And that was when I learnt why he had made that remark, very sad.

From conception to birth, it was nothing but hell in my soul. There were questions with no answers, no one to talk to and every attempt to flatten the house of the beast was hindered by his barking mongrels. When my mother asked me who was the father, I told her it was for an employee in the office of Mr. Hannikim. Since my mother saw him as "big shot," she didn't say anything. I had a feeling that the thought of a connection with the "intelligent, respectable member of the community" meant he was someone of "high class" That was the world my mother lived in, respectful of so called intelligent people with big jobs. Little did she know the turmoil I was in, wondering myself who was the father, the employer or the employee; sickening.

This time around mother didn't take me to the doctor neither did I go on my own. Frankly, I didn't care. It was hell all around me I had no peace in my soul, just a hunger for revenge. Revenge was my pain killer. And I didn't want the brethren at church to see me "in the family way" again so I stopped attending church. The second half of my school fee was not paid in full so I used the occasion to stay home; discouraged and feeling like a total failure. Living in a one bedroom house with my mother, expecting my second child was a far cry from the life I had dreamed of; the Champion of the family with a career in Gospel Singing and taking care of everyone in a big house.

NINE

Sister Lyn had now moved away to another community and Sister Love who by now had two children herself, was occupying the little flat vacated by Sister Lyn that was held by Brother Victor till he left for England. If mother buried her pain in a song, Brother Phil sure did show the weight of the stress. His eyes were always red like he needed to sleep and his feet wearily dragged his little body.

The more the family increased, the less likely it seemed that much was coming in from Overseas. Everything that came in went as fast as butter in the sun. Our Sister in England had a large family. Both brothers over there had families of their own too, so the little they could afford to send mother hardly gave her a good night's dinner because it was constantly being used to help cover the needs of the ever increasing family. We had lots of fruit trees and ground food but everything was seasonal and none of us had a paycheque at the time except Brother Phil. Later my sister picked up a job at a furniture store. I don't remember ever getting any money from Mr. Dawson because I was living at home with my mother and he had his family, but I remember him bringing me a nightgown and some baby clothes. My poor mother was so distressed with conditions around that one day I heard her said, "Louise sent for me in England and because of the two of you I didn't go because I know your father wouldn't like that, and I didn't want anyone taking advantage of the both of you and look at the thanks I get." "A Shopkeeper begged me for you; a Doctor begged me for you; a Teacher wanted you; your Godmother wanted you, and I held on to the both of you . . ." According to Sister Love, everybody wanted me because of my brown skin and my long hair apparently they had never seen anyone like that. I fought the tears and stood speechless, but it's a burden I have always carried. Maybe that's why protecting her from further pain and doing all I could for her was always paramount. But it sure gave the appearance that I didn't care about her and all I was doing was adding more stress on her. Seeing my mother hurt in that way was very, very difficult it made me want revenge on that beast even more. At the same time I wrestled within myself to understand how that could have happened to me on my way home from Prayer Meeting; almost like I was questioning God. I wasn't coming home from a party or club or some place I wasn't supposed to be so it didn't make sense and I don't think I have ever understood it.

The agony I bore from the time I found out I was pregnant up to the birth is not something that I can clearly put words to; all I know it was nine months of hell, turmoil, rage and anger. And the daily devotion mother conducted every morning and bedtime became moments for me to wander off in my private world of horror and shame. Even though I continued going to church on and off afterwards I was never the same. Something bigger than me was eating away at the very heart of my soul and I was way too ashamed to talk about it. But when I realized I was pregnant I stopped going to church. I bottled everything inside of me and kept a calm composure to remain a solid rock for my mother but that took a lot of strength. Underneath I was falling to pieces.

One Sunday evening while Convention was going on at church, Mother returned home much earlier than usual. I was playing baseball with other children in the neighbourhood. When I asked her why she was home so early she said she had a strange feeling that I would be having the baby that night. She was right. Hours after she returned, she led me through a successful delivery.

I don't remember whether the midwife was called, or if she got there or not, nothing. Delivery was quick, seemed the force from my anxiety gushed out the baby. I don't even remember the pain. Whereas a mother should be excited at the birth of a child, not so for me; I was scared as hell! The moment he came out my eyes were busy studying the features. The forehead was no mistake, but I wanted to believe my mind was playing tricks on me. But there was no doubt, the baby was the seed of the rapist; and just as he had exclaimed: "it's a boy." That was another blow. I remember staring at his forehead instantly when mother placed him on the bed beside me. The forehead could not be mistaken but I hoped in my heart that Mr. Dawson would not realize it so I could keep my shame under the rug. I even thought that the baby was far too young his features hadn't developed yet so I must be wrong. I held to that belief firmly; at least for a while; but I knew.

The rapist lived nearby and Dawson met with him at his house frequently so he must have gotten the news and came flying. I distinctly remembered him holding the baby's fingers and scrutinizing them over and over and kept saying, "these fingers are not mine, these fingers are not mine; all my children have a certain shaped fingers." I could feel my body shaking like a leaf but I didn't say a word, I was more concerned how the child would get a last name so I anxiously turned his attention towards the birth registration at the Post Office in my hope to snare him before the baby's features began to become more visible. There was no way under the sun that I could tell anyone I was raped I was too ashamed and scared. When the date was arranged, he decided he wanted to name the child but I had one name in mind so he gave two; and for whatever the reason which I can only guess; or, may be just my bad luck, one of the names he chose was his boss' name. I didn't say a word. Needless to say I felt raped again, "the beast" had exclaimed "it's a boy" and now by a twist of faith the child was getting one of his names, and there was nothing I could do.

Ironically, he was an adorable baby and it was always fun to watch Colin enjoy the company of his baby brother, hugging, kissing and playing nose to nose with him. At times he would sit down and demand that I put the baby on his lap. And when I fed the baby, he stood by to get his leftovers. Even when I bathe him he was there beside me. The pure innocence of a 2-year old baby who now saw himself as a bigger brother and the joy of seeing how he interacted with his little brother leaves a lasting memory; a very pleasant one.

In spite of all that fun and laughter and trying to act normal, I wondered what the hell would happen when the baby grew up and it became clear that something went wrong in the "father business." "How would I be able to distance myself from the memory?" Worst of all "would anyone believe me?" The shame and the thought that no-one would believe me was enough to silence me for life. In fact the experience in itself is a life sentence with no chance of a parole.

I didn't deserve what happened to me. I didn't. I was not a rude child. I got a chance to return to school and the very person that gave me such a wonderful Letter of Recommendation, turned around and knocked me down, my God! "Someone so close to the family, who knew the hardship we faced, went out of his way to make sure he hindered my progress for the rest of my life?" "He destroyed the little life that was counting on me to return to school, get an education and help him, he destroyed my mother, he destroyed me and on top of that he made sure that as long as I live I never forget it. "What a punishment!" "How can anyone fight that?" The look in my mother's eyes, the weight on her face, the experiences she shared with me, the thought of learning how brothers and sisters had to be sent to live with relatives. It's not being able to have a good night's dinner, my little brother sent away to live with extended family briefly and me in the house with two children before I was even old enough to take home a pay cheque.

I was a child who was very observant. I picked up on everything. I could read my mother like a book. And even though half of her communication was done with her eyes, she understood without my telling her that I wanted to know, so bit by bit, from time to time, she'd share what was on her mind. From what I have learnt through what she shared, and for what I have witnessed, one thing was absolutely clear; I would never ever add one more ounce of stress on her. But in the end, I inadvertently made things worse by my silence, shame, and my desire to protect her from anything that would cause her more pain. And that hurts. My best was not good enough.

One Sunday night, when the baby was about six months old, after mother left for Night Service and both babies were asleep, I got dressed and popped in church briefly. My guess is I was hungry for church and I wanted to show that my heart was still there. But I was ashamed so I didn't stay long, plus the babies were left unattended. I doubt my mother realized at the time that I was there, but she was still at church when I left.

On my way home I heard the sound of the drums playing some fiery revival choruses at another church. Even though I was anxious to get home, I could not resist stopping there too. It's not that I couldn't help it, I thrived on it. Whether it was a Gospel Song or a fiery Gospel Service, anything church was like a vacuum, it drew me to it and pulled me in. I could never resist the force of it. As I approached the door of the church, the Spiritual Leader moving under the anointing of the Holy Spirit moved towards me at the door with a spear pointed towards my chest. A member pulled him back and then the congregation formed a circle around me and began speaking in tongues. I had known the Leader from my eyes were at my knees. He was a deeply spiritual man. I heard him prophesied once that the fishermen wouldn't be returning home from sea, and they didn't; so I knew he was gifted. After they were all done speaking in tongues and the circle was broken, if there was anything more that went on or was said, I have no memory of it because I left in a hurry to get home to the babies. I don't recall having a conversation with mother about what transpired maybe I was asleep when she got home or I simply didn't see the need to mention anything. Ironically, I learnt many years later that within minutes after I left my mother at church that very night, Mother Burkely, spun her around and prophesied, *"sudden death, how prophetic that would prove a few hours later!"*

The following morning between 3 and 4 am was devotion as usual, Mother on her knees praying for the entire globe before venturing outside to start her day. By now, I was the only one left with mother in the house. Sister Love had taken over the little bamboo house vacated by Sister Lyn;

and my brother was spending time with a family member due to financial hardship. As she drew to a close and I felt her fingers on the bottom of my feet, I knelt beside her with the babies on the bed, and we sealed devotion with The Lord's Prayer.

It was unusual for mother not to have started the day hauling a few buckets of water from the pipe then gathering firewood to heat the oven or store under the house for rainy days. She had planned to do her Monday washing by the river, but I didn't know. After making a mug of peppermint tea for the both of us, she loaded a wash-pan of laundry on her head and left for the long walk to the riverside. I could only assume that she got tired of hauling water; but at the same time she always tried to help me because she said I had the boys young and putting extra strain on my back to lift the weight of the bucket to my head could affect my back later in life. She knew what she was saying.

Not long after mother left, while the babies were still asleep, I decided to haul 6 buckets of water to get a shower, shower the babies; do their laundry and to make sure the drum was filled with water so my mother wouldn't need to haul any for a day or two. In between trips I would check on my babies to make sure they were asleep. At one point between trips, I distinctly remember stopping to use the outdoor latrine. It was anything but a moment of relief. I felt a strange feeling as swarms of black bats began circling me, some almost flying in my face and I remembered having a very strange feeling like a weight coming down on me, almost like a heavy burden, like something was going to happen to me. I had never ever felt that way before, or since then.

When I made the next trip of water, my brother-in-law, Sister Lyn's husband, popped in as he usually does form time to time after a graveyard shift to see mother and Brother Phil before going home. He was like a son and a brother so even though he and Sister Lyn had moved away he visited regularly especially after the graveyard shift at the Sugar Estate. I clearly recall telling my brother-in-law that very morning that if he saw Mr. Dawson to tell him that I wanted to see him because I felt strange like something was going to happen to me. I remember, I remember, I remember without a shadow of doubt I remember. I will never ever forget that as long as I live.

Sometime later my brother-in-law denied being there much less me saying that to him, but I am one hundred percent sure that I asked him that very morning to tell Mr. Dawson because I knew that as comrades they frequently met at "the beast's" house. And just as I said that to him, Brother Phil turned to me in front of him and said, "And you know child, it's funny you would say such a thing, because Cousin Richard told me he dreamt your father last night and he gave him five shillings and told him to use it to help you." Anything about my father always left me with a smile so that's what I did. I laughed and told Brother Phil that my father was trying to help me even from the grave because he saw that I had the babies young and I didn't have any help. After that I went up the hill singing away joyfully. It was like getting a letter from my father. Always happy to hear anything I could about my father. When I returned with the last bucket of water to take my shower before the babies woke up, I went to check on them again before I took my shower. I never got to shower. The older baby 2½ years old was missing.

I didn't see my brother-in-law around, he must have left. I ran down to Brother Phil's house where he and his friend Mass Lucas were smoking tobacco in the kitchen. The baby wasn't there. I ran back up to the house thinking he might have curiously wandered off to the outdoor toilet house but he hadn't. I never thought of his father going to our house and taking him out of bed because to this day I have no recollection of him even as much as coming into our yard, much less entering our house while mother and I weren't around. I ran around to the nearest house and then finally I made my way down to "big yard" that's the yard where Cousin Richard lived; the same cousin that dreamt about my father giving him 5 shillings to help me the night before, the very home where my ancestors lived until they died.

As I got closer to Cousin Richard's house, I could see my son's back, with his feet swung around his father's neck at a distance walking away. I ran and caught up with him at the far end of the house near the kitchen.

Realizing I was calling out to him as I got closer, he turned around to face me then kept walking. I was mad with him for having gone into our house and taken him out of bed while he slept with his brother so early in the morning and I demanded that he gave him to me so I could feed and bathe him before the younger one awoke. He couldn't understand why he could not be allowed to keep him. I tried to grab the baby from him but I was no match for him. He held him high around his neck. He was around 6' 5" tall. We argued for a while and then I tried to grab him again. This time he hit me with either a piece of stick or a sugar cane. I looked around for something to hit back at him but it was just the grass all around. I grabbed at the baby's feet again and he swung the wood at me again. I ran down to the kitchen to find a piece of stick or kitchen broom, anything that could hit back at him but there was nothing.

Just as I was walking out of the kitchen, I saw a little kitchen knife about the length of a pen on the counter; big mistake. I'll regret it for life. I took up the knife and went back to face him in my attempt to get the baby and to use the knife as a defence, to scare him off should he swung at me again with the stick. Picking up the knife was a mistake I'll carry for the rest of my life. Every day I regret not having just left him with the baby, go back home, take my shower and maybe by then, he would bring him back. Apparently I was in such turmoil over the rape that I had no rational thinking. The last attempt to grab the baby from off his neck, he swung at me again with the stick and in return, I swung at him with the little kitchen knife. After that, I noticed that he took the baby from around his neck and began to put him down. I ran, thinking he was putting him down to tackle me. I knew at 5' 3" I was no match for his height so that's why I ran and hid behind a pile of bushes in the lower level below the lane. I stood there for a while but there was no sight of him coming after me, so I began tipping on my toes while looking around to see where he was lurking to hit the hell out of me. I cautiously moved towards where we were standing because I could see the baby wandering around aimlessly.

As I stooped down to pick up the baby, I saw Samuel lying on his back with his arms stretched out by the side of the house at the other end from where we were standing. I was frightened. I noticed a speck of blood like ink from the tip of a pen on his upper chest and his eyes were blinking. I looked at the knife in my hand and to my surprise there was blood on the tip. Whether in shock or fear I don't know, but at that point I threw the knife away and ran with the baby on my side to call Brother Phil.

Brother Phil and his friend Mass Lucas (Samuel's step-father) were still in the kitchen smoking their cigar. I hurried him to come with me to see what he could do for Samuel. When we got to him, his eyes were still blinking but he wouldn't move, he just laid there. Brother Phil frighteningly turned and looked at me, "Sister, what did you do?" I was numb, speechless, in shock, I don't know. I had no idea whatsoever that the knife had caught him until I saw the speck of blood on his shirt as he laid there, which in turn led me to look at the knife in my hand and then I saw the blood on the tip of it. I had no idea with me being so short and he being so much taller how and when the knife grazed him. I do recall swerving at him after he launched at me with the stick the last time; but I still to this day didn't realize that the knife caught him.

Whether from shock or not knowing what to do, neither of us touched him even though his eyes were still blinking. It was the last I saw of him. Inconceivable! I really thought that the ambulance would get him to the hospital and he would be okay but as I stood there speechlessly looking on, and the crowd began gathering around, I heard a female voice said, *"is air get into it, if them did cover him with a piece of cloth him wouldn't dead."* I don't remember what I thought or felt at that moment. I just stood there speechless almost like I was planted there. I don't remember who Brother Phil sent on the 3 mile journey to get the Police and the Ambulance. We never had phones back then and only that big shot man had a car. Typical of Brother Phil, he was concerned for our mother. He sent to get her from the riverside.

It seemed like the news began to spread at the speed of lightning because before long, a crowd began to gather. And I distinctly remember a lady looking nine months pregnant and carrying a baby on her side crying mercilessly for me. With every wail she made, she looked at me and called my name. I remembered staring blankly at her but I knew I was in shock, so even though I might have been staring at her I doubt I even realized it. And I don't know how I got back over to the grounds of Brother Phil's house but I got there, and I just stood there. Nothing else, I just stood there; without a word.

My cousin Rowena never left my side except when I sent her to collect my slippers. I was still walking bare feet even though I had two children and I was saving my only pair of slippers for when I could start going back to church. Standing there in the midst of what felt like a huge circle getting wider and wider with the baby on my side, something was bothering me. I desperately needed a shower. I could smell myself. The last bucket of water I carried, I was supposed to use it to take a shower but I panicked when I checked on my babies and found one missing. Even though I stood there for quite a while before the cops arrived, it never occurred to me to take a shower instead of just standing there. It's like I was glued to the spot, just looking on blankly. I never got the chance to shower. I have no memory of how or when Colin was taken from my side or if his 6 month old baby in bed was left unattended. I have no idea who went to get the Police. I only recall standing there in the middle of the circle with my cousin Rowena like a rock next to me.

TEN

The crowd that descended on the five acre property that Monday Morning gathered like bees on a honeycomb, and even though I was in the midst of it looking, none of the faces registered. It's like I was staring into space. The only faces I vividly remember were the brethren from church, my cousin beside me like a rock, my mother as she pierced through the crowd to get to me, and the unforgettable horror on Clare's face as she wailed with the baby on her side. The bawling from the church brethren was gut-wrenchingly riveting. Sometimes I wonder where Sister Love was, or if I had seen or even spoken to her, I just can't remember; but thank God I don't. I wouldn't want to live with the agony of that look on her face in my rear view mirror.

My mother arrived before the police. As she pierced her way through the crowd, it was obvious they were clearing a path for her. Our eyes kept looking at each other as she made her way up to me. She looked so weary as though she hadn't eaten since we shared that cup of mint tea and the one cracker earlier. Or maybe she was just barely making it to ask me what happened. I could only look; the crowd was hushed as she drew close to me. We stood face to face in the middle of the circle. The sight of us at such a poignant moment seemed to have left the crowd speechless; you could hear a pin if it dropped. Before I could finish my statement her arms swung backwards. She was about to hit the ground, but they caught her. It was unlike me who loved my mother maybe more than I loved myself not to extend my arms to catch her, but I couldn't. I could only look. She fainted before me and I was too helpless to help her. All I could do was say to them, "hold her for me." It was the last I saw of my mother that morning. I don't want to imagine the state of shock I faced, that would allow the person I loved so much, to faint before me and not reach out to help her. I don't want to think about it, not for a second.

There was no sound of a Land Rover rolling down the hill. Maybe the sound was drowned out by the crowd, but sometime after mother was taken away I distinctly remember a brown skin man in civilian clothes with a slight dip on one side walking up to me. He rested his arms on my shoulder and kept saying, "She's insane, she's insane." I don't remember whether or not he told me that I didn't have to say anything. And I'm sure it wouldn't have meant anything to me at the time. All I know is that the moment he approached me and rested his hand on my shoulder and said I was insane, I instinctively knew he was from the Criminal Investigation Department (CID), and relayed everything that happened to him right there. The only thing I wasn't forthright with was the knife. I told him I didn't know where it was. Up to that time I didn't think I would be taken away on the capital charge, I thought they would just see the whole thing as an accident. A passerby in the lane who recalled seeing me standing there which was about the time I ran thinking Samuel was coming after me when he lowered the baby to the ground from around his neck; led the Investigators to the area and they readily assumed that the knife was thrown somewhere there and they were right. And later, said passerby claimed to be a witness to the incident, the only so called witness for the crown, but he failed them.

I could smell myself. I wanted to shower so badly but Detective Montgomery said my dress would be needed for evidence so I'd have to wait until I got to the Police Station. If only I could get to shower, I felt so horrible. And I don't think I really believed that Samuel was dead, because I had absolutely no knowledge that the knife even caught him, much less to be told that he was dead. I really thought that once the Police arrived and he was taken to the hospital that he'd be okay. It wasn't until someone remarked that it was air that got into it, that if he was covered he wouldn't have died. And even then I didn't think I could fathom what I heard because it couldn't be. There was nothing to warrant what happened. It wasn't intended to be. It was senseless to believe what happened. My only intention was to ward him off with it in case he lounged at me again. Every day I regret picking up that knife. Another thing that was frightening that morning was a plain clothes officer who came along with some long silver looking poles. My eyes enquiringly followed his every move until he was out of my sight. I just didn't know what to make of those poles. I didn't believe he would hit me with them, but I felt uneasy because I just couldn't understand why he would even come with those things. I recently learnt that they were used as poles for his camera to take pictures of the position of the body. I am glad I didn't know that at the time. I didn't need to hear that.

When Detective Montgomery guided me to the Police Land Rover, I climbed on to the back, stood up, looked around on my church family swarmed around the jeep like they wanted to get on with me, and said to them, "Don't cry, pray for me." I honestly don't know where those words came from, much less the strength to utter them, but I had to say something. They were looking on like the disciples at the foot of the cross on Crucifixion Morning.

When I look back at everything that morning, I find it a little strange that after being away from church for so long and the very night I decided to go and take a peep a little bit, and even proceeding to stop at another one on my way home, that I'd face a murder charge the following morning. I often wonder if something triggered the memory of what happened to me that fateful Wednesday night after I left Prayer Meeting. I will never know. I'm neither God nor a Psychiatrist; nor was there one on my defence; nor did I say a word to my Lawyer that I was raped 16 months prior to being charged, or, that the baby is the product of a rape. Only God knows how that happened to me, but I think a monster went down that wasn't standing before me or I was insane as the officer declared; because even now, over 40 years later, I don't feel a burden for what I was charged for as I should. It's like I was told that I did something that I have no knowledge of. And the rape has left me so numb, it's as though no other pain gets so deep. I don't understand it, which makes it very, very hard to explain. And it frightens me, because one could easily get the impression that all I talk about is the rape with no remorse for a life that was snuffed out. Nothing could be further from the truth. Absolutely nothing! My husband will never hit me again, the Divorce Court settled that. The High Court settled the trial even though that will never bring my son's father back, but the shame and hurt from being dragged and treated like an animal and left stained for life never goes away. It is something that I must face every day. And that's what I mean when I said no other pain that I feel has robbed me of life more than the rape. All my troubles follow after that downfall and I live it every day. It never goes away. And by talking about it now I hope to have healing. I want to live now in freedom. I have never had that.

By the time I arrived at the Police Station, another large crowd congregated right in front of the station helplessly looking on in disbelief, some softly saying, "But is a little girl!" It was a small community station with a couple of holding cells separately at the back of the station. But they didn't lock me up; I stood beside Detective Montgomery at the Guard Room, and the crowd stayed all day looking on. I thought I'd be allowed to shower but apparently the conveniences weren't there and I'd have to wait till I got transferred later that evening. It was horrible. I desperately needed a shower. A little relief came when the said detective led me to the staff bathroom where I was able to lactate. I was a nursing mother; my baby was only six months old.

Another great soul I'll never forget when I got to the station was Inspector Palms. The moment I got to the station, like a scared father, he began to make plans for my accommodation. I could hear him on the phone in the office frantically talking to the station where I'd be transferred to . . . *"Get a mattress, get a mattress, we have a little girl coming down."* They were the kindest words of the day. I've never ever forgotten neither him nor those words of hope. And I always remember Detective Montgomery sending to get me patty and cream soda but I couldn't eat. I could do nothing except to gaze blankly on the crowd that gathered before the station. Maybe I was nervous because they were making arrangements to transfer me to another station and I was scared to leave them. And I couldn't show it for it was embedded in me to always remain strong for my mother, or maybe at the time too, I was insane as the cops had said, I don't know. I do know that I didn't want to leave the company of those two caring cops, Detective Montgomery and Inspector Palms, I was dead scared; so while Inspector was arranging for the next station to have a mattress ready for me I was a nervous wreck but I didn't show it and I didn't say a word.

I had some unexpected visitors that same day. First, was a group of girls from my High school, and among them was a face I recognized very well but I just couldn't remember her name. As they approached the counter I was leaning against with the Officer beside me, the student that I readily recognized stepped forward and said, *"Mi Granny said she want to hear directly from you what happened."* With the officer still standing next to me, I told her everything exactly as it happened. To this day, forty years later, she is the only person who has forthrightly asked me what happened, except for my mother at the scene that morning and my Lawyer. And incidentally, the grandmother she spoke of was Hezekiah's grandmother; the young Pastor in Church who everyone felt was my first child's father.

Before I was transferred I had another visitor; one I did not expect, "the beast" that raped me. There I was standing by the Guard Room with the Officer next to me, my eyes blankly fixed on the crowd; my thoughts a million miles away; the death of my child's father; my babies; my mother; badly needing a shower, and at that frightening stage of my life, the wretch with his eyes wide open coming to ask, "Elisabeth, how did you let this happen to you?" My God Almighty, I wondered if money and power had destroyed his ability to have any shame. I was so shocked at the nerve of him that I don't even have any memory of him walking up the steps to the Guard Room. I only remember easing away from the counter and turning my head slowly from left to right, and staring at him. As soon as I did that, he straightened up himself and turned his face away. I could spit on him! I knew he left at that point but I don't even have any memory of him walking down the steps to leave. It took many years to understand why God hadn't struck him with lightning right there at that very moment. But he had a better plan for him, one that would have him on his behind for years rolling from side to side without feet so he could think of what he did to me before cutting him off the face of the earth. The Crucified Son was right when He said: *"Whosoever shall offend one of these little ones who believe in me, it would have been better for him that a millstone (A BRICK) were hanged about his neck and he be thrown in the bottom of the ocean." (St. Matthew 18:6.*

Today when I see how offenders are privileged to have trained professionals working alongside the advocate to dig deep into one's emotional baggage, given the same help, one would have seen what had been destroying me and might have been able to pluck it out. Instead of the Investigating Officer saying I was insane a lot more would have been learnt and the real criminal would have been thrown behind bars. I bore my pain alone. Maybe I carried too much and I exploded. I guess I'll never know

As I stood by the station that day, interestingly enough something gripped my heart like only a mother could experience. The sight of an innocent little baby practically dragged from his mother's breast, cradled in Mr. Dawson's left arm as he gingerly tried to manoeuvre the motorbike with his right arm, leading the infant away from the home and the family he knew for the first six months of his life, inflicted a blow that not even time can heal. That was my baby, but I was powerless to do anything, other than to look. But to see Mr. Dawson stepping in and taking responsibility in a time of crisis even though he doubted the child was his, adds credit to the man and his character. That to me was the epitome of fatherhood at its very best. He earned my respect. I do not ever want to try to imagine the agony of big brother, 2 ½, when he woke up the following morning and realize that his brother and Mommy didn't come back and Daddy is gone. Too much. Too soon.

I stood by the Guard Room all day at front desk with an officer leaning against the counter beside me and Inspector Palm busy on the phone in the background making arrangement for my accommodation elsewhere. Later in the evening when I was transferred, I got the feeling I was sent there because of the conveniences, and maybe the nature of the offense necessitated my being at a more suitable location.

I don't know if I was scared or it's more like I didn't know what to expect. I do know that leaving the company of the officers that I had spent the earlier part of the day with was very unsettling. Even though the conveniences weren't there, they were very compassionate, and for that I wanted to be around them.

There were only two cells on my side of the facility separated by a bathroom between. It seemed they were used for females only but except for a very brief occupancy in the adjoining cell, I was there alone for the most part. My cell was big and spacious with a huge mattress but no bed linens. Maybe they thought I would use the linens to harm myself. The cell bars were kept locked, but the door was left unlocked. It was frightening, but I recognized that I was given preferential treatment and I appreciated it. I didn't worry about my clothes that hadn't come yet, I was just thankful to be able to have a shower.

The roughest times were the first few days and nights, horrible. I couldn't eat and I had difficulty falling asleep. In fact I was afraid to fall asleep, because as soon as I did, it was nothing but nightmare, nightmare; nightmare. I always dreamed of a body wrapped in white sheets lying on a piece of board across from me. Never saw a body, but just the way the sheet was wrapped around on the board next to me, it gave that appearance. I mean it would happen so fast after I fell asleep; it's like it was on standby just waiting to be a nuisance to me. It was punishing.

After that period passed and I managed to fall asleep, it was another issue, my babies and my mother. I was so used to having both babies in the middle of the bed beside me and my mother on the other side from them, that I couldn't imagine what it must be doing to my mother with just Colin 2½, alone beside her. That must have destroyed her. No wonder the two of them were like peas in a pod till her death. That's exactly where it began.

I don't recall crying, or worrying about my dilemma. I don't know why. And I never gave any thought about serving time in prison. I don't know how to explain it because I can't understand it myself. I felt like I was told that I was charged for something, that I have no knowledge of doing. But my son lost his father and I am deeply sorry. He needed his father. And there was nothing under the sun to warrant that. He wasn't a bad person, he didn't have a bad temper, we've never fought before, mot even argue. He just got defensive when I demanded the baby and we ended up in what was suppose to be nothing but a "grab and take" exchange and it turned deadly. I am truly sorry. But I have no knowledge of how and when the knife caught him, so it's hard to feel responsible for something that I have no knowledge of. If that's what insane is, then maybe I was, but I just don't know if I was or not. To me it was more like someone saying I did something that I have no knowledge of, and it would all clear up and go away once I explained what happened. It never crossed my mind that I'd be arrested.

While I was in custody I was very concerned about my family. I didn't worry so much about the baby that was taken away; at least he was gone to a more stable environment, but I wasn't sure my mother could withstand anymore. And I was concerned for 2½ year old Colin when he wakes up and finds that Mommy and "Chucky, Chucky" aren't around and his daddy is no more. Dear Lord, I wonder what he remembers about that day. Sometimes I wish I knew. I had no space to think of myself and what my outcome would be. It was too much to process.

A couple days later, I had my first visit from Sister Love. From my recollection, she was the only family member to have visited while I was in custody, a smart decision I thought because two people I didn't want to see behind bars were, my baby brother and my mother. I didn't want to see my mother faint again before my eyes and I couldn't help her, and I always told my little brother I was going to be the Champion of the family so I didn't want him to have a picture of me in his mind behind bars in custody. Thankfully, the cops only kept the grill locked and left my door unlocked for the whole time I was in custody.

When the young Asian Officer walked up the steps and announced I had a visitor, I quickly got to the door with my hands holding on to the grill as if to find the strength to boldly stand. It was Sister Love. Luckily her friend Patricia was with her because she did so much crying, she needed an arm around her. I don't recall us having a conversation. From the moment she looked up and saw me, her head went down. She stooped over and sobbed uncontrollably. Again all I could say to Patricia was, "hold her for me". To see my Sister cry like that was devastating. At home, when she had a toothache, I stayed awake all night and cried with her too, eager to share the pain just to make it lighter for her. We were always at each other's side, always there for each other in every situation even though we had separate friends. If she was sad, I was sad too. Even though I was the younger one, I always feel the need to shield her. Now for the first time, I could only watch helplessly. I couldn't allow her to tell mother she saw me crying, it would hammer away at whatever little strength she had left. And it was important to me that they saw me strong for their sakes even if it was just a show. But the sight of my sister slumped over sobbing uncontrollably, unable to climb three steps to the grill of the cell door so I could even touch her, much less talk to her, is a memory that could be resurrected even hearing her voice; and has left me with a feeling of deep compassion for her and a tendency to shield her so that I never see her reach that point again.

One Officer, Constable Binns, brought me snacks when he learnt I wasn't eating much, one brought me some well needed toiletries and another brought me a book. They all did what they could to keep me cheerful but it was a very difficult time for me. I couldn't sit still much more to relax to read a book, so it sat there on the mattress like a little company at nights. In the days I mostly stood by the grill at the door just to see the Officers go by. Their chit chat strengthened me and kept my thoughts from straying. Each one passing by would encourage me with the all too famous quote, "Don't worry man, you gawna get off."

I needed something more than that. Nothing I learnt from Reverend Black's RK class in High School was coming to mind; nothing from church; and nothing from Sunday school. I just could not think. Mother had sent me a Bible with Sister Love but all I needed to keep me was a song or a verse of Scripture that I could keep repeating to myself. That way, I wouldn't have to worry about making an effort to focus on reading. Even that was stressful. I would rather be standing by the grill looking out into the world or talking to someone.

A sign of deliverance came one night when I remembered the very first memory verse that Hezekiah taught me in Sunday school, *"It is better for a man to bear the yoke in his youthful days."* I didn't remember where in the Bible the text was taken from. All that came to mind were the words as in the case of some of the Prophets (eg. Nahum & Obadiah), not much is known of them, just their message so that we can focus on the message and not the Messenger. That was my turning point. It turned out to be the best thing I learnt in Sunday school and it came to my mind at the perfect time. That's why it's good to read the Word, because that's how God communicates with us; through His Written Word. Suddenly I began to fantasize years ahead. It was a big boost. That was written for me. I got so excited that I started to imagine how everything would all be behind me someday and I would still be young enough to raise my children and help my mother. And even though at the time I didn't know what yoke meant, I replaced it with my own dilemma. And with that, came the urge to start reading the Bible at once. Suddenly the Bible my mother sent me became the best thing I ever received in custody. For days I searched through the Psalms eager to find a few that would address my situation, something I could hold on to and say repeatedly. Any form of prolonged reading would leave me thinking and wandering off into space. I had to avoid that. I needed to find Psalms that could help me in my situation, but also ones that I could memorize quickly and recite in my mind continuously whether I was eating, drinking or talking, and on those sleepless nights when I lay alone in the dark.

There were no outside breaks but with the privilege of an unlocked door, there was lots of fresh air. My connection to the outside world became the cops who I saw on a daily basis when they passed by to check the male prisoners on the far side or when they went about their daily routines; so it was very important that I had something engraved in my memory so that even when I was standing by the grill looking outside I could still be reciting over and over to prevent me from wandering off. I combed through the Psalms on a daily basis looking for more power and strength to add to my memory verse from Sunday school. Eventually I found myself returning to two Psalms: Psalm 46 and Psalm 51. The first seven verses of Psalm 46 blew my mind; I couldn't believe it. It felt like

I was drowning and someone threw out a life jacket to me. The Psalms reminded me that: *"God is my refuge and my strength and that He is present with me in my trouble, so even if the earth and the mountains around me got thrown into the sea; He is in the midst to help me, all I needed to do was to be still and know that He is God."* It was clear that God was on a rescue mission for me. Psalm 51 became my cleansing Psalm with a promise to blot out my transgression, wash me with hyssop and deliver me from "blood guiltiness" while Psalm 46 was a promise from God to deliver me no matter how grave the situation seemed. Within a couple of days I memorized both of them and was able to put the Bible to rest. Truthfully, during the whole ordeal I don't recall reading anything more in the Bible since I memorized those two Psalms, except for when I was out on bail and Mother and I would have the occasional devotion.

From the day I memorized those two Psalms; to the end of the trial and through the appeal, I never stopped reciting them. Forty years later, I still do, even though it might not always be on a daily basis, but often enough so I never forget them. I am convinced those Psalms delivered me out of trouble. And in addition to them, I had a few lines of prayer, *"Lord, if you deliver me, I will serve you; I promise you."* That was always my prayer, nothing else. No "Our Father" or "The Lord is My Shepherd", nothing; just the two Psalms, my little prayer, and my Sunday school memory verse, *"It's better for a man to bear the yoke in his youthful days."* They occupied my thoughts so much that at times when I pause to speak to someone or stop to eat it felt like I was getting in my own way; even when a female was brought next door for the weekend for some misdemeanour I was very upset. She was so loud and vulgar that she interrupted my ritual. It was "good riddance" when she left.

The food was good, three hefty meals a day but I worried about what my mother and my son were eating. And I couldn't understand why inmates were not allowed utensils, it made no sense. "'What could I do with it except use it to eat with?" Anyways, one of the cooks managed to sneak in a little plastic fork for me. It stayed with me throughout my residency in custody. I never thought that a little plastic fork could be so indispensable. That's why years later when a UPS store clerk in America told me that her Mom died, but what was upsetting, was when she went to clear out her storage and found that her mother had paid the storage company thousands of dollars for years just for storing nothing but a pile of extra plastic containers, I could empathize with her but I couldn't comment; I remembered the importance of my little plastic fork in custody.

ELEVEN

At my very first Court appearance I was accompanied by one of my very favourite officers, the very one, who was the first to arrive at the scene. I was so happy to see him. He came to get me from the station that I was transferred to and we rode together to Court. He was like my Guidance Counsellor. Before we arrived at Court, I asked him if he thought I would get bail, he suggested I asked the Judge to grant me bail. In retrospect, he probably was just boosting my spirit when he encouraged me to apply for bail, because there's no way I could be facing the capital charge and stand before a Judge unrepresented and be successful in acquiring my own bail. Anyways, it was my first experience in learning how to address the Judge, "Your Honour."

After the charges against me were read by the Judge and I was asked how I plead, I said, "not guilty" as the Officer had explained to me; then in my childish voice following the "not guilty" plea, I said, "Your Honour, can I please get bail?" He sharply replied, "Application not considered." His answer was so sharp I felt ashamed for asking him. I had naively associated his gorgeous black and white priestly attire with compassion and warmth, that he wouldn't have a mean streak in him so his reply really injured me. I just didn't get it. I thought, why on earth would any reasonable thinking person want to keep a little girl with a 6 month old infant and a toddler locked up behind bars? If he had given me an explanation, it might have been easier for me to take, but to have fired back at me like that I felt ashamed. I kept a brave face because I couldn't let my mother get a glimpse from anyone in Court that I appeared weak, but I was shattered. And it was at that moment that I got a glimpse of what I was faced with. Apparently someone in the Court didn't hear what I said to the Judge because Sister Love used to tease me that she heard that I asked the Judge for a snow-cone.

Except for my first Court appearance, all trips to and from the Courts were carried out by Corporal Viscount, the singing Cop. I always look forward to my Court appearances. I saw it as a time to dress up and go for a ride in a motorcar even though it was just to go before the Judge. I realize now, how irresponsible it was to have felt that way given the seriousness of the offence, but at the time I was only thinking of being able to "dress up" and get out of my cell for a ride.

Corporal Viscount never wore his uniform but he was always neatly dressed and he loved to wear sandals. His feet always looked like he just had a pedicure. Even from the confines of my cell whether I saw him or not, it was easy to tell when he was around by the sound of the sandals flopping on his heels. The little open side two-seater green mini wagon he used to transport me to court was so tiny and so low, that every corner he took I could almost touched the ground, but I didn't think he realized because he was always humming all the way to Court to keep me cheerful, and he seemed so professional that I didn't get cozy enough to ask him.

It was either the second or third Court appearance that I was assigned a Court Appointed Legal Aid Attorney. And I don't remember if that so-called bucket nose witness for the crown went on the stand, but I remembered seeing Brother Phil on the stand at some point in his khaki shirt and pants with his "felt hat" in his hand glancing over at me pitifully. I guess to show respect for the Court, he took his hat off. His eyes were so red and he looked so much thinner, I was sure he'd been sitting up at nights with Mother. Apparently because I had gone to call him, he was considered the closest person to being a witness but it was his only appearance seeing he was my family. I am sure my brother was counting on being on my defence team.

If appearance meant anything at all to the Courts, there was no way under the sun that the Court Appointed Legal Aid Lawyer they assigned me stood a chance of successfully defending me before that well groomed priestly looking Resident Magistrate. The man appeared lackadaisical and unprofessional. His taupe coloured suit was so soft that the pants couldn't even hold the seam. When I looked at the Judge so handsome in his priestly black and white attire and then to see what the Court gave me, I didn't think any Judge would even bother to hear his application for bail much less to consider it so it didn't surprise me when Your Honour denied his application for bail. The man didn't fit. Even if all we had was one dress, we always had it looking its best. My mother's only white dress for Church; Prayer Meetings; Funeral; Concerts; Crusades; Convention and wherever else, was always clean with every pleat in place. I returned to custody without bail feeling like a convict. All I had going for me up to that point was the support of my mother and the church with Prayer and Fasting, the Cops who were rooting for me from day one, and the two Psalms with my Sunday School Memory Verse and my little prayer.

I have no memory of where and when I first met my Queen's Counsel Barrister-At-Law whether it was in Court at bail hearing or in custody; no memory of the bail hearing; no memory of being jubilantly lifted out of Court when bail was granted; no memory of how long I was incarcerated for; but if I were to guess I'd say about 2 months. I am sure I had more than enough on my mind and the shock of everything knocked me out, especially after it seemed like I would have to settle for a Court Appointed Legal Aid Lawyer. That blew my mind. But I vividly remembered being in the Recreation Booth at the Police Station with my Lawyer and the family friend who had retained him, and a few cops. And I remembered that we were there because my Lawyer had just gotten bail for me and he wanted to "have a drink" as he called it, with the staff for their hospitality towards me. I guess too that he was so excited to have his application for bail granted on his first appearance that what followed I presume, was a marketing strategy for future referrals.

I distinctly remember rushing off to see my baby afterwards. The memory of him cradled in Mr. Dawson's arm as he gingerly rode by the station was tough to deal with when I was incarcerated, and I knew it destroyed my mother, so I was anxious to see him. When I got to their home, he was resting comfortable in his little makeshift outdoor bed between the kitchen and the house while his step-mother was in the kitchen which was a good sign. She had him in her sight. But I remembered getting a bottle of feeding from her to feed him and the darn bottle was so hot I kept moving it from hand to hand. When I poured it out to cool it, steam came out of it. My baby couldn't have been more than 8 to 9 months old. When I commented how hot it was, she remarked, "that's how Sonny's children are, they like hot food." It would be 15 years before I'd see him again. That will haunt me for the rest of my life because as a mother I can't help wondering what else happened to a defenceless little baby, but I couldn't help myself at the time and my mother was in no position to cope with anymore. However, to be fair, those two people did for me what I couldn't do for myself for 15 years and they deserve my gratitude. And furthermore, they are his parents; they are the ones who raised him from he was 6 months. He carries Mr. Dawson's name and rightfully so. That "garbage bag" that hauled me like a dog on a leash in the woods and forcefully stuffed itself in me has no right to fatherhood. He is a criminal even in his grave.

Initially, there was not much time for my older son when I got home. I needed to be at the scene of the incident with my Lawyer. It was very punishing to be re-living in detail everything that happened that fateful morning, especially with my mother right there with us wearily looking on. As he strolled across the area, up, down, and around making notes, taking measurements, instinctively I knew he had begun to prepare his case and he was in a battle to save my life. I was dead scared but I couldn't show it, always had to be strong for my mother. It was even scarier knowing that the victim's family just lived a few doors away and they might want retaliation. That was nerve wracking. As I watched my Lawyer scoured the area for every little detail in preparation for his case, it was only there, at the scene, that I began to get the true sense of the immensity of what I was facing. I don't think it was real to me before. But to have just been released on bail, and then faced with all that on the very same day, overshadowed my release. He wasted no time chipping away at the Crown's so-called witness as he combed through the scene making notes. Referring to the witness, he said, ""*That mother . . . er, the amount of conviction he has for rape is longer than my arm, wait till I catch him in Court, I'll rip his little . . . to pieces.*" Pointing to an area of the scene he said, "Anyone who can tell me they saw what happened from there must have been looking down from heaven." The man was like lightning and thunder, but I soon realized that like an Actor, it was definitely his Court Room personality: to conquer and destroy. It was clear that I had a thorough methodical and aggressive fighter; never doubted his ability; my biggest concern was how he would be paid.

When he was done at the scene, he turned to me and said, "Little girl, you need to tell me the truth. If you lie to me, you jeopardize your own life. Tell me the truth and I'll fix it for you." I heard him, but I had something far more pressing on my mind that I needed to ask about ever since the incident. *"Can I still be a Christian?" I asked him.* I had waited so long to ask someone, that I really couldn't answer him until he first answered my question; it had been chewing away at my soul ever since I was charged. Even to get the question out was a relief, though I was terrified of what the answer might be. I don't think it occurred to me that he was a Lawyer, not a Pastor. He turned with his eyes fixed on me and said, "One of the biggest Ministers in the United Kingdom was once charged for murder." There was a long pause; a silent one. It seemed I had carried the weight for so long that it took me a while for his reply to sink in. I didn't comment. But given the situation at the time, I am sure there was a feeling of relief; I just didn't know how to show it. I even wondered how he knew that because some of his choice of words earlier didn't sound like he was religious, so, I quickly associated his Queen's Counsel (Q.C.) title with one who had studied in the UK and had some knowledge thereof.

The fear of getting hurt while I was home on bail was very real; in a way I missed the security I had from the custodial staff. I was even afraid of going to fetch water. My cousin Rowena really scared me one day when she saw one of Samuel's brother coming, "Look who is coming, look!" The kerosene pan with the water almost fell off my head. My neck hurt me for days. It seemed I had pulled a muscle making such a sharp turn. He was close to me, and I was too terrified to even say Lord have mercy! Luckily, he passed by without a word and we have not seen each other since. Months later I was not so lucky when I came upon a younger brother, luckily Sister Love was with me, he was cordial with her, but from the look he gave me, I knew that I had to watch my step.

It was understood when bail was granted that the trial would proceed at Circuit Court (High Court). I was home, but I was fretting. At the crime scene, I overheard my Lawyer telling my mother £600 for the bail hearing, not to mention the cost of going to High Court for trial. I didn't recall ever seeing any £20 or £50 notes from England. It was usually £5 or £10. "Where on earth were we going to find £600 to pay a lawyer?" "Was he asking us to sell the four leaking sheets of zinc on the roof?" The few buyers that came along sometimes to get a few limes hardly got three dozens. The few coconuts we gathered for cooking oil was just for a few nights dinner. The bunch of green bananas we got every now and again was just enough to cook for a couple of night's dinner. The nesberry fruit tree would never be able to produce £600 worth of fruit. The little pimento we sold in the summer was just to help us get by; coming home on bail to face the depth of the financial strain that was placed on my family when we could barely find food to eat made me want to curl up in a corner and hide.

Aside from going to fetch water; the Grocery Shop; and meeting with the lawyer, I don't remember what else I did or what was discussed, my mind was in turmoil. In fact, I don't even recall saying much and no one asked or talked to me about anything pertaining to the incident. I don't think my family wanted to stress me anymore and for all they were going through themselves, maybe they just didn't know what to say. Everyone was going through hell. At times my mother and I would sit under the nesberry tree for hours without a word; just sit there like a mother hen protecting her chickens. Not only was the rape destroying me, now I was on a murder charge and we didn't even have what to eat much less to find money to pay lawyer.

On one occasion while Mother and I were lounging under the tree we got an unexpected visitor; the man that raped me. Something must have been bothering him; but how could that be, he had no conscience. "Imagine the man raped me and had the gall to come to the station the day I was charged to ask me what happened; now I am home on bail curled up under the tree, my mother and I sitting there, didn't even know what to say to each other and he's coming to visit my mother like I am supposed to think that he cares?" Well small correction, he didn't come to visit my mother, he came with a suggestion. In my state of mind I don't know or remember what I thought at the time but I clearly remember him suggesting to my mother that they found a way to get rid of the witness because he could be detrimental to my case. My poor Christ like mother who had never even uttered the word "dam" out of her mouth must have been so shocked, she immediately replied, "No teacher, my knees and my God will take care of him, I don't want any blood on my hands." His visit didn't last long after her reply. Of course he never said a word to me and as far as I was concerned, I didn't see him. The man either had no shame or he was confident that he was untouchable. He knew if I dared to open my mouth no-one would believe me. I would only embarrass myself further, or, he would use his influence to grind me to powder the very way he was suggesting to mother that a way be found to eliminate the witness. That son of a bitch! Thank God for my mother. Me in trouble already, now he wants to get my mother's hands dirty too. What a bitch!

I guess when you're a child you think as a child, because for quite a while I use to think that maybe he redeemed himself by his willingness to go the extreme in order to spare my life, without even realizing that the same thing he was suggesting for the witness might have been used to apply against me had I gotten him charged for rape.

Each time I was due to meet with my Lawyer, the arrangements were made ahead with Mr. Bartlett who had retained him. He would either pick me up and take me to him, or arranged with me to meet him at his house and from there he would take me over to my Lawyer. There wasn't much of a serious case preparation until it was getting near to the trial. It seems I was just always sitting there waiting for him to finish in court and began wagging a sheet of paper and rambling about his Secretary's spelling and typographical errors, then off in his car with me to a club.

On almost every occasion whenever we met for case preparation he closed the evening off by "going for a drink" which was a little uncomfortable because I always felt like a misfit in his circle of friends. And besides being introduced to them as his client, I never had anything to say because I felt like a misfit among them so I was bit shy. The first time he stopped at a club with me, I was served a red drink that looked like tomato juice. When I asked him what it was, he said "Bloody Mary". I had no idea what that was, so I didn't drink it. But the thing that concerned me mostly was how he would introduce me to his colleagues as his client and how he was going to get me off "scotch free." From a Lawyer's point of view, it might have been illustrious to his profession to be able to defend me on the capital charge and be "cock sure" he could win; but at the same time I felt uncomfortable being constantly introduced to his colleagues as his client. I don't think he realized he was hurting me and I didn't think I had the right to tell him what to say and what not to say but I felt he was advertising the charges against me to all of them. Anyways, I knew nothing about the law, never had to retain a Lawyer, I was just there to listen to him and take his advice. My life was in his hands. He came highly recommended by Mr. Bartlett, a friend of the family, as a top Q.C. Advocate, the son of a Baptist Minister. If left to us, we would have to settle with that Court Appointed Legal Aid Lawyer who couldn't even get me out on bail so I was extremely grateful to be blessed with him. It was just a little uncomfortable for all his colleagues to be hearing that I was facing a murder charge . . .

TWELVE

Once after leaving the club, he stopped by what looked like a home, saying we had to make a brief stop. When we entered the house there was a lady sitting behind a desk. He handed something to her and then something was handed to him. I proceeded with him and he turned a key in a door. I don't remember what else I saw in the room beside a bed when he unlocked the door. I was too shocked. I believe I became grounded to where I stood by the door looking on in shock just like the morning of the incident when I just stood there stoically. I'm sure I was still frozen by the door when he rested his attaché, undid his tie, proceeded to undress, and got into bed without saying a single word. I never had a clue where I was going, never been to a place like that before, didn't see it coming, didn't expect it and I never got the impression he was attracted to me. He led me to the river like a donkey and I drank.

My God Almighty, I had a 2 ½ year old son; a baby from a rape who was just 6 months old when I was charged; I was on a murder charge for the death of my 2½ year old son's father; and the man defending me was now taking me in bed. After standing there for a while looking like a zombie I had no choice but to shyly crawl up on the bed beside him. I was tired and needed to sleep and it seemed he had fallen asleep, but I was dead wrong. The thing that bothered me was the idea of having sex so soon after giving birth; the baby wasn't even a year old. It didn't make me feel good about myself, but my life was in his hands. And I am sure I took into consideration that my family was very poor, we didn't have enough money to pay him, yet he was still proceeding with my case. It didn't make it right but if I resisted what would happen to me? Would he abandon me, abandon my case, return me to the Court Appointed Legal Aid Lawyer who could not even get me bailed and run the risk of a possible prison term leaving my babies and me to suffer even more? You be the judge. And the truth is I don't think at the time it mattered what he did, I didn't have any feelings. I hardly spoke. I was very complacent. I listened, heard and followed but do you think I really had any feelings left? For God sake I was on a murder charge after a vicious rape that left me with a child and I still didn't get the chance to flatten the house of the son of a bitch. So how does feelings come into that? Tell me.

Compared to the way I was treated earlier, the man treated me with respect and dignity. He didn't haul me like a dog on a leash from his car in some bush neither did he pull me onto the bed beside him so I could never ever accuse him of rape. And after two or three meetings, it was something I came to expect each time we met, for the entire period that I was on bail. I can remember times when he fell asleep how I would just lie there and stared at him. I just had a strange feeling almost like a premonition that he wasn't going to live long. He had a temper, he drank, he snored and he had small bones with poor muscle tone. My premonition would prove true years later.

Whereas he took me by surprise initially, the relationship ended up taking the form of a consensual one. And by the time the case reopened in Circuit Court, it was a full blown relationship and I was visibly pregnant; expecting his child, my third at barely 18 years old and still living at my mother's house. I was caught in a web that was spinning out of control. My God!

Before the case proceeded in Circuit Court I told him I was pregnant. When I told him I was pregnant he said, *"Little girl, I can't own it I would lose my license to practise law and my wife works at the Head Post Office so I won't be able to send you any money."* To be fair to him, I don't remember if he said his wife was the Head Post Mistress or she worked at the Head Post Office. I didn't say a word, and I wouldn't have known what to say.

He was my Lawyer, my life was in his hands; I had no say. Furthermore, that was not the most important thing; my freedom, my mother and my two boys were my main concern. The case was scheduled to be in Circuit Court at the next session and so far he only got a £120; that was more to worry about than being pregnant because even though he was sleeping with me, the thought of him abandoning my case because of insufficient funds worried me.

Circuit opened with an impressive Guard of Honour Parade. Law and order was on display under the imposing statue of one of Jamaica's National Heroes; they might as well have named the Courthouse after him. The cops looked stunning in their white helmets, matching white tunics with glistening silver buttons and red belt over red seamed black pants. Their black shoes were almost as shine as the buttons on their tunics.

Whether I was asked to for protocol reasons or as a friendly gesture, I don't remember why I went back to the station where I was incarcerated on the morning of the trial. But whatever the reasons were, it was a strategic move because I clearly remember walking through a throng of bystanders curiously looking on from the Police Station to the Courts with female Constable Kendall walking beside me. They must have anticipated the crowd. We talked all the way from the Police Station to the Courts. The crowd was sombre and I could hear a few sighs and groans of sympathy. There was no looking to the right or left just straight ahead while trying desperately hard to engage my mind with the conversation so as to avoid any eye contact. The green and white fish tail dress with matching hat that Sister Louise sent from England to wear for the trial would have been the perfect fit had it not been for my pregnancy, but it did little to hide it; which I was sure had many wandering. I had no time to focus on myself.

This was a Courthouse unlike the local Resident Magistrate Court. I was totally fascinated with the language of the Courts and the way they addressed each other. They were all so proper. I hardly recognized my Lawyer in his robe and white wig with the twirls coming down on either side of his face. In the R.M. Court, they referred to the Judge as "Your Honour", in Circuit Court it was "My Lord and His Lordship". Lawyers for the Defendant and Counsel for the Crown were referred to as Counsel for the Defence and Crown Prosecutor/ Crown Counsel." Addressing each other to the Court they would say, "My Learned Friend". To this day, I have no idea if the Courtroom was full or empty or any knowledge of who was there or not. My eyes were focused on the Court proceedings and on the men in their robes and wigs. There was nothing intimidating about the Court, I was more curious to learn everything and I felt like I was part of the body of an arena that I could work in for life. And as I look back now, I have to wonder if I was fully aware of the charges against me or, if I was more like a young law student studying the intricacies of Court proceedings. I was so fascinated with the Court's attire, their mannerism, and order; that I believe that's all I was focused on and I instinctively knew it was a profession I could have been excellent at.

I was seated in the defendant's booth directly behind Counsel for the Defence and the Crown Prosecutor. The panel of 12 jurors fittingly sat to the left of His Lordship with their eyes seemingly fixed on me. Whether the single so called witness against me was destroyed in the local Courts or if he even took the stand at Circuit Court, I do not remember but I do recall my Lawyer telling me that he did a background check and found that he had more convictions for rape longer than the length of his arm so he couldn't wait to catch him in Court. My Lawyer was brilliant, aggressive and very persuasive; a great advocate.

When the victim's mother took the stand, it was gut wrenchingly riveting. She cried her heart out. It was very, very difficult to see her like that. Samuel was her favourite son. They played and laughed like two kids. All through her testimony, my eyes were stoically fixed on her. To see a warm, fun loving jovial lady in tears like that ripped my heart out. No mother should have to go through that. I was so sorry for her that I kept gazing at her hoping my pain would ease hers, but there was no such luck. For a person who could neither read nor write, when she took the stand she spoke with power and conviction.

There was no mistake in that Court as to who she was; the sorrow and grief she brought was enough to identify her. Yes, she wept bitterly throughout, but she stood her grounds. When she was asked if she saw the accused in the Court today, with my eyes still fixed on her, she pointed directly across to me sitting in the defendant's dock and said, "Yes sir, there she is over there, she was a greedy little girl, she had milk at my house every morning on her way to school." My heart sank. She couldn't contain herself. I sat there stoic with my eyes lethargically fixed on her. I looked, I saw, and I heard, but I believed I was either blank or didn't fully acknowledge what was really happening to me. She was forceful and strong with her testimony, but it was her tears I thought, that was enough to convict me.

If there was anything left in me, when she took the stand, she tore it all out. When she was done, I was just an empty shell looking on trying to keep poised. I didn't see my mother or any of my siblings but I knew they were there and I couldn't allow my mother to hear or see me falling to pieces, I had to be strong, so they could draw from my strength. But it was the one point in the proceedings when I really felt like a hole was punched in the case against me.

A mother's tears are an effective weapon, and her tears really pierced my soul. She was just too nice a person to have had to weep like that. If my Lawyer tried to punch a hole in her statement, I have no memory of it; I was too devastated. Before she testified, I was so fascinated with the order and mannerisms of the Court that I wanted to be Judge, Court Stenographer, Lawyer and Prosecutor, but my dreams evaporated when she took the stand. Even when I was acquitted, the dream could not stand up to the weight of what I would carry for the rest of my life.

It was brilliance at its best as the Crown Prosecutor Dan Clarkson addressed the Jurors and presented the case while periodically turning around to look at me with those big bulging intimidating eyes. He spoke eloquently and that really impressed me, always like to hear someone with good command of the English Language, it lifts me to a higher level of myself. But his power of persuasion to convince the Jury of a guilty verdict was too much. I thought he was so heartless trying to put away a little girl with two young babies for life. And I'm sure he must have noticed that I was pregnant. I couldn't understand his reasoning for making me out to be a murderer instead of it being an accident.

Whether the case was wrapped up the same day or the next remains vague but when Court recessed for lunch and I walked outside, a member of the Jury said to me, "Little girl, how did you let that happen to you?" I don't remember what I said to her or if I even replied because I don't think I knew what to say, but when I told my Lawyer he was encouraged. He thought it was a good sign that the defence could get an acquittal, but when the case was given to the jurors, they returned a guilty verdict breaking down their verdict in ways I didn't understand. When His Lordship sentenced me to eighteen months I thought my Lawyer was through fighting, but even as I was led away to a small back room in the Court, I could hear him arguing to have me sent to the Juvenile section of the Women's Prison. He knew I was pregnant and I'm sure my pregnancy was on his mind. His petition to have me placed in the Juvenile section was granted but the sentence would be reversed eventually.

At the end of the day, an officer escorted me back to the very cell I had been in before bail, pending my departure to begin my sentence. It was hell. I don't think it ever occurred to me that my Lawyer would have lost, he was always "cock sure" of an acquittal the first time around. I'm sure he was just as devastated as I was. He had to be, I was carrying his child and I was now Government Property and he had a license to protect; but it was my mother and my babies that devastated me. *One officer brought me toothpaste and other toiletries he thought I might need to take along with me. In addition, he brought me a Guinness stout and said, "Look, it could be worse, you're very lucky; before you finish drinking this stout you'll be free again; eighteen months is nothing."* Another jokingly came to congratulate me for "winning the case". He called it, "getting away" in light of the short sentence. To me it was like leaving my mother and my children for eighteen (18) long years. And what bothered me was the thought that I'd be sent off to some other place to serve the sentence, leaving the men and women in uniform that I had come to know and trust. That was painfully frightening. All I wanted was to be left alone so I could drown myself in my tears but it was uncharacteristic of them to allow me to wallow in despair. They had all been my extended family from day one, always there to cheer me up.

I missed the Cook even before I was taken away. I always look forward to seeing her three times a day and getting the latest scoop, plus any little thing I needed she would always get it for me. The sound of Corporal Viscount arriving for duty in his flip flop sandals clapping the back of his heels and humming was very soothing. When Mrs. Kendall was at the Guard Room on duty, I felt like Sister Love was around. They strengthened me. A simple thing as a nod and a smile meant a lot to me. Bottom line, they had all been family to me and I didn't want to leave my family. And that's why even now some 40 plus years later, whenever I am in the island and I pass by I always drop in to say hi even though they're no longer there.

I don't remember exactly how long I stayed with them before being taken away to start my sentence; and I don't remember if my Lawyer came to see me after the trial or before I left; but I remember leaving the facility with an officer sitting with me in the back of what looked like a huge open bus, escorting me to the Women's Prison. I can never remember the name of the Officer who rode along with me, but I have never forgotten how calm and reassuring he was. It was like taking a long ride out on the countryside with a friend and talking, just the way they treated me during my tenure in custody. But when we arrived and they handed me over to the Matron of the Prison after entering through what appeared to be a never ending set of locked gates, I felt like they had abandoned me. It almost felt like I wanted to blame them for taking me there but I knew they were just doing their job. And deep down inside I knew they were very sad for me.

THIRTEEN

I believe I arrived at the Penitentiary on a Friday evening. The Matron's paperwork at the Admissions Office seemed more like a waiting period at a hospital emergency. After that I was escorted to my cell. There was one inmate per cell. And apart from going to church on the premises, the weekend was very quiet so I thought my sentence would be spent locked away in the cell and I would get plenty of rest. But the possibility of my baby being born in prison was a constant worry. My mother delivered my two sons. I wondered if anyone would be as tender with me as she was and how I'd get to make preparation for the birth of my baby.

Contrary to my idea of being locked up in the cell all day getting plenty of rest, Monday morning was to be the first day of work. And even though my lawyer had argued in Court for me to serve my sentence at the juvenile section of the Women's Prison, there was no such thing at the facility. It was so intimidating to find myself among women so much older; some of whom it seemed could have been my grandmother. On the other hand, I was surprised to find some of the most beautiful and intelligent women at a place like that. That was a shock. I expected to see the worst of society. And even more surprising to me were those who were second time offenders for the capital charge and one who was a third time offender. If they were unhappy, they certainly didn't show it. There was one inmate that I was drawn to, a very Christ like lady; I wondered what on earth led her to be there for the murder of her husband, but I didn't have the courage to ask her. I was afraid and she was a very tall lady with a fair amount of weight, but I always wonder what became of her. And maybe that's why I always yearn for a Prison Ministry, because they were not all cold hearted, they slipped up and I could tell that some of them needed an understanding ear, a voice of hope and something more to look forward to other than just church on Sundays.

I don't remember at one point I was given a set of ashes coloured cotton dresses, whether at the Matron's office or from the Corrections Officer who checked me in. But I clearly remember that the waist was large enough to accommodate my growing belly. The Monday morning we were escorted to what looked like a large concrete building shaped like a tent where there were a lot of wash pans filled with clothes to be laundered by hand. My guess is they were the uniforms of the male prisoners. I was standing over my wash pan contemplating which piece to start washing; they seemed so big for my little hands. As I stood there pondering, the other inmates were busy at work. An Officer walked briskly over to me while I was contemplating which piece of clothes to start washing, I thought she was going to scream at me for just standing there, but instead, she stopped me from working. The Matron, she said, had just been informed by my lawyer of an appeal in my case. I could not be allowed to work and I had to change back into my civilian clothes immediately.

Less than 72 hours after arriving to start an eighteen month sentence, my status was reversed from Prisoner, to Appellant. The Inmates were shocked when they returned from work later and found me in civilian clothes. They all wondered how my lawyer could appeal an 18-month sentence on the capital charge. With everyone thinking it wasn't a smart thing to do; silently, I began to question his decision too. "What was he doing?" I thought. "Was he crazy?" "What if they gave me a longer sentence?" I was so frightened and confused. It didn't make sense either that they still kept me confined pending the outcome of my appeal. Why couldn't I await the outcome of my appeal at the station where I stayed previously? Why keep me sitting down in my civilian clothes looking; no one to talk to about anything? I just sat outdoors day after day and wondered. I wanted so much for them to return me to Palm Springs Police Station where "my family" was. For sure, they would explain things to me;

I trusted them. The uncertainty of not knowing what to expect almost seemed harsher than just doing the eighteen months and getting it over with.

So much was bothering me; the possibility of my child being born in prison; I worried about my sons; and I ached to be so far away from my mother. She delivered both my sons, now I don't know who would help me and if they'd be as patient and gentle. There were times when I even wondered if they were putting anything in my food that might affect my baby. All sorts of things went on in my head. How would the baby be provided for, would they take it away? The inmates were even more concerned, I was like their daughter. One began drilling me on spelling after learning that I was a Spelling Bee Contestant. It was all I had to look forward to: Spelling and going to Church. Night after night from behind her cell doors, Cynthia threw some of the most difficult words at me. When she asked me to spell "Czechoslovakia" I failed, and after that I lost interest. On top of everything that was going on in my life, it was a sad reminder of my fifth-place-finish a couple years earlier and how disappointed Teacher Hollinger was. Failure is not an option for me, it's a huge blow.

No matter how I tried not to think of the appeal, the uncertainty of not knowing what the outcome could be was worrisome. With so much on my mind I wasn't even capable of fathoming at the time that my Lawyer was doing all he could to make sure our child wasn't born in prison and possibly run the risk of jeopardizing his career. It wasn't until many, many years later that it occurred to me it might have been the reason behind his vigorous pursuit for an acquittal. God bless him! God bless him! God bless him!

With nothing to do in the days while other inmates were working, I tried to study the Corrections' Officers' duties to see if it was a job that might interest Sister Love. They didn't seem to have much to do other than walk around with a million and one key and handcuffs guarding inmates and for the most part sat and talked about their trips to Miami and what they bought for their homes. It was a good job. I stored all I could in my head to share with my Sister. It gave me something to do and kept my mind occupied.

On one occasion an inmate wanted to comb my hair. I never liked anyone touching my hair, but it was so boring that I agreed to let her. The very same night I dreamt a man looking furiously at me. He asked me if I couldn't comb my hair myself. Amazingly, the man bore a striking resemblance of the same photo in my father's passport. It was the first of two dreams I had while awaiting the outcome of my appeal.

The second dream I had, I was washing my hair and showering out in the open air. It's like I was showering and washing my hair all night in my dream. The morning I woke up there was a sense of relief, I felt very light and I had a strange feeling that something good was going to happen to me but I didn't know what.

Later that day, I was sitting down in my little orange and white polka dot dress some distance away from the matron's office. "Appellant, Appellant," the Matron called, "get dressed, your lawyer is coming for you." I had won my appeal and was free to go home. My Lawyer's efforts had paid off. The Correctional Officer walked me to my cell inside where I got dressed, picked up my belongings and left a free woman. I don't think at that moment I had fully grasped what just happened and what it would mean for me, but I am sure I was happy to be going home to my mother. And even though I was nervous when I learnt he appealed, I came to realize the importance of living without a conviction. Without an acquittal my daughter would have been born in Prison and my children and I would not have had the opportunity to call Canada our home, so what he did for me went far beyond an acquittal, it has given a whole generation a future they may not have had otherwise, and it happened because he dared to believe. I am forever indebted to him.

I thought I left my troubles behind when I won my appeal and was on my way home but the devil wasn't through with me. Apparently he wanted to leave me with a scar to look at for life. While Mr. Bartlett was taking me home in his old cream coloured fish tail Zephyr motorcar, the door swung open. I tried to reach for the door so I could close it but on my third attempt I fell out before he managed to apply his brakes. It happened directly across the Rod Nellston Police Station. For a split second I must have lost consciousness because I vividly remember getting up, brushing the front of my dress off and said, "Let me see if I am dead." My guess is I was about six months pregnant at the time, but being incarcerated for so long before I got bail and again while I waited the outcome of my appeal had robbed me of my sense of timing so I can only assume that by the time I won my appeal, I was about six months pregnant. And according to the driver behind us, he saw my attempts to close the door and anticipated my falling out. Without his attentive driving skill I might have been killed. The staff at the Police Station ran out with alcohol and poured some on all three wounds. It was the third and final set of Police Officers that I came in contact with since my ordeal began, and it left me wondering if God had an array of angels in uniform all along my way to protect me. Incidentally, I still have the three marks on my body, two on my arms and a pancake size one on my leg. I didn't understand the importance of returning to the hospital to have them dyed as the nurse had advised me to. But I am glad I didn't return for that dye. I see them as a constant reminder of the barrage of tribulations that God has brought me through.

FOURTEEN

I doubt my mother was aware that my lawyer had launched an appeal, because first of all we didn't even have enough funds to cover Bail Hearing and Court cost. She was shocked when Mr. Bartlett pulled up with me in his motorcar. Ironically, when I arrived, Brother Phil was telling her the dream he had the night before that I came home covered in blood.

My little brother who was never one to say much, turned to me one day after I got home and said, "How comes you are like that?" Considering the mess I had just gotten out of, he wondered how I could be left pregnant. I didn't want to tell him the whole story so I told him I ate a whole loaf of bread. Sister Love never said much either but I knew she was hurting for me. I learnt to read her eyes. By the way she stared at me one day I knew she was deep in thought, then in a pitiful way she shook her head and said that during my ordeal, *someone remarked that I was well made.* I knew exactly where she was coming from.

I don't remember at what point my Mother enquired who the father was, but when she asked, I told her it was the Lawyer's. She didn't comment, but I had a feeling she was proud to know it was a "high class" person. I didn't bother to tell her that he said, he couldn't own the baby because he could lose his license to practice law. She didn't need any more stress. But it bothered me one day when I went to purchase something from my Shopkeeper cousin and she frowned at me and said, *"you mean with all the hell you just got out of you're pregnant again, which man you think is going to marry you with three children for three different men?"* I could only stare at her; if only she knew.

After sharing my observation of the Corrections Officers' duties with my sister, she applied and was accepted. But she had three children and soon I'd be having my third too, and our mother at her age couldn't handle so many grandchildren. But the opportunity for my sister to leave the country for the city would open the doors we needed to escape the life we lived in the country. From the start, mother decided that I would join her six months after I had the baby, because after all I had been through, the best thing that could happen for me was a change from that environment. I was too uncomfortable being left alone with the victim's family living so close by.

When my sister sought the help of a cousin nearby, she was successful but it didn't come easy. A busy-body Cousin-in-law who had nothing better to do after her husband left for work than to go from house to house and chat people's business, tried to sabotage our efforts to get away from the country. She told the cousin that my sister asked to keep the children, *"Let them stay there in their shit!"* Thank God Cousin Wynnette didn't listen to her. Through the help of Cousin Wynette my sister could leave to do her training and find greener pastures and I got to join her 6 months after my baby was born. And I am proud to say, that today, the two children are respectable Civil Servants with the American Government. Mother's Prayer and Fasting had the power to cut off all our enemies, plucked out all those who plotted against us, and destroyed anyone who stood in our way. "Every time!"

As the saying goes, *"after a storm, there must be a calm."* And so one glorious evening in March,1970, God closed the harshest chapter of my life with a little bundle of joy weighed six pounds four ounces. The first question I asked my mother after I heard the cry was, "what kind is it?" I wanted a girl this time because I had 2 boys and God answered my prayer. Then mother said something which remains a mystery to this day. When she delivered her she said she saw the number 3. I have no explanation for that but she is my third and last child. I am sure God knew I could not handle anymore, but what I would like to remember is my state of mind at the time of her birth knowing the hell I had just gotten out of; the thought of planning to leave her at 6 months; and the knowledge that she would not be allowed to carry her dad's name. There's got to be a reason why I can't remember, it had to be hell on me. But regardless, this baby came to represent the rainbow after a storm. God had not left me. There was hope.

Up to the time of her birth I never told my mother what her dad said about losing his license to practice law if he owned her so whether mother wrote or telegraphed him after the baby was born I don't know, but I am sure she got the news to him because I remember receiving a telegram from him saying: "Congratulations on your bouncing baby girl". That was it. We never received a Penny.

The very thought of planning to leave my 6-month old baby and her 3½ year old brother to go out and get food on the table for them was extremely stressful given all that I had just been through. Another thing that was difficult to envision was the idea of leaving the older child who by then understood much more, what was going on. His father died, Mommy was away in jail, his brother was taken by Mr. Dawson, Mommy came back, had a baby, now Mommy is leaving again. I can only hope to God that Colin has no memory of life between 2½-3½ it would scare the hell out of me. It was far too much, too soon. And the harsh reality of planning to leave them with my mother at a time when she herself needed to be comforted was devastating. It went against everything that I stood for. The only thing that wasn't too bad was that Dawn weaned herself from breast milk and had begun taking substitute. Everything else was unbearably difficult, at the same time I had to try to keep a brave face so mother wouldn't worry too much.

On the other hand, getting me as far away from home was of paramount importance. Our house was just a couple houses away from the victim's family. It was uncomfortable and I am sure it bothered mother, that's why in a way I thought Chase was lucky to be in a more stable environment.

There was a major hurdle to get over before leaving to join my sister that I never had time to give much thought to because of the court battle. But ever since my lawyer told me he wouldn't be able to own the baby because of his licence to practice law, I knew I would eventually face a big problem getting her birth registered. As was the case in the old days, the 90 days deadline for registering a birth was closing in on me. I had no idea I could have registered her in my name alone and I still hadn't told mother what her dad told me. All I could think of was getting someone to do it for me and I had to get it done before leaving to join my sister. I wrote to one of the officers at the station who always went out of his way to make sure I got the little necessities I needed while in custody. For a long time he didn't reply and I wrote again. When he promised to meet with me to discuss it, I deliberately met with him at the Post Office where Birth Registrations were done; time was against me and I had to get it done before leaving for the city. He debated it for such an embarrassingly long time that I began to get scared. At times during the conversation I would burst out with laughter to give the Postal Clerks the impression that we were having a friendly conversation. He was definitely not happy doing it, but I could tell he was sorry for me. The three month deadline for registering her birth had either passed or was close to the deadline so I moved her date of birth two months later to avoid getting in trouble with the law. Several years later when I took her to meet him I learnt that he died after a tragic car accident. He never met her and Dawn didn't learn who her biological father was until she was 29 years old. I was ashamed to tell her because I knew it would have opened up a whole can of worms and I wasn't ready to go there; far too deep.

I left home to join my Sister without ever returning to church. Too much had gone wrong with me. I felt like damaged goods, and I blamed them for all that had befallen me for nearly 25 years. It may not have been fair, but it was how I felt. I couldn't understand how they were such spirit filled, holy-ghost powerful healers, able to see what's going to happen to others; yet they could not save me. There I was a very active little girl in the Church, Sunday school and occasionally the Basic school. How could they not see that something was going to happen to me? My God I was there moments before, the very night I was raped; and the night before I was charged with the capital offence, I popped in briefly, and no one could help me?"

"How was it they were able to prophecy another's danger but not mine?" Well, I didn't blame God or myself; I blamed them; the Church. I blamed them and I stayed away. I blamed them for how stained I felt; I blamed them because I felt that something very precious within was stolen; I blamed them because I didn't feel like I felt before troubles showed up on my doorstep; I blamed them for everything under the sun that happened to me. Each time mother would say to me remember the church, I would say to her, 'what did they do for me?" It doesn't make sense now that I would blame them; probably in my childish mind it was all I could think of saying to alleviate the pain; but that was how I felt for almost 25 years towards the church I attended from dusk to dawn Sundays, Wednesday Night Prayer Meetings and the Healing Services on Mondays. Now, when I look back, I don't think deep in my heart, the question was really what they did or didn't do for me; or should have seen and didn't see, it was more my soul crying out in despair for the child in me who was robbed of her childhood and chopped down before the world got a chance to see the light in me. And that still hurts. Silently.

By the time I arrived in the city to meet my sister, the seat of the pantyhose had almost reached my knees. Words don't justify the sight of it; a camera would. Putting on a pair was a first time experience. I had no idea it was too short so while it kept riding down I kept pulling it up with one hand while the other hand hauled the grip (suitcase) behind me in the blazing sun through traffic and stoplights to meet my Sister. I felt such love and warmth when Sister Love met me; I could tell she was anxious for me to get away from all those memories but she couldn't help curling up into laughter when she saw me walking like my knees were joined together.

The first thing she counselled me not to do was to go around greeting everyone. As a little country girl I respectfully greeted people whenever I went by. Sister Love said, "cut that out." Learning to cross the busy streets with those fancy streetlights was a big difference from country life where there was only one light post at a major intersection, and a flashlight or bottle torch lit the rest of the way if the moon wasn't shining.

The first time I mailed a letter I dropped it in a resident's mailbox not realizing that it wasn't the regular mailbox. Truth is I didn't know any better. Back home in the country the Postman brought in a bag of mail each day from the main Post Office to the local, where they're alphabetically sorted and collected by the Residents. We didn't have the luxury of having a mailbox at home.

Our little home was a rented one room in a large house. We shared the same bed just as we did back home in the country with our mother and brother. All the tenants in the home shared the single bathroom and kitchen. A friend of my Sister joined us later to find a job in the city and was quite comfortable setting up a makeshift bed on the floor. Everyone was always on the lookout for an opportunity to leave the country for a more prosperous life in the city.

The Landlady, Miss Mack had 3 little children, 2 boys and a girl in the home caring for because their parents were in America. One of them, Paul, became very attached to me and I was fond of him but he was about the age of my son, it was very hard for me to forge a bond without feeling the pain of practically walking away from my own children. And with so much baggage it was difficult for me. But I've never forgotten how sweet he was and how much I wanted to love him.

I didn't have much. Not everything I brought from the country area was suited for the city, so for a while I shared my sister's clothes. One day we were out shopping for a few things when we came upon Samuel's younger brother selling pants length. But unlike Samuel's older brother who passed by me months earlier when the bucket of water almost fell off my neck, the younger one spoke to my sister but from the look he gave me, if my sister wasn't beside me I might have fainted. I never passed that way again but it left me with deep appreciation for the opportunity to have moved away from so close to his family.

Times were tough. When a friend of my Sister visited, I secretly borrowed $25 from him to send to mother to help feed my children. I didn't have it to repay him. Each time Mr. Dylan visited and asked about the money; I gave him the same story I made up, that I had sent it in the mail. Poor Mr.Dylan was such a dignified and trusting soul that he just kept hoping to get it, even wondering if it was stolen in the mail. Little did he know that it was never sent in the first place because I never had it. Many, many years later when he was doing mother's eulogy I remembered the $25, but I didn't bother to resurrect the subject and I was always thankful to him for not mentioning it to my Sister. I didn't need to cause any more embarrassment on my family.

Thank God for the Oprah Winfrey Show. Mr. Dylan $25 used to haunt me, but it got much lighter when I learnt that there were others in the same shoes; waiting for money that was supposed to have been sent but never was.

While I was trying to find a job, I sought help from Dawn's father, he didn't send me any money, but he arranged for me to get a temp job at the Land Tax Office through his friend. Within a few days I began working; never sat an interview, just reported to my Supervisor and started working. As soon as he arranged for the job, he found his way to the little room my Sister and I shared.

One Saturday night, we heard "bang, bang" at the door and then his voice called my name. I recognized his voice and so did my Sister but I didn't answer. My Sister, not knowing "what's what," looked at me with a frown and said, "Go on out with the man". Understandably so, she knew he was the father of my child; and he just got me off the capital offence; but she didn't know the whole story. I hid from everyone what he said about losing his license to practice law if he owned the child; the whole family had just been to hell and back with me they didn't need anymore; much less to have the audacity to tell them that he said he couldn't send me any money through the Post Office because his wife works there. No little sister wants to say those things to a bigger sister much less a Christian mother, I hid everything. Well, that is until later when my mother needed to get her blessed at church and didn't see his name on the Birth Certificate.

After a few bangs and no response, he grumbled and left. I imagined he grumbled that I owed him my life, but I knew he would just be taking me to the club in the company of his "learned friends" to have a drink and boast to them that he "got me off the capital charge scotch free" and then off to a motel. I wasn't used to that type of life, and I was embarrassed over the way he treated my pregnancy, even if he couldn't own her, a real man, I thought, would have made every effort to contribute to his child's well being. My God, it was only out of fear for my life and to get away from the environment why mother shipped me off to my sister in the city when my baby was only 6 months old. The first 6 months of her life was especially difficult because she weaned herself very early. Every Penny was spent on the case. There was nothing to buy even a can of Baby Supplement. Getting her a tin of feeding was pure hell and when we did; we had to stretch it so it could last a long time. Luckily Sister Love had a little girl 9 months earlier so my baby was able to get some "hand-me-down." The morning when I was leaving them to go to my sister, I looked at my 3 ½ year old and my 6 month old baby and I wondered what on earth mother was going to give them for lunch; I was so frightened. She had practically borrowed from the whole community to make up my bus fare.

I was in no position mentally to leave my mother and my children. I desperately needed their love and warmth to help me heal. The trial was over but I was a total wreck. No one knew the hell I was still going through. A baby at 14; then a rape; followed by a child from the rape; then a murder charge for my first son's father; and a third baby fathered by my lawyer by the time the trial was over was enough to blow my mind. Although I must admit, when I was penning the memoir and Dawn learnt of the night he came banging and asked, *"Mom, what if he had brought money that night?"* I didn't have an answer. But even so I questioned his timing and the hour of night and there has never been any doubt in my mind what his intentions were. A £5 a month from him could have gone a long way to getting a little cornmeal and a pint of cow's milk to make her a little porridge. She was the tiniest little baby, all because of malnutrition.

Even at age six, she barely looked like 3 years old with few strands of hair on her head. My son could eat crushed boiled bananas but she needed baby food and we couldn't afford it.

Whether it was the Collector General's idea or my Supervisor's idea I don't know, but I remembered my Supervisor trying hard to keep me on the job as long as possible. When the work was running low, he would say to me, "Don't rush take your time, do you want the Collector General to let you go because there's no work?" Little did he know my heart and soul wasn't into what I was doing. I just wanted to be away from everyone and everything and frankly it was very boring going through those huge logs everyday writing, writing, and writing. I had no patience; didn't fit in. I had a lot on my brain. All I wanted was to be by myself far away from everyone and everything and just sleep for about a year undisturbed. I was driven to do things so the children could survive, but I myself was having a hard time coping and functioning normally.

The slightest thing was extremely stressful for me. It wasn't a matter that something happened and it was over and done with, I was in real pain while pretending to be normal. No one talked about anything with me. There was no professional help. If only I could be somewhere close to my babies where I could see them, even at nights and go to work the following day; that might have helped a little but to just leave them like that after being up and down and away for much of the year then come and have a baby then leave them again; "it was hell." . . . For my older child, it must have been so traumatic. Being joyful and happy, working with others just did not fit in the equation. I couldn't wait for the end of the day to get away and be by myself, but many years later it occurred to me that even the Supervisor Mr. Bellamy must have known something and was doing all he could to keep me earning an income.

When my mother was ready to have Dawn blessed at church and found her birth certificate bearing another name instead her father's she was furious. When she wrote to me saying she didn't understand, only then did I explain to her what her father had said about losing his license to practice law if he owned her so I asked a friend to put his name for me because I thought I wouldn't have been able to register her birth without a surname. That was the end of the story. It was never mentioned again but I'm sure all those things weighed my mother down. And she knew I had no more space left inside of me for anything more, so she closed down and so did I. It wasn't until a few years later that I learnt from my daughter's father that I could have left the space on the birth certificate blank.

To this day I do not know who was chosen to be her Godparents. To avoid the subject I never asked my mother, and up to the time of her death 25 years later she never mentioned it, so my daughter never knew who was chosen to be her Godparents. But I have always told Dawn that even though we never knew them, her dad has children out there, one daughter I heard is a lawyer in America, DNA could easily bring them together. I hope I live to hear that some form of communication is established between her and her siblings. She deserves to have her sister. I won't be around forever. Having her would help.

FIFTEEN

Life in the city seemed enticing, but trying to fit into a world that I wasn't mentally ready for was frightening. Time alone, a much slower pace, space and years of therapy was what I needed; not to have found myself in a city as busy as New York after experiencing so much turbulence. I was only 18 years old!

I struggled from job to job for quite a while. After recalling my fascination with my Shorthand and my Court experience I decided to go to school for a course in shorthand, typing and bookkeeping with a view of becoming a Court Stenographer. Of course, it didn't take me long to realize that my brain must have taken leave of my senses because I left two babies with my aged mother and they all needed to eat and wear clothes, plus my brain couldn't take anymore. I remember completing about three journals of shorthand homework while on holidays.

My Shorthand was very good. The typing was not as good as it seemed, my fingers rambled like my thoughts but my teacher had no idea until she started going through word by word. The 60 words per minute she thought I was averaging looked more like 35wpm. I could manage Shorthand because I could do it alone in silence; the Typing was noisy and required too much attention; I could not cope. Many times when I knew my Sister left for work I would return home to sleep. I couldn't handle the pressure of school, work, and the thought of practically walking away from my babies leaving them with my mother; on the other hand maybe they were therapy for her but only sleep could help me.

My whole family was so shattered from all that had transpired, I don't think anyone had time to realize that I was in no position to help myself nor my children so soon. And now that I have time to reflect, they just didn't know much at all; all they knew about was the murder charge. They didn't know anything about the rape and the shame I was carrying; no one knew that Dawn's father said he couldn't own her and what I had to do to get her birth registered; so they probably thought I was getting money from her "rich" father for her.

I was the twelfth of thirteen children, with eleven of us remaining. Being the youngest sister and the only half sister, I felt like a failure and an embarrassment to face so much while all the others had a clean slate. I couldn't go to a Christian mother with things like—the child I had before was not for the person I said, it was for his boss who raped me. I couldn't go and tell them that. I couldn't tell that to my siblings. Not even if Jasmine was around I couldn't tell her that, but I guess nothing of the sort would have befallen me had she been around anyways. Everything happened so fast, I had no time to deal with one issue before another came crashing down on me. The easiest thing for me was to tuck myself away in the little one room my sister and I shared, that's where I felt safe. Outside, I felt like everyone knew about my past and all eyes were on me, that's why the space and time alone locked away in our little room was so important. That's not something I could explain to anyone because I didn't understand it myself. It just felt safe to be alone in silence. And maybe that's why I didn't attend my Sister's "Passing out Parade," the weight was just too much for me to bear. I was afraid of the world. But I was happy for her; particularly when she told me that when she made her salute the Governor General joked that she was the tiniest of them all.

About a year and a half later one Sunday, I went with my sister to visit a friend from the country who was stationed at the Police Barracks. While we were visiting I met a persistent young officer named Douglas, a recent graduate who was determined not to take no for an answer; he seemed like the answer to my prayer. Even though I was pretending not to be interested, a part of me was telling me he could be the answer to my prayer because I wouldn't need to be afraid of retaliation from Samuel's family anymore, he would protect me. There were no cell phones and we never had a home phone so I must have given him my address because within a few weeks he started visiting. It became clear as we both began to have visitors that my sister and I would eventually move on.

Douglas suggested we moved in together but I didn't feel ready even though I needed his protection. I had nothing, no money; I was still wearing some of my Sister's clothes. Every Penny I could put my hands on went to my mother to help care for her and my children. It wasn't much but it certainly was better than sitting down back home just looking at each other and waiting for Sister Louise to send money from England or for Brother Phil to squeeze himself to nothing trying to feed all of us.

Despite the pressure from Douglas, a few months passed and I still didn't want to move away from my sister, even though we both needed our space. He probably saw the inconvenience and capitalized on that by constantly pressuring me for us to rent an apartment together. I needed the security but I was always afraid one thing would lead to another and I didn't want anyone else knowing about my past. Furthermore, I only knew how to wash and clean. I didn't know much about cooking. The little I learnt came mainly from Sister Love's practical experience at class when she studied Shorthand and Typing. And during the time we lived together I learnt a little more and how to use gas stove. The few lessons from mother though well intended, wasn't much preparation for living with a man because there wasn't much to practice on, and meat and fish were not luxuries that were easily affordable.

One day when Douglas asked me to make some fish soup, I served him in a big white Pyrex dish, large enough to accommodate the length of the butter fish. When he asked me if I couldn't cut the fish I didn't comment. Truth is I didn't know I was supposed to cut it, and it didn't occur to me to do so. What I needed was rest; space; time alone; my family; years of therapy to sort out my mind and then a typewriter to sharpen my skills, not a marriage minded man. It was hard trying to forge a relationship when I had the weight of the world on me, and so much to hide.

When his power of persuasion for us to live together was finally realized, he celebrated the occasion by making a small deposit on a Smith Corona Typewriter for me which cost $161.00 with monthly payments of $12. It was a bit much for me to carry from my on and off temp jobs and all the responsibilities I already had.

Our first home was a room in a tenant house where the owner also lived. Beside our room was another couple. We all shared the same kitchen but we each had our own bathroom. Sharing a kitchen I thought was a good idea for me. I could learn a thing or two from the other lady. One day when she made a very fancy salad, I swore I copied everything mentally. I tried making the same thing one evening to impress Douglas, hurrying to make sure I got out of the kitchen before she gets home in case I didn't get it right. Just as I was putting the finishing touches she popped into the kitchen with her eyes wide opened and said, "Miss Elisabeth, what you doing?" I bolted out of the kitchen so fast with my Pyrex dish, but it seemed Douglas didn't know any better, he cleaned the plate. Since then I stayed away from the kitchen when she was around. Whatever I had to whip up, I whipped it up fast when she wasn't around.

I started missing payments on the typewriter; the installment was too much for my budget. When Douglas came home one day and found large shoes prints leading from the walkway up to the front steps, since "jealousy" was his "middle name" he became suspicious. I made up a story but he later found out that the typewriter was seized that very day. He didn't understand why I couldn't make the payments. As I said earlier, I didn't tell him about my children because I was always afraid one thing could lead to another and there was no way under the sun I could allow anyone, no matter how close, to know about my past. But as a cop, he had many friends and co-workers and he was always curious to know why a squad-mate who was my sister's friend always said he had something to tell him but never did; and of course I always pretended that I had no idea, so that was a strike against me because we were all from the same home town. Something didn't add up but he couldn't put it together.

When Douglas brought home a friend who readily recognized me and asked, "How did that thing go with that guy?" I almost dropped dead but I blinked my eyes fast at him and he got the message and never mentioned another word. Douglas never missed a beat, he caught on, and he always wondered what "thing was that with the guy" that his friend's friend asked me about but he never got a clue. Each time he tried to find out, I managed to wiggle my way out of it, but throughout our relationship he drew reference to that man's comments; the mystery behind the typewriter being seized; and what that squad mate always wanted to tell him but never did. The combination of all the coincidences heightened his suspicions and laid the foundation for doubts and mistrust. And later I would lose the privilege I had of going to see my mother and my children alone.

Until we were separated, I was never allowed to travel alone to see my mother. When I asked a friend to urgently send me a telegram saying my mother was sick just so I could get some time alone with my family, he traced the telegram and realized it wasn't from my mother. He came along with me. That man belonged in the Criminal Investigation Unit, he shouldn't have been just a regular cop; he was too clever. Just before our very first trip, I broke my silence about two children, no mention of the one by rape who was living elsewhere, in case he scornfully walked away and left me.

I don't know if he was digging for clues or what, but the very first thing Douglas did when he went with me after meeting my mother and my children, was to take a walk out to the shop. Alone. My heart almost stopped beating. Would someone tell him about the trouble I was in? I stared at him when he returned trying to detect any change in his facial expression, but there was none. Thank God! I survived another one.

Back in the city, when he suggested we move from one community to another I welcomed the idea. It was someone he was well acquainted with he said from his hometown. The street was somewhat calmer and it impressed me to be a nicer neighbourhood. The facilities were basically the same so I reckoned that he probably just felt at home being around someone he knew from back home.

Well, from day one, the landlady made my life the living hell. It took quite a while for me to learn that her niece had a son for Douglas. He never once talked about Luke so I really didn't know, and it wouldn't have mattered. It could only make me feel a little more secure to know he had children before he met me too but he never talked about his children. I wasn't from their home town; didn't meet him in his hometown; never knew of mother or child; but clearly this woman's loyalty was to her niece even though their relationship was long over. She was determined to make my life the living hell. Her resentment towards me intensified when I began wearing what appeared to be an engagement ring. Actually, it was a little silver coloured plastic ring that I retrieved from a little bag of popcorn. It got to the point where I couldn't take it anymore and Douglas had no desire to move. As far as he was concerned, I was the bad one. I decided to settle the matter once and for all quietly to get her off my back.

One day when she left to sell all the used clothing she collected to the little poor people in the country, I poured water in the burners of her gas stove. That night when she got home and for almost a week later, she couldn't do any cooking. It was a thrill to see her enjoying some of the agony she had put me through. Douglas devilishly looked at me and said "I bet you did that". I didn't say a word but it certainly got Mrs. Vain off my back for much of my remaining time in her house. It wasn't over anyway because she wasn't the only one after me. She had company. A worse jezebel!

The first visit Sister Love and Sister Bev made together, I didn't know what Sister Love sensed, but she made a remark and like a mother hen protecting her chickens, I guardedly said, "Mother hen won't step on her chickens." I always try to hide things out of fear that she might share it with mother and cause her to worry more than she should, but that Sister knew me like a book. She had the eyes of an eagle; she could spot a grain of mustard seed in the grass from a distance. I couldn't fool her if I tried.

The truth is, not only was the landlady a constant sword in my back, Douglas' mother was another one I had to contend with, so it was always one or the other. Both women knew each other from back home, and from the time we went to that house of hell to live, almost every month she invited herself. She always arrived close to the middle of the month, and she would never leave until he got paid on the 29th of the month even though we lived in a one room with one bed and shared conveniences. Douglas slept at the front of the bed; I slept in the middle; and his jezebel mother slept behind me. And to make matters worse, no matter how hard I tried to be nice to "that woman" and God knows I tried; she always had a complain to make to her son about me when he got home, even though she knew he had a bad temper. When she was successful in getting him upset with me, she would turn to me and said "you love Douglas too much you love him more than you love yourself." "That witch!"

A couple years later I learnt from Douglas's cousin that his mother found out about my past problems with the law from the very first time she visited and so that was her way of instigating a separation. And one of Douglas's eight (8) brothers later confided in me that his brother was a mamma's boy from birth because of his remarkably handsome looks and very light complexion. He said Douglas was never allowed to walk outdoors when it was wet and muddy. It was always their responsibility to take him around on their backs, get him inside without any mud touching his feet and served him mint tea, so he grew up being a rotten spoiled mamma's boy who could do no wrong, his brother said, so his mother would forever be a thorn in my side because I had her baby. I guess those were some of the reasons why we clashed some Saturdays when I made my Saturday evening beef-soup, because it's made with pumpkin and I love my pumpkin and his mother told him not to eat pumpkin and he should wear purple and white. But I was young and in love, trying to put the past behind me and looking for an opportunity to get my children a home I didn't see any mountain that we couldn't climb. Love is certainly blind.

I think a rock rolled off my back when we moved out of that house of horror. The very same week we moved, I landed a job in the Claims Department at a Health-Insurance Company. So far that was our best move. It was a very fine home with lots of beautiful flowers and a well manicured lawn. A Police Officer and his wife decided to sublet a room in their beautiful home and we were fortunate enough to get it. Being the extremely clean person I am, I saw it as the perfect match.

A beautiful green and white chenille embroidered bed spread Sister Louise sent me from England graced our bed, which sat in the middle of our little one room. And a friend who visited regularly always said our room looked like a palace, so it surprised me that the landlady found fault with my sweeping. Each time I swept the leaves and placed them in a drum for burning she turned it over to see if there were gravel among the leaves. I knew we wouldn't be there for long when I cleaned my kitchen one day and leaned the mop against the refrigerator. The refrigerator was part of a kitchen set (stove and fridge) that she bought in America. That made it iconic. It never ceased to amaze me how our own people could get a little six month visa to go to America, work their butts off either as a domestic help or do a little live-in-companion job and then return home looking like a movie star and behaving like they were some Stenographer at Buckingham Palace. And if they ever manage to bring home anything from America, my God it's like a prized trophy. How times have changed! I guess children do grow up . . . Eventually.

As expected our time at that home was not as long as we wanted to but I got a very good break. Apparently Douglas didn't want the higher rank officer to see how he lived, so his mother never visited when we lived at that address. I thoroughly enjoyed my privacy and I wished she could stay away forever but I knew that like a wart, she'd be back.

Getting a job was difficult. Keeping one was even harder. I wasn't ready for responsibilities. I just couldn't cope. Sometimes a job lasted only a week. When I landed a copy typist job at a Teacher's Credit Union, I made so many errors; every second sheet of paper was folded and stuffed in my drawer. It didn't even dawn on me that they could be easily found. One Monday morning when Miss Drew handed me the news that Mr. Hilton, the Manager, found a multitude of paper in my drawer, she remarked that if I had thrown them away, I would still have my job. I just could not think clearly. Another job I picked up at an office, when I typed a letter and presented it to my boss she found that the only piece of information in the second page was a letter line for her signature. The letter was perfectly done but it left no space on the first page for her signature so I made a dotted line on the second page with her name in bold caps underneath for her to sign on the line. "What if the client called to say they lost the second copy, what do I send them, a line with my signature?" Good point. Instead of doing it over or simply say I'm sorry, I told her it wasn't my fault. I was fired. Before I left that evening, I searched the Yellow Pages Directory and called all the Human Resources Departments of the various banks, every single one. Within five days, I was working in the International Department of a major bank preparing foreign drafts. I remained in that job until a few years later when I ran away from Douglas; my body couldn't take the beatings.

Our final move before we purchased our home was just across from where we were living at that cop's house; a corner lot with two semi-detached 3-bedroom houses. Here we had our own separate entrance, own conveniences and exclusive privacy. The $80 per month rent was a bit high considering our gross monthly income, so to help with the expenses we sublet two rooms, the front and the back to two separate tenants. We stayed in the middle room nearest to the bathroom. To create a balance in the house and to get some assistance with the cleaning, since it was a very large unit with a living room that looked like a banquet hall, we rented one each to a male and a female.

Like Douglas, Mr. McLean was a cop. He took the front room, Joyce took the back room and the bathroom separated our room from Mr. McLean's. It was a match made in heaven with one little itch. Mr. McLean from time to time had a male visitor and Douglas detested that especially because we all shared the one bathroom. In my opinion, Mr. McLean was an extraordinarily clean person, very professional and we got along very well. When he cleaned it was like having a house opening view, everything done to perfection; what he did in his bedroom was none of our business. He was a good decent respectable man who always met his obligation on time and months later when we got a helper both of them had a wonderful relationship. Charlotte had an uncanny ability to make him laugh every time and I enjoyed that because I didn't have that in my relationship. Somehow I always sensed fear and the need to be always on guard.

Shortly after we settled in, an old Sister-in-law paid us an unexpected visit. Apparently she had gone to visit my mother before and didn't like what she saw. Miss Inez pulled me aside and said, "Elisabeth, you need to do something, Miss Len is old now, and she is struggling with your two young children and can't even afford to feed them properly; Dawn is very tiny for her age and all she's getting to eat is crushed boiled banana." While she was talking to me my eyes wandered around the banquet hall living room thinking that Miss Inez might be thinking I am living in a big three bedroom house in the city while my poor mother is left to struggle with my two children. I could only hope that she noticed it was shared accommodation and the living room was empty so she wouldn't leave with the wrong impression. We had just moved from a one room and trying to settle in a little place more accommodating, paving the way I thought that would allow me to ask or suggest that my children join us even one at a time. Now there was no such thing. No time, had to act immediately. I simply made up with Miss Inez to bring Dawn for me since she was younger and showed more signs of malnutrition. I didn't share the conversation with Douglas, I was afraid he wouldn't agree, he just thought my Sister-in-law dropped in for a visit, end of story. Since Miss Inez would be returning with her soon, and I needed to pave the way for her arrival, I concocted a plan which could be speedily executed.

One morning while we were having breakfast, I began sobbing uncontrollably. When Douglas asked me what happened, I told him that Miss Inez was very concerned about Dawn's health because the little I send was not enough for mother to feed them well. He suggested we ask Joyce to vacate the room and bring her home. Little did he know that I had already made plans with Miss Inez to bring her, in fact, when Miss Inez visited I didn't get the impression that she was merely telling me I needed to take Dawn, it was more like putting me on notice that she'd be back with her in the near future so she made it very easy for me to say bring her in two weeks and then create the scene at the breakfast table that morning to pave the way for her arrival instantly.

I put on such a show with my tears while we were having breakfast that he couldn't say no if he wanted to. But there was a deal, Dawn's surname had to be changed, he didn't want his friends to know that he was with a woman who had children for another man. In two weeks she was back with her. One hurdle down, but there would be several more rivers to cross, I had only just begun.

I was thankful that Miss Inez had the courage to step in and take a stand. I was so caught up in my own little world at the time, slowly scheming my way through, that it probably would have taken me much longer to take her away from my mother. I am indebted to Miss Inez. Like they say, "the chip doesn't fly far from the block". Miss Inez is Brandon's mother, the very nephew who I could depend on any day or night when I wanted to go to church. Now, it was his mother stepping in to straighten things out for me when I couldn't even think. Beloved Gospel Singer, Janet Paschal puts it this way, "God puts special people in our lives for a reason." God bless her! I could do well with a few more "Miss Inez" along my way, maybe someone who could take over my life and ship me off to some form of therapy.

No woman in a right frame of mind having three children would consent to one child undertaking a change of name in order to be accepted by a spouse. I realize now, that all I was doing was just trying to escape my past. I was in no position to make decisions; I needed help; but it was a vivid reminder of a remark my shopkeeper cousin made when she noticed I was pregnant with a third child after the trial, *"Which man you think going to marry you with three children for three different men?"* "What if he knew I faced a murder charge for my son's father? What if he knew I was raped and had practically abandoned that son? What if he knew Dawn wasn't even carrying her dad's name because he feared losing his licence to practice law?" "When you're living beneath such a pile of rubble, maybe the most secure place is just to stay there so no one will know; and if you do escape you mask everything by pretending that nothing ever happened." I think that's what I did for a very long time. Fear and shame silenced me. Nothing ever happened. No-one would ever found out.

Dawn joined us when she was about 3½ years old, but she could easily have passed for a two year old or less, barely any hair on her head. The little I could send to mother wasn't enough to feed them well but she was a remarkably brilliant child. Grandma's home tutoring had already prepared her for 1st grade. I took her to work with me until I could find suitable help, but travelling on a bus with her was like a Spelling Bee Contest, she spelled and pronounced everything in sight and was equally good with writing and counting.

It didn't take me long to find Charlotte, a God sent woman with an infectious smile and a mother's heart. Charlotte had two children herself, but according to her when Johnny became a Police Officer, she didn't measure up to his standard so he abandoned her and their two adorable children. Charlotte was nothing less than a sister to me and a mother to Dawn. Even when a letter came for me from my mother, she would hide it under my pillow because she knew how jealous Douglas was. She could be trusted. We really loved each other. Dawn was really in good hands. Four days a week; three hours per night, I sweat overtime at the bank for the $1 per hour overtime to help with Charlotte's $15 per week pay. I believe there were three of us in the department with helpers at home so we mastered the art of stretching the work so we always had some for overtime.

Just three weeks into the little home kept Basic school, the teacher sent a note home with Dawn, recommending that I placed her in a more advanced school because Dawn already knew everything she was teaching. A co-worker with two girls attending Alpha Kindergarten Preparatory School recommended I enrolled Dawn there. Douglas demanded that she be registered in school bearing his surname: he didn't want anyone to know she wasn't his child. Luckily there was no request for a Birth Certificate because a change of name required a marriage certificate for the Deed Poll and we weren't married yet. Before the end of term Dawn was voted Form Captain. Mr. McLean used to say, "Dawn is so brilliant she has got to do Political Science." To "daddy", it was all about his pride, getting her surname changed. Top priority!

Nothing ever came easy for me. I was making decisions and taking actions that I wasn't capable of. Shortly after Dawn left Mother, I started facing a barrage of letters from her, horrified at the nerve of me to take Dawn away and leave Colin alone. But she would never understand, so the only thing I could say to her was, if I took them both, I wouldn't be able to work. But even that didn't matter to my mother, if I couldn't take both of them, I should have left them together. I was torn. Every letter was a reminder of the many instances Colin had been robbed of the people closest to him and left alone: the morning his father died; his brother taken way; me taken into custody; and now I've taken the one sister he had been so close to; he sits alone and scratches until he bleeds. It was hell all around me. Little did she know that many times I felt like running back home to her and just curl up under the bed; the thought of having to make some of the decision I made frightens me even now. But I was trying my very best the only way I knew how. That's why even years later when I heard that some people thought I was strong as a rock and there were those who thought I was cold and did not care; they didn't understand. I always had my plate full. I had to block some things to survive. "Don't forget, in the midst of everything I had the lives of three little ones and an aging mother to worry about." "There was never any time to think of myself, never." "My life had been nothing but one dilemma to the next." "It was hell all around me, all the time." "I often wonder how I survived without losing my damn mind."

There were co-workers who found me extremely moody. Others just didn't know what to make of me. Even two auditors sitting across from my desk at the bank once, asked me to stop the humming while my fingers clicked away at the adding machine, I apologized and kept going without the slightest idea, until I held my head up and found them staring at me. I'm sure my humming was a form of tranquilizer for me. In my Probationary Report Mrs. Adams stated that I was smart but I resent being spoken to: little did she know the weight I was carrying, plus a very ugly side of Douglas was surfacing that concerned me but I needed the protection, and frankly there was no way out for me, I couldn't return to the country.

SIXTEEN

Douglas and I were home alone one rainy day when he surprisingly walked out on the veranda and said he had something to show me. It was an engagement ring. We had outfits custom made for the occasion but we had to settle for a dinner for two because we just could not afford it. The following day when a co-worker noticed it, she wondered if the ring was blessed. Poor me, I had no idea that the Pastor should have blessed it. But back then Policemen were getting married like wild fire, practically every week there was a wedding; a Policeman marrying a nurse or a teacher, so I guessed when I landed a job at the bank; that qualified me. He was thinking too about purchasing a car but I suggested to him we paid down on a home instead because we couldn't live in a car. He agreed. Since we were considering a home, we decided that we wouldn't go on a honeymoon and instead of renting a Hall for our Reception we would use our living room.

Ever since I moved from the country, I was drawn to a particular church in the city. Bethlehem Tabernacle Church along with its neighbouring Catholic churches brought together an audience from various communities every Sunday in a section of the city so heavily trafficked, that without the churches in the area, that busy part of the city would be like a place without a soul. I chose that Church for our wedding because the Pastor impressed me as being very warm and caring. After Service on Sundays, he went straight to the door where he shook the hands of each individual. It made quite an impression on me. It wasn't just a hand-shake, he had a contagious grin, always had a kind word and seemed to know everyone by name, that's why when I approached him with the intended date and he told me the line of marriages he had lined up for that day, it didn't shake me one bit because I had long decided that whenever I said "I do" he would be the one administering the vow.

My next priority was to retain a Soloist. I knew exactly who I wanted. For years I had watched him sang Moon River at the Annual Beauty Pageantry. No matter how busy his schedule was, no one else would do, even if I had to change the date to accommodate him. Of course I had no idea how to reach those big important people, but a co-worker at the bank had contacts. From the day he agreed to sing at my wedding I believed I was ready to get married that same day even though "Moon River" would not be his song of choice for a wedding. Frankly, I didn't care what he sang as long as I had the privilege of having him sing at my wedding; it was all that mattered.

Whenever the budget allowed us, we treated ourselves to an evening out, usually once or twice per month. One of Douglas's favourite spots was a club where he watched girls danced seductively. I found it beautiful to look at and very entertaining. I can still see Queeny in her lilac silhouette gown gracefully gliding across the stage like a ballet dancer. "I enjoyed every minute of it and I didn't regard it as a sin." After two or three times though, I got tired of it; wasn't my style. The dancing was done in good taste but something about the environment and the crowd it attracted was just not me. It's like something inside of me was fighting against me being there. My comfort zone had always been church from dusk to dawn.

On the contrary, I enjoyed attending the Miss Jamaica Beauty Pageantry every year. I wouldn't miss that for love or money. And I was quite comfortable going to see Mo-Town Artist Marvin Gaye perform at the National Stadium. I loved Marvin Gaye. And when he sang "Let's Get It On," I loved him even more. That night with the National Stadium packed to capacity, as Marvin bellowed "Let's Get It On", the women in the audience went wild. I don't think there was a single woman in her seat when he took his shirt off and threw it in the audience. It seemed like a million hands reached for the shirt. My knees went weak. I would have been satisfied to have caught a piece of the thread that sewed his shirt. It's a moment in history that I shall never forget as long as I live. Each time I hear the song, *"Let's Get it On"* I relive the moment with the same passion and intensity I felt that night. As far as I was concerned, he came to sing for me and he delivered with every fibre of his being. I have never been to another performance of such, but I don't need to. The memory of that wonderful night is enough to last me a lifetime. And I hope when Jamaica celebrates its 50th year of Independence in 2012, that history will be kind to the memory of this great legend's visit when they rewind the tape.

When I visited my mother with the news of my wedding, she suggested that I "travel out" and get some experience before jumping into marriage. Secondly, because Douglas shared the same astrological sign as a cousin who used to beat his wife mercilessly, she was very concerned. The cousin's wife walked in a crouched position as though both feet were broken at the knees as a result of a beating she got for peeling the "boiling bananas" too deep. As a result, my mother forbade us to marry anyone who was born under that astrological sign. I was too concerned about the prospect of getting married to a cop and having all the protection I needed. But had I listened to my mother, my body would not have taken so many beatings. My mother's motto was always to use one good to cover ninety nine bad, so for her to use that story as a metaphor, I can see now that she was trying to steer me clear of any situation that might lead to trouble again, even if it meant applying a little astrology.

Looking back now, I realize that, while I was trying to forge ahead my mother was still traumatized by what I had faced just five years earlier. I don't think I was in any position whatsoever to make some of the decisions I made in the first ten to fifteen years following all the trauma I faced by the age of eighteen. Nothing I did made sense, I was simply trying to survive, to put the past behind me, but there was a lot more, deep down inside of me that desperately needed therapeutic help. Sadly, it wasn't until I began to put everything on paper that I realized how far I had sunk.

I don't recall being hit before our marriage but I'm sure there were many instances and I blocked them out because I earnestly wanted to carve a new path. The Officer we shared the house with wasn't thrilled about us getting married and I don't think he was present, he vacated his room for the day so we could have full use of the house but he didn't attend; neither was my landlady who vowed not to attend because she thought he had a very bad temper and there was a real possibility he might hurt me. According to her, a leopard never changes its skin. Yes there were moments of jealous rages, but I interpreted them as him loving me so much that all he was doing was protecting his property. In my mind, that would all go away once we were married and he felt more secured. Dead wrong! False security! It was the typical thinking of an insecure 23-year old woman with more skeletons in her closet than a grave yard, trying desperately to move forward whatever the cost. *"Sometimes when we are in a relationship, we choose not to see what is really happening, we do everything to see it the way we'd like it to be because we don't want to believe it. It often takes someone on the outside to steer us, and even so, we often refuse to accept the truth. Clearly I was planning for a wedding; not a marriage. All the signs were there not to proceed. I ignored the red flags, blinded by a sense of urgency to wipe away the past and unite the family. I needed my son to come home."*

When I asked a co-worker to purchase a pair of sandals in Miami that would match my engagement outfit. The very night I took it home, Douglas held it up before me in the bedroom, sliced it to pieces and then burnt them despite my pleas to give it to my mother who only had a pair of sandals that was barely kept in place around her big toe and a pair of church shoes that went to the shoemaker practically every month for repair. I realize now that it shouldn't have passed that point; he could have sliced me instead. There were no such thoughts at the time, just a desire to move beyond. I was convinced marriage would make things right. After all I had been through in my short life, tying the knot seemed like a way to step out of the past and embrace a new era. He loved me, I loved him, and we could overcome anything, or so I thought.

Working in the International Department at the bank allowed me some well needed overtime. There were always a lot of branch copies from drafts to be filed at nights. Even if they could be filed in the days, they were set aside for overtime at nights. It was a means to assist with wedding expenses and to help pay Charlotte. Lunch time when other staff members were ordering their expensive $3 lunches, Michelle and I opted for a 60¢ patty and lemonade and now and again her mother treated us to some fried fish and bread.

After several months of careful planning, the big day finally arrived. The skies in magnificent blue and white and the sun warm as can be expected in a tropical climate. My mother along with family members and friends arrived late the night before. Very typical of my mother, she had an assignment in the kitchen for each guest she brought, not realizing that a hotel was doing the catering. My son dashed into my arms, climbed up to my neck and rested his head on my shoulders. When I ran to awake my daughter, all hell broke loose. It had been nearly two years since they were separated and hadn't spent much time together since. I couldn't contain my emotions, I ran for the bathroom. Just to see the both of them playing happily almost in the middle of the night was a reminder of the devastating loss they suffered when I took one and left the other. Silently I vowed "So help me God" to change that as soon as I "tie the knot."

Except when Charlotte was around, Mr. McLean didn't laugh much but when he did it was contagious. On the morning of the wedding, I heard him laughing hysterically in the kitchen, I was still in bed, when I went to enquire he could hardly talk. Douglas decided that morning, for the first and only time ever, to make breakfast and brought it to me in bed. And that triggered the biggest laugh around the house on my wedding day between my landlord and Mr. McLean; to them it was just a farce. For me it was a pleasant surprise, one in which I indulged myself if only for a day, no time to think negatively, certainly not the day I was going to be a princess.

For my special day, my beautician who was married to a cop herself, made a part from the crown of my head while sleeking down the hair on both sides with two curves resting just above my eyebrows allowing the crown of the veil to anchor between the parts with layers of spiral curls dropping to shoulder length. Except for La Fay's of Jamaica Beauty Salon in Canada, no other beautician I knew of at the time had the magic touch to leave a woman looking as glamorous as Mrs. Allen of Le Julie's Beauty Bar in Jamaica. After leaving the Beauty Salon I was escorted to the home of my Give-away Father to be dressed by his wife. Mrs. Chronicle sensed I was a nervous wreck. The truth is I hadn't eaten all day, something was bothering me. I could only have a sip of the coffee she gave me. I remember thinking, what if anyone showed up and tried to stop the wedding. "Could there be anyone among the guests who knew about my past?" I had to brush that aside, that was the devil trying to spoil my dream day. I felt like a Princess when Mrs. Chronicle was through dressing me.

For my dream day I chose an A-line cut sheered back long sleeved white silk dress with the front of the upper half adorned with French guipure lace to match the floor length head piece. From the moment I stepped outside of the dressing room to the waiting car, motorists halted to get a peep at the bride; I had finally arrived. I had silenced the critics. For those who said no man would marry me because I had three children by three men; for those who felt I'd be stuck in the country bare feet with three children; for all who had written me off; this day was for them. I was the center of attention! We didn't have a lot of guests with cars so the best man took us to the church then dashed inside to join the wedding party.

Clasping a bunch of lily of the valley bouquet in the arms of my Give-away-Father; my maid of honour followed closely behind guiding the hem of my dress in a stunning floor length yellow chiffon dress with matching hat. The moment I stepped inside the church I could hear a guest softly saying "The bride is here." The organ prelude was like the sounds of angels singing. As we marched down the aisle to meet my prince, my eyes went over to the upper right hand corner for a quick glance at the man I had watched for years singing Moon River at the Miss Jamaica Pageantry; but on this very special day, this glorious occasion, he was serenading us like only he could, with the song of his choosing, *"We've only just begun."* Seconds later another quick glance at him and a gentle smile conveyed my gratitude. Dawn and Colin curiously looked on; no one had bothered to seat them. They couldn't be contained. For all the times together that they had lost since Dawn joined us, they were left alone to have their freedom that day running around in the church playing hide and seek.

As I approached the altar, the wedding party formed a semi-circle with my husband in the center facing the Pastor that I love so much in the gap of the semi circle who was about to join us in holy matrimony. The bridesmaid in their sea blue chiffon gown and matching hats with white bouquets set the tone for a sombre moment. I could not wait to say I do.

Anxiety and excitement gave me the chills but there was never any doubt in my mind that I was in love with my husband, I made the right choice and I was in it for better or for worse. Pastor must have sensed I was a nervous wreck. Just before I signed my name he smiled and said, "Mrs. Holyday, you can relax now. "Did I hear right, Mrs. Holyday?" Wow! I was ready to spend a lifetime with my husband to love and to honour, in sickness and in health, till death. That's how I wanted it, for life. I know now that either my heart and emotions controlled my brain, or I was looking for a safe haven. With all eyes fixed on us, we strolled down the aisle to the sweet sound of another selection by the soloist *"She wears my ring to show the world that she belongs to me."* That's a moment I'll never forget. My husband seductively turned his eyes, looked straight in my eyes and said, "Kiss me". Mr. Junior sealed the moment with his camera. The day belonged to two people only. It was ours to lavish in and we did! That evening, as the car slowly made its way with the bride and groom home for the reception, it seemed like the whole community lined the streets eagerly awaiting a glimpse of the bride. It was hauntingly beautiful. I felt loved by the one I was in love with. I wish it had lasted.

After changing into a one shoulder yellow and white floor length dress copied from the Miss Jamaica Pageantry years earlier, we opened the dance floor with my two left feet trying not to trip and fall. It was my first time dancing in my life.

Among the guests were two photographers from the evening newspaper, I basked in their attention. Days later the newspaper featured it as, "The wedding of the Week" Beneath the photograph of the bride and her maid of honour was the caption: "Two Beauties". It was the dawn of a new day and in my mind, the sky was the limit.

It surprised me that after the reception and we were lying in bed, that my husband would use such a glorious occasion to reprimand me for dancing with my Give-away-Father. It seemed so unfair. Mr. Chronicle and his family were very dear friends of ours, it was his wife who dressed me at their home, we took photos on the lawn, we travelled together to the church; He escorted me down the aisle where he gave me away to him, that wasn't fair to neither of us. And he said something else too which I regarded as a big joke, but it later proved to be the case; *"Your going out days are over now."* I have no recollection of being taken out by my husband since the day we got married, except when I went to see my mother and my son.

Since we were saving for our house, we opted instead to spend the time together at home. It was the best three weeks of our marriage. If that was extended through the marriage we would still have been married today. "What a pity!" It was all I wanted. When I returned to work, one cold hearted co-worker who was not invited commented there was no need for a honeymoon the honey had already gone out of the moon. We had lived together before we were married.

There was a time after my marriage when I felt that if ever I had a chance in my life to feel like a little princess, my wedding day gave me that but the nightmare that followed completely erased that thought.

SEVENTEEN

The first priority after my marriage was to get my daughter's surname changed as my husband had requested; mine was to bring my son home. I turned to the only Lawyer I knew to get the Deed Poll done on Dawn's name; her father. And because of our connection I knew he wouldn't charge me. First he asked me for my Marriage Certificate and then turning his face aside, he said "Did you bring your daughter's birth certificate?" "Yes sir." I said. But I thought, shouldn't he be saying "our daughter?" He inspected the Birth certificate and surprisingly, he remarked that she was born March—. When he noticed the male name on the certificate and our daughter's last name, he lifted the birth certificate from his desk and held it up to the right of his face and said, "What's this?" I pretended that I didn't know what he was talking about and addressed the date of birth by letting him know that the three months deadline for registering her birth had expired or close to expiration when I registered her birth so to avoid any legal ramifications the only thing I could think of was to move her birth date couple months ahead. He was still staring at me while holding up her birth certificate as if I hadn't answered the question; so sheepishly I said to him "I had to beg a friend to sign as father for the baby so her birth could be registered because you told me you couldn't own her because you would lose your licence to practice law and you couldn't do any transaction at the Post Office because your wife was the Head Post Mistress . . ." (To be fair to his memory I don't remember if he had said she worked at the Head Post Office or she was the Head Post Mistress). "You could have left it blank," he said. I didn't know I could do that. I wished

157

he had taken the time to tell me that upfront as he did when he explained to me why he couldn't own her. Her correct month of birth would have been on her birth certificate. The Cop I begged was so hesitant to do it for me that when he eventually met with me I deliberately met with him at the Post Office where Birth Registrations were done and it took everything in me to convince him to help me. I had no idea I could have left it blank or registered her in my name, he didn't tell me and I had no one to ask because I didn't tell anyone what he said. I kept everything to myself. It was my first time seeing him since the night he knocked on the door so it surprised me that he remembered her date of birth. It wasn't until I left the office that it dawned on me, that mother had advised him when Dawn was born and he had sent me a congratulatory telegram.

The Deed Poll was done free of charge as I thought, but I truly expected him to give me a little cash for her, at least no one would have known because he wasn't sending it through the Post Office, I was right there in his office just the both of us, but he didn't. All he did when I was about to leave was walked me to the door with a hand resting on my shoulder and told me to give the baby girl a big hug and reminded me that the birth certificate should always be left attached to the deed poll; and whatever his reasons were I don't know, but I clearly remembered him cautioning me never to have a joint account with my husband.

As I revisit things now years later, there's a part of me that would like me to think that I probably made a mistake, that maybe if I had gone to the door when he came banging that night he might have given me some cash for Dawn or he would have found a way to be involved in her life and she would have had a better life, I just don't know. I remembered him talking about getting me into Law School in Barbados during the time he represented me, it seemed that's where the Law Campus for the University of the West Indies was at the time; but I had a lot on my mind, I couldn't see beyond what was happening at the time. And when he came by that night all I could think of was him returning to pick up from where he left off and I didn't want that life. Maybe I question myself now because of the way my marriage turned out, but I knew I did the right thing; he was much older, he had a family, it couldn't be anything more than an extramarital affair and I was a teenager with 3 children, no help, and a lifetime of havoc facing me.

It would be a dream come true to see Dawn get the chance to meet her brothers and sisters. She has children and is very anxious to know her roots, especially after learning that her father died from heart failure. I did call his home and briefed his wife after learning of his death years later, in the hopes that Dawn could meet her siblings. But after she learnt how old I was when I had Dawn, she commented that I was old enough to know what I was doing at the time so she had no interest in the matter. I never called again.

EIGHTEEN

I began to notice some changes in my husband's behaviour about a
month or two after our marriage. He was always late getting home when
he worked the 7-3 shift but I didn't pay much attention because he always
talked about stopping to play a game of poker. When he began coming
home, getting dressed and leaving without having his dinner and returning
home at around 11pm it bothered me but I didn't say anything because he
had a bad temper. When he became increasingly jealous and was quick to
explode over simple things, I couldn't understand it.

When a bridesmaid from our wedding party started avoiding me
or pretending she didn't see me, I confronted her head on, that's when I
learnt that when my husband delivered her wedding cake he apparently
fell in love with a tenant and had been visiting her home at nights, leaving
moments after the 10pm alarm went off. It all added up. Before long the
tenant moved a couple doors away from our house, it seemed her landlord
wasn't comfortable with Douglas's behaviour seeing we had just gotten
married and she knew both of us.

As newlyweds facing the prospect of owning our first home, I was far too
excited to see any mountain that we couldn't climb; but when the Real Estate
Agent came to get both signatures as required in a Joint Tenancy Agreement
and I made my way from the kitchen to meet her on the veranda and my
husband said to me, *"You should be in the kitchen at the back"* that floored
me. I didn't see it coming, didn't know where it came from, and I certainly

didn't expect it. We weren't even married a year yet, just a few months. Up to now I don't know what I did to deserve that. I can only guess that he expected his mistress to pass by and he didn't want her to see us together on the veranda. It was such a blow I didn't get a word in before the Agent shot back at him, "Mr. Holyday, I came to get Mrs. Holyday's signature". After I signed she said, "May God help you" and she walked away.

With a new home in the works and all the expenses that comes with it, my firm belief was that there was no space for her and she would just fade away when she found out he had nothing to offer her. My marriage was my only glimmer of hope at the time to move forward and put the past behind me, I wanted it to work, I wanted to get settled so I could bring Colin home, I wasn't going to have a nervous breakdown over my husband, I didn't have the energy to fight anymore, I was very tired. And quite possibly, with all I had on my plate, maybe I felt I had no choice but to sip everything to create a new life for myself and my children.

Earlier when we took a trip to his hometown, I met the sweetest, most innocent looking little girl I had ever met living with her Mom and Grandmother very close to his parent's home. The little girl kept a thumb in her mouth and a finger stuck in her navel, her back almost protruding through her little tummy. Her Grandmother hinted to me that she was my husband's child but he refused to own her, immediately I thought of Charlotte our helper with two adorable children how she said that when Johnny became a cop he abandoned them because she wasn't good enough. I promised her to do what I could and I left with enough information to expedite the process. Before long, the little girl was Jillian Holyday with her Birth Certificate bearing her dad's name, Douglas Holyday. Only when I penned this article around 35 years later that it occurred to me that I did it for her but I didn't do the same for my daughter; but I don't think at the time I even knew that it was possible, much more to have gone to the Registrar's Office and have the name of a father placed on a child's Birth Certificate without even a Letter of Consent. And even so, with Dawn's father being a Lawyer, I doubt I'd be that brave, furthermore, I wouldn't dream of doing anything that could jeopardize his license.

I didn't get the impression that Douglas fully understood the consequences of his actions because Jillian was the darling of his heart when she joined us later and I never mentioned a word to her. And the truth is, as I was getting her papers done; in my mind I was clearing the way to make it easier to bring home my son too. Those were the issues I focused on, not my husband's infidelity; at least not yet.

Eventually, with a wife and a mistress living on the same street a couple doors away from each other that even my daughter knew of, was a real test of faith but I couldn't dare say anything. It was very humiliating when Dawn told me one evening that daddy took her down there and Valerie gave her Milo and crackers. And it seemed the only way for him to stay in control was to always find a reason to pick a fight with me. On my way home from work one evening, as I got off the bus, I saw him coming towards me. I smiled thinking he was coming to meet me. Instead, I was greeted with the full weight of his fist in my forehead so hard that I slumped backwards to the ground. According to him, I was too late getting home. It wasn't possible for me to have been home earlier unless I took a helicopter. He battered me all the way home.

Another beating came when I was preparing his uniforms for drop off at the Cleaners and found condoms in his pockets. After confronting him, I threatened to throw them out on my way to work and then hurriedly left for work with them in case he tried to take them away from me. He caught up with the bus at one of its stop. When he realized I was on the bus, he beckoned to me. As soon as I got off, in full view of a bus full of passengers he began battering me mercilessly while everyone looked on until the bus drove off. Charlotte took one look at me when I got back home and graciously took the day off to spare me any further embarrassment. While he was serving and protecting the public, he was destroying his wife at home and there was no one to turn to. One cop was a tenant, another lived across the street. Timing was everything, I had three little lives to protect, and a mother I loved dearly. The wrong move at the wrong time could plunge me six feet six inches; into my grave. Returning to the country was never an option, too much pain and I would just be looking for the chance to have "the beast" roast in his house. I had to find a way out, I just had to hang in there and be patient.

It was common to finish working overtime, walking up the street and find him lurking behind a post to see if I was getting a ride or talking to anyone. Sometimes if he was at home and heard a car coming, he would climb above the door and peep over to see if it was me getting a ride from anyone. It was a nightmare. Many times I wanted to laugh when I saw him getting down off the stool but I wouldn't dare. It wouldn't have made a difference if it was a co-worker, male or female; his philosophy was that one could be acting on behalf of a lover, which was so dumb because the price I would pay would not be worth the ride.

On many occasion when Dawn came home from school, Pastor was there counselling us. Poor thing, she always said, "Mommy, think I don't know you're complaining on Daddy?" With Pastor Shepherd's busy schedule, I always wonder how he found the time, but he was always there for me in an instant when I called. Always.

Things got so bad or maybe his conscience pricked him so much that he made a mountain out of everything. A pair of sandals I asked the GM's Secretary, Margaret, to buy in Miami for me came long after our engagement. It was the perfect match for our ivory and red wine outfit but it came long after the engagement and the big splash we wanted to have but couldn't afford. The very evening I took it home, my husband told me he was going down the street to play a game of poker and he didn't want to see them when he returned. I pleaded with him to let me keep it since we still had our outfit or even give them to my mother for church, but he just smiled and went away. I knew that was a deadly sign; him smiling when he was angry? Deadly combination! But they were still there when he got back, I didn't know what to do and I just could not bring myself to destroying them when my Mother would have loved to have them. When he returned from his poker game, I was lying in bed. He walked into the bedroom with a knife in his right hand and the sandals in his left; held the slippers up before me; sliced them diagonally; then he walked out to the gate; threw them in the garbage bin; poured kerosene oil over them; set them on fire; and while the fire was raging he sang. When it was all over, he returned inside the house and got into bed. Neither of us said anything to each other, and if I thought or felt anything I do not remember, but it had to be scary and the memory of it is still terrifying.

When I cashed a Foreign Check for a customer without holding funds against the account so she could clear her shipment on the wharf; weeks later she returned with half-a-dozen underwear from her shipment for me. Like mother, I learnt to put aside the best for "special calling" (special occasion). For months, they sat in my drawer untouched until I was being fitted for new uniforms. I had no idea that my husband had been keeping tab, patiently waiting for me to wear them. The day I wore one, when he got home from work, he headed straight for the kitchen where I was preparing dinner. *I froze when he dashed into the kitchen and said, "Holyday, let me see the draws (underwear) you wear to work today."* I tried to explain to him that I wore one because I was getting fitted for new uniforms, but before I could finish explaining he ripped it off right there in the kitchen; grabbed the others from my dresser drawer; went straight to the big garbage bin by the gate where he treated them just the way he treated the pair of sandals months earlier; threw them in the garbage bin, made a fire in the bin, and watched them burn while he sang. It grieved me.

For a man who always cursed me and told me that when he met me I only had five underwear as though I could wear more than one at a time; one would think he would appreciate me having a few extras. Sometimes I wonder if he would have done that if he knew that three of the five he met me with were from Sister Love when I was moving out to live with him, and the other two from a batch Mother got from Sister Louise in England and she downsized them for me when I was leaving the country. And I wonder if he would have done that if he knew that my mother used to collect flour bags from the shopkeeper, soak out the marks with kerosene oil and used them to make panties for me. *The pain I feel here; is enough to make me end the story right here; but if it can help one person; then maybe it's worth it.*

I became so afraid of the man that I dread leaving work not knowing where he'd meet me and beat me. He wasn't only beating me; he now turned on my daughter. She brought a friend home from school while Charlotte was out and attempted to light the stove by using sticks of matches. He took a cane and attempted to hit her. When I blocked her with my body, he pushed me aside and repeatedly spanked my little five-year old baby that looked like three. I tried to grab her again but only after I heatedly told him I was the one who felt the pain and brought her into the world did he let go of her. I could tell he was frightened I may blurt out that she was not his child. "And so help me God that's exactly what was coming next!" I had to soak her in warm water for days. I had never seen my child cried so much. It was as though she couldn't cry anymore. Years later, my daughter still had cane marks all over her feet. That was the beginning of the end. The following evening I got home from work he was sitting with her in his lap on the veranda. I wanted to vomit. He was just sitting there holding her so I would think he was sorry. "Rubbish". If I had taken a ride from someone he would have dropped her so fast to beat the hell out of me. His little game didn't impress me one bit. From that time, I didn't think he deserved her calling him daddy. And they were playing once when I heard him say to her, "anytime your breasts start showing I am going to beat you on them because it would mean you having boyfriends." So help me God, I had every intention of chopping his hands off at the wrist while he slept if he ever did that to my child. Period! And that's when I knew that it was time to start thinking of moving on, because I knew as a Cop the Law would crucify me for him.

Sister Love visited frequently and that was a big help but I hid everything from her. I didn't want her telling our mother; it would kill her. To have just gotten off a murder charge a couple years earlier and now living with a husband who was beating me, it would have been easy for her to think the worst. My mental well being largely depended on knowing my mother was okay. It would have been easy for me to lose my strength if I knew she was falling. I lived for my mother and my children. I was tired of calling on our Pastor just about every week, but he was all I had. He once said to me that of the six hundred plus marriages he had officiated, we were closest to him because of his constant attention to us.

All the people I knew were his friends. My only visiting family was Sister Love but I didn't want to bother her; afraid she'd worry my mother.

My landlord despised him and the Officer living in the front room kept to himself. Across the street from us was another Cop and his wife; lovely couple. They religiously observed the Sabbath but never interfered. Many years later when I saw him in America, his first words to me were: "Holyday, what a way the man could beat you?" He should be ashamed of himself. I wonder what would happen to me if my Pastor had turned a blind eye on me like he did. If that was what "serving and protecting" was all about, he should have resigned from the Force. If my husband was a civilian they would have shovelled him up a million times, but he was one of their own, a member of a very loyal fraternity that serve and protect each other. That neighbour certainly was not an asset to his profession. Thank God I had a chance to see the other side of some who to this day I regard as my family, had it not been for them I would have been left with a bad taste in my mouth.

Going back to the country was never an option. I didn't want to see the rapist, and didn't want to raise my daughter around him. I was still in this first year of my marriage and was hopelessly in love with my husband. I wanted to settle down and get my son home but I couldn't wait for the closing deal on the house, I had to run. Divorce was never a consideration; running away yes; but never a divorce. I expected my marriage to last for life.

With all the skeletons in my closet, and the fear of being alone I thought if I hung in there everything will work out in time, and we could live happily ever after. I was always daydreaming, maybe that kept me sane. Whenever my husband hit me, I looked way ahead and imagine how wonderful everything would be ten years down the line; how I'd be living the good life and all these things would be behind me; had never dealt with the present. There was never anything in the present to live for. Fantasizing how bright our future would be was an escape. I lived for the future. I believe now that it was a divine way of maintaining my sanity. But my husband's lack of respect was killing me. The humiliation of having his mistress a couple doors away, beating me in front of Dawn, our helper, people on the street; life began to zap all the energy out of me. At times I felt like I was just hanging in there for the sake of my children, my mother and the chance to run away with Dawn. At work I joked a lot trying to cover up my pain; other times I was moody, withdrawn or I hummed all day but I felt safe at work. The moment it was time to go home, I was a nervous wreck. And from all that I had been through, Douglas beating upon me was like peeling the skin off my body. Dear God in heaven!

My mother once told me I could sit on my pride but should never walk on my dignity. On Sunday September 8, 1976 less than 2 years after our marriage, there were talks earlier that day between my husband and "his friend of convenience" who owned a red Subaru car about a trip to a Mineral Bath. Douglas never had a car. He drove the Police Land Rover while on duty. The Mineral Bath they spoke of was only a few minutes away from where my mother lived. I wasn't invited even though my battered body needed the bath more than they did.

When my husband was picked up, the car went in the direction where his mistress lived a few houses away. I deliberately positioned myself on the veranda to see what was going on. Would they really have the audacity to pass by the house with her? A few minutes passed, then they whisked by, I didn't want to believe my eyes. Totally abandoned; that's how it made me feel. I thought, in addition to all the beatings and the humiliation of a third party just doors away; now a mineral bath on a Sunday minutes away from where my mother lived while I was left to press his overalls for a marijuana raid the next morning; I'll be damned!

We had only been married eighteen months, divorce was never a consideration. I made it an evening on the veranda, deliberately to see if they would have the audacity to use the same route on their return or if they would show me a little respect. Several hours later I guess I wasn't expected to be there, but I was, looking into every car that went by, seething with anger while giving the appearance of one lounging on a Sunday afternoon. When the red Subaru drove by; my hair stood up; and I waited. The car stopped a few houses down within the perimeter of where the third party lived. In the meanwhile, I was getting very impatient. I had been sitting there for hours waiting for him to return. He was going to be on the offensive, I knew him. He would try to find some fault or get angry about something even if he had to scheme it.

The overalls hadn't been pressed. I was too frustrated, really didn't care. As far as I was concerned, whether he went on a marijuana raid or not, I couldn't care less. If he had the gall to leave with his best friend and his mistress in front of my eyes after bluntly discussing their Sunday trip to the mineral bath in my presence, "why the hell should I care about him and his overall?" Furthermore, as far as I was concerned, the only person who benefitted from his marijuana raids was his jezebel mother. She had to have her big bottle of over-proof white rum stuffed with marijuana every month for her asthma. She treated it like "American Express" never left home without it. Only God knows how she managed to stomach that stuff. I tried making a cup of tea with it once just to see what it tasted like. The thing didn't just make the house stink; it left me feeling like I was walking in a pile of flour and one foot felt shorter than the other.

When the car left from his mistress' gate it cruised to our gate. He alighted and walked passed me without a word. Somehow I was thinking he might have brushed things off by saying they didn't bother to go or something. Even if it was a lie just to make me feel a little better. He didn't. A couple minutes went by and I began to put the lounge chair away when he aggressively asked "Did you press my overall?" as though I was his dam maid. With all the anger, the rage and the bitterness that consumed me; and all the strength that I could muster, I said to him, "Fuck Off!" "And let me make it very clear, I have never regretted saying that to him." If my going out days were over, then why should I cook, clean and wash while he sports his mistress. He didn't say a word. Deadly! As soon as I was finished folding the lounge chair and ventured inside, he knocked me down with a punch in my chest. Before I could raise myself up, he stomped into my chest with his shoes. When I tried crawling under the bed, he pulled me out, lifted the heavy typewriter and dropped it on my chest. Thank God, my daughter slept through the whole episode, not a pretty sight for a six and a half year old. Blows were landing all over me; blood was running down my face; an eye felt like it was punched in; a tooth felt like the nerve was shattered; (Years later I needed a root canal) and I couldn't see very well. With my clothes practically ripped off, I stumbled to the gate and over to my civilian neighbour (not the cop across the street) who rushed with me to the University College Hospital. Hospital records may indicate the 8th or 9th depending on the time I was seen or admitted.

Along the way to the hospital, I couldn't stop vomiting. Mr. Hamilton pleaded with me to tell the doctor who beat me but I was afraid. I was all my children had and I wanted to live for them and my mother. The doctors tried hard to get his name, but I couldn't, too afraid. I remember being taken for X-ray. When the results came back 5 doctors circled me. One looked at the others and said, "How comes her lungs is like that and she doesn't smoke?" A second x-ray was requested but I don't remember anything else except waking up in a hospital bed in the morning with bandage over one eye and excruciating pain from the eye and all over my body.

I was never told why they found my lungs so black but many years later, I managed to put two and two together when I worked for a famous American Writer/Author in New York City who was suffering from emphysema. Mrs Trilling told me her father wasn't very educated, but he told her that each time he saw her put a cigarette to her mouth, he felt like she was putting a nail in her coffin. My husband was a heavy smoker, so maybe I was the recipient of second hand smoking and it might have made my lungs black at that time.

If my Sister knew what had happened to me, she'd be sure to tell our mother and I did not want my mother worrying anymore. She had been through enough. So when the nurse asked me who she should notify, I asked for Pastor. His reaction when he saw me, told me I was in bad shape. I was only given three weeks at home to recuperate. The glare from the sun made my eye feel like it was being sucked out of my head. If the days were bad, the nights were worst when the lights were switched on. Months later it still felt like I was carrying a load on the affected eye. And even today, 35 years later, the glare of the sun or snow is still stressful on the eye.

I was in the hospital when Dawn awoke the following morning and found Daddy cleaning blood stains off the wall. Being the inquiring child she was, she asked about the blood and she said he told her that it was mosquitoes he killed on the wall. When I got home from the hospital, instinctively she knew what had happened. And according to Mr. Hamilton after he left me at the hospital and returned home, he went over to see my husband; but his knocks on the door went unanswered. Later when Pastor asked him where he was at the time, he said he went to the bank to get money so that he could come to see me. Lie. In my opinion, he thought Mr. Hamilton came back to tell him that I was dead so he had began to plot his defence. I barely had the chance to say thank you to Mr. Hamilton before he left the neighbourhood, he told me that my husband harassed him in an attempt to lay false charges against him.

When Sister Love visited, she had her suspicions but out of fear of her telling mother, I believe I told her someone threw a stone in the bus which caught me in my face. She had no idea I was badly beaten and hospitalized. I'm sure she didn't believe a single word I told her; she knew me better than any other sister. I couldn't fool her if I tried but I just could not imagine my mother hearing that my husband was beating me after having gone through what I went through just barely 5 years earlier. I realize now that it must have scared the daylight out of her, and I was scared too, but with all the bad memories back home, I didn't want to turn back and I dread sending my daughter back to stay with my mother out of fear "the beast" would target her next.

Three weeks later just before I was schedule to return to work I missed having a frying pan smashed in my face because I decided the Friday that my body could do well with a sea bath. Even though I took his best friend's cousin along in case he thought Dawn would cover for me, it didn't matter. Apparently he passed by on duty while we were out and geared himself up for my return; so while I was in the kitchen heating our Thursday evening leftovers for supper he headed straight for the stove and grabbed the frying pan. Thankfully, I was always on my guard and there was an exit door leading out to the open yard.

No matter how happy I pretended to be at work and I really put on a show, I dread going home. Getting off that bus was nerve-racking, I could be beaten right there on the street if my husband felt I was late. My co-workers suspected that I was being beaten too but I denied it. One day one of them just plainly said to me that my eyes looked like I had been crying all night; I told her my husband gave me a lot of jokes and we were up all night laughing. Everyone in the department raised their heads and looked at me. I never had enough time to think of anything better to say.

Leaving the island was my only way out. My Landlord had a friend in Canada who could send me an Invitation Letter but aside from a letter, I needed airfare and 60 Canadian Dollars. Once I secured those I made plans with my Sister to leave as though I was going to work and she would pick up Dawn in the evening from him when I didn't return home. But looking back now, it wasn't a very clever idea; I should have left with her. When one lives in such fear and uncertainty, plans made hastily are bound to cause havoc.

NINETEEN

On the night before I left for Canada, we had the most passionate intimacy. Little did he know I was doing it with vengeance, I had a plan to execute, and like Judas, I was using the only weapon I knew best to inflict the betrayal of a lifetime that could never be forgotten; and I was doing it with his favourite pleasure; sex. The following morning, armed with my documents stuffed in my underwear, I lovingly prepared his breakfast and left as though I had gone to work. I landed in Canada 9pm that night. It was a plan lead by my wonderful landlord who had a friend in Canada, but my freedom would not come so easily.

When I contacted my Sister, I got the news I feared. Douglas refused to hand Dawn over to her. As much as I dread going back to him, I had to get my daughter, there was no way out. But since I had resigned my job, I stayed for a few weeks to earn some cash in case I needed a place to live when I returned. On my way to work one day, I saw a red car behind me looking like the red Subaru Douglas often borrowed from his best friend. I ran as fast as I could and hid in a gas station thinking it was my husband coming after me. While I was hiding it occurred to me I was in Canada; not Jamaica.

I think I was stressed out over my daughter; she was only six and a half and only a few months earlier he caned her when she brought home a classmate and they tried to light the stove. Charlotte was no longer with us. Douglas fired her because she was late one morning, but I had a feeling he got rid of her because we were close and his mistress was only a couple doors away. My nights were restless. I had no choice but to trust my gut feelings that he would love and care for her since he was going to use her as a bargaining chip. And the truth is, even though he mistreated me, there was a special bond between him and Dawn.

Apart from wanting to know my whereabouts and if he would be joining me, not much was said when I contacted him. It seemed he just handed the phone to Dawn, and immediately she asked, "Mommy, why didn't you tell me?" I froze. Little did she know I made plans with my Sister to get her when I landed in Canada but "daddy" refused to hand her over; I didn't have an answer, and I couldn't tell her I didn't want "daddy" to know and she would have told him, it wasn't the time for that. All I knew, if I had to face death, I had to return for her, I was all she had, the only parent.

Almarine's home was one of fun and laughter. They had all night parties every weekend. I wasn't a dancer, wasn't into those things, but I had fun seeing friends coming together and having fun; that wasn't something I had ever experienced before wholeheartedly since I left home with my brother and sisters. I even met a dentist who was looking for love but that was the farthest thing from my mind. I was a pillar of stress. My daughter was on my mind.

After a Saturday Night Party ended and all the attendants left; we were about to retire to bed early the Sunday morning, but there was a knock at the door. I went to get the door thinking someone had left something but somehow I got to the door and just stepped back; never felt like answering. I turned away and told Almarine to get the door.

As Almarine got to the door and asked who is there, a voice replied, "Immigration." I slipped into the living room which was about 3-5 feet from the door and sneaked underneath the couch. Two officers sat on the very couch I was lying under while one stood at one end. My long hair must have been showing because Almarine began to throw the cushions behind the couch as if to make room for the Officers to sit but she was actually covering my hair. Another undocumented friend who ran to the back of the house was caught and deported. I was so very sorry and I'm sure they blamed me. After a short visit they left a message with Almarine for me that my husband sent them to get me so I needed to return home, which was useless because I had already booked my flight to return home. Only God knows how I got under that couch. I made so many attempts after the officers left to fit underneath it again; but I couldn't. God must have known that I would need to return to Canada someday to find refuge for the family and if I was deported, we wouldn't stand a chance.

I have no concrete evidence of how Douglas got information on my whereabouts. I did call him after learning from Sister Love that he refused to turn Dawn over to her but he didn't get my phone number or address. But according to his best friend, when I didn't return home from work, and the hospitals found no trace of me, he casually mentioned to Douglas, "I wonder if Holyday went to Canada" and that innocent assumption led him to check with the Passport Office which confirmed that I had gotten a passport recently, and the Airlines confirmed that I left on a flight to Canada. Douglas then called my landlord with a changeover voice, pretending to be Sister Love, got the whole scoop and then burst out in laughter. That mischievous act almost cost me my sister. She felt that I jeopardized her by revealing everything to Douglas when we reunited, when in fact it was he who told me how he tricked my landlord. Douglas never disclosed how he was privy to such detailed information from places like the Airline and Passport Office but I hope they have corked all those holes now; at least for the sake of a woman who might be running for her life.

The next time I contacted my husband I confirmed the date I would be home. He met me at the airport alone and like a hypocrite, I attempted to greet him with a kiss to get a feel of his mindset, but he turned away. Of course, I could afford to take that chance, airports are crowded, and he couldn't punch me over in such a public place. Surprisingly, he had lost a considerable amount of weight and looked very sad but he was not one to be sorry for; he could floor me with his fist in a split second. I was just thrilled to see my daughter who was more interested in what Mommy brought for her.

"And To my surprise, despite all Douglas's 'weight loss and looking sad," even though he could have waited till I got back he took possession of our house during my absence and his mistress was there with him." "And without any emotion at all, the following morning when we awoke, he showed me a bottle of water mixed with bleach that she used to clean the bathroom. It's as though he was talking about my sister." The grace of God must have been present with me because I didn't say a word in English, not one. But the whole idea made me feel like I wanted to stick my face in the trench at the back of the house and hide from the neighbours. And to make matters worse one of the neighbours was someone I had gone to High School with.

We had moved miles away, his mistress didn't have a car, the only possible way for her to have gotten there was by my husband, and that's why I have never had any animosity towards the lady. I blamed my husband one hundred percent. While he was sending Immigration for me in Canada, he had her in our house. At the same time in my sick mind I thought he must really love me to have gone to such lengths to get me back. And with that belief, was a strong determination to have my marriage succeed; bring home our children, and make our home one big happy family. I really wanted that.

By the time I got back my Sister had left for America. It was so strange. Except for when she left for College, the three of us were like peas in a pod. Now she was gone. No one to fuss over me, style your hair this way; wear that colour; put a bracelet on that hand; be careful when you go to the country; no one to visit me regularly to keep an eye on things. I never pictured myself being at a distance from her. Now I had to look out for myself. But I'd be okay, I thought. Small correction, a leopard never changes its skin.

TWENTY

Our home was in a new developing neighbourhood. There weren't many houses around, and the few that were there were far apart from each other. We were lucky to be sitting between two neighbours who had already taken possession. I shamefully introduced myself to them the following morning.

The soil all around the house was dry with scattered patches of weeds. The backyard was so uneven it looked like a ravine below a mountain so I was very eager to establish a lawn. I had no idea what I was getting into when I undertook such a project. The yard practically became one big swamp from the constant watering and trying to establish a weed free lawn was back breaking. Varnishing the window blinds and painting the exterior walls of the gate were a lot easier. But I will never forget the gratification and the feeling of accomplishment when the lawn and flower beds were established. And the diamond cut wall fencing with two lions perched on either post at the gate drew so much attention it made it all worth it.

Moving to a new community much farther away, meant we had to make changes. For Dawn in particular, leaving Alpha Kindergarten Preparatory and all her friends was a big disappointment; but at least she was able to make friends with kids of both neighbours. At our previous residence she was the only little child, that's why when she brought home a friend from Alpha and Douglas caned her because they tried to light the stove I was very mad because she had no-one to play with at home except the both of us and she didn't understand the danger in striking a match.

For a while things were relatively quiet on the home-front, Douglas and Dawn played like two kids. It was laughable to see him dressed to go out then turning to her and said "D, how do I look?" Larry and his fiancée joined us briefly while their house was under construction. They were an exceptionally funny couple. They played and laughed a lot. You could always hear Winsome saying, "Larry, stop it." Their presence really helped to keep the tension down. Larry had a car and they were best friends so that kept them busy. I loved that. The less he was around; the less likely there would be any fights. He loved to play poker and gambled the horses but it didn't bother me because Larry was fairly intelligent so I always believed that he was just tagging along with my husband and that it was only a matter of time before he influenced him to stop gambling.

Brother Sylvester, my husband's brother, joined us soon afterwards. He had been living in England for over eighteen years but when the Courts imposed a hefty child support fine on him, he couldn't afford it so he found his way back home to his motherland. The fines must have been really astronomical for him to decide to return home because he was a hurting man and it was clear that he missed his children. For a while though, it seemed our home would become a house of friends and I was able to focus my attention on getting some finishing touches done and get the lawn established. I even tried a little farming which I learnt from my mother by digging a hole and placing three goongoo peas (pigeon peas) in it, covered it with water then filled the hole with dirt. Within a year, the tree grew and flourished right in time for Christmas dinner for the neighbours and my family.

If only Brother Sylvester and Larry could have stayed; life would have been better. But as new homeowners with four mouths to feed and one income; after three months, my dear brother-in-law had to return to the humble beginnings he had left in the country almost nineteen years earlier. It was a big loss for me. I loved the way things were when he and Larry were around; no fuss; no fights; no quarrels and whatsoever my husband might have been doing outside went unnoticed.

Things got pretty bad before I got a job but I blamed myself. I was in a good steady job when I ran away so now I must stand the consequence, however, I could go on fasting but my little girl didn't deserve to go hungry again. Douglas paid the mortgage but nothing else seemed to matter and he ate out most of the time; I suspected at his mistress' house and sometimes he would take home a box of dinner for Dawn. At times he stayed away up to three days which was just fine with me. I would rather be hungry and not be beaten up than have a belly full and worry about being beaten, so even if his time away bothered me a little, I could live with it. On one occasion, times got so hard, that one of my neighbours gave me a bit of cheese, a little rice, and the head of a pickled mackerel. It wouldn't make for one of Martha Stewart's cuisine but it put something in our bellies that night and I have never forgotten her thoughtfulness.

Eventually, I got back in the work force, this time at another bank working as the Manager's Secretary. I've always loved working in the banking industry, particularly dealing with numbers; however, I welcomed the opportunity to be the Manager's Secretary. We made a good team.

One of the first things I learnt when I started was that my Canadian Manager had zero tolerance for tardiness, which was a little awkward for a people who were accustomed to being late for work and using a shower of rain as an excuse to call in sick. And it was rumoured that he fired 13 tellers in a single year for being late for work. I had no intention of being added to that list so I made every effort to be at work every morning before my boss so he could never keep a tab on the time I arrived. In turn, he placed a clock on my desk for me to keep a record of late arrivals, but he soon found out that was not an assignment I was comfortable with. With the sense of pride that came with owning my own home, my self confidence soared and my hunger for more out of life grew so I was determined to be always on time for work.

My efforts to be punctual had its drawbacks. Douglas's ugliness began to resurface. There had to be more to my reaching work on time every morning. One morning while I was at work, he walked in, past my desk without a word and went straight into the Manager's office. After a considerable time behind closed doors, he left just the way he came in. My boss never discussed the details of their conversation, but when he inferred if I'm sure I wouldn't like to return to Canada with him and his wife, I realized he sensed that things weren't looking good at home.

I was so ashamed to have my co-workers see my husband walked in and left without speaking to me. Being a very private person, I had never taken my problems to the office. I often boasted about him to mask my pain, so his behaviour that day showed that there was trouble in paradise. I knew it didn't sit well with him when he did the 11-7 shift and I was leaving for work when he was getting home; that to him was like losing control but I was just trying to keep my job.

To tighten the grip on his authority, he turned back on his way to work a Saturday afternoon and demanded that the heavy royal blue wall to wall rug be pulled up out of the living room; rolled up; and be placed in a corner before he returned home. There was no reason for such nonsense except power-play and I wouldn't dare argue with him; or else . . . The mahogany furniture that sat on the rug, especially the buffet and the 36inch wood frame TV, made it extremely difficult, but that was the point, to punish me. For all the time I spent at the house after that, the carpet was left rolled up in a corner of the living room; nothing said, no further instructions, it just sat there while the beautiful mahogany furniture sat on the bare concrete floor.

Before long, the beatings resumed. It seemed to me he was just waiting for his friend and his brother to leave. It had been such a good break for me; I was beginning to feel like it was a thing of the past. Call it short-sightedness if you may, but I was excited about my home and the prospect of moving ahead in life. It was challenging yes, but I was in a fight to save my marriage. I saw potential. We were on the right path, young newly-weds, two professionals; a cop and a banker with a daughter in private school was a dream come true. I really wanted it to work. I was hungry for that little bit of fresh air to glow and grow with my husband, however, the vision was mine alone; he had other plans with someone else. It left me on pins and needles whenever he got home; I never knew what to expect. The expenses of maintaining a home I was sure would settle him down, but I was wrong. The effects of a third party put a strain on me. He was always angry when he got home, like his conscience was bothering him, so whatever antics he could employ to make him feel and sound like an authoritarian, he employed it.

One morning after he battered me and went outside, I could hear the neighbour enquiring at him how I was doing. "She's doing fine Mrs Hall, just fine," he assured her, with his photogenic million dollar smile; "how deceitful!" That is why around 17 years later when a close family member told me that her husband told her that if his family were to desert him, he could kill off the entire family and no-one could find out who did it because of all the mystery movies he watched; I made it my business to tell someone else in case I'm not around.

My husband could beat the hell out of me inside, and then walked outside and smile with the neighbour like all was well. And *"no-one would ever believe"* until I ventured outside. The very morning he smilingly told one neighbour I was fine, a few minutes later when I walked out in sun shades, Mrs. Hall didn't need to ask, she just disappeared. They all knew it was my way of hiding the black and blue marks around my eyes.

In one instance just to spite me, he locked me out of the bedroom the night and didn't open it until 8am the following morning, the exact time I was supposed to start working. The pain in my heart that morning found its way in a song as I bellowed out, *"PLEASE RELEASE ME LET ME GO, I DON'T LOVE YOU ANYMORE."* It was a weapon I used with every power that I could muster from my diaphragm. Not even Percy Sledge could have done it better. It was all I could do to fight back. After my daughter left for school, my body took an unforgettable beating. The song had the intended effect. Whether I was afraid of losing my job or didn't want to be home alone with him, I don't know, but I went to work; presumably looking very dishevelled because the moment my boss spotted me coming he met me and led me straight into his office. Without a word or any question, he offered me the next two days off with pay. "I felt like I needed a month in bed."

As usual, Pastor Shepherd was always there for me but I left with Dawn before the week was over. My friend had no accommodation for two so I took her to an aunt not very far from mother. I felt better leaving her there so she wouldn't be near that man who had raped me. Many years later, she told me my aunt's husband exposed himself to her and when she complained to my aunt she was accused of being "chatty, chatty" then she woke her up early morning when it was still dark and while she prepared her husband breakfast, she sang to her:

"You talk, you talk too much, you talk about people that you do not know . . ."

No wonder she couldn't talk about it until many years later. My aunt never had the gall to confront the animal she had under her blanket; she took it out on her little defenceless seven-year old grand niece. And what made it even worse, when Pastor took me back home, out of fear that I may soon have to run again, I took a week or two before I went for her: that's what makes it so much more painful for me even now.

I use to wonder why my mother's only living Sister at the time of her death didn't come to her funeral; the answer was in my daughter's story but I didn't know until many, many, years later and only then did I understand what she really meant when I went to get her and she ran to me and said, "Mommy, Mommy, I thought you weren't coming back for me." I didn't know, I didn't know, I didn't know *the sheet my auntie was covering with was dirty."*

I lost count of the number of times I ran away from my husband, could be six to seven times yet he always searched for me and took me back home. Each time he seemed so sincere. On one occasion when I ran away near the Christmas holidays I didn't see the possibility of getting even a candy to my mother for her and Colin. Dawn needed a doll for Christmas as well, and we needed food. I needed to get to the house when my husband was at the station. So bearing in mind that his platoon had to be on parade before he actually went on duty; I called the Station, found out when he would start duty and executed my plan.

Just about the time he was scheduled to be on parade I got to the house via taxi, knowing that if he tried to make it home right after getting on duty it would take him about thirty five minutes. And there was a lot to get done quickly so I chose the side door in case Douglas pulled up at the gate, I would have enough time to run up and over the hill at the back. After I surveyed the scene, the first thing I missed was the sight of my flourishing goongoo peas tree which at that time of year was usually laden with peas ready to be harvested for Christmas dinner. Only the stump was left. He had chopped it down. Like the saying goes, *"You can't catch quakoo, you catch his shirt"*. But that was just fine with me, the house was still standing; there was food in it; and that's where I needed to get to. I was on a mission and the taxi meter was running round trip; no time to waste.

My neighbour had no idea I never had a key to get inside my house, so when I asked to borrow her machete, she freely handed me just what I needed to get the side door off. I emptied the cupboards and the refrigerator; sold the 36 inches Zenith Television to a cop who was in the market for a Cabinet TV; and last but not least, with the help of a dearly-beloved brother in law, I managed to get my wedding ring sold for a well needed $80, the equivalent of one United States Dollar based on the current rate of exchange at the time of this writing. It was the best Christmas I ever had during my marriage. And the $80, though not much meant more to me at the time than what the rings represented.

Later when Douglas found me and brought me back, he jokingly said if he had been around when I was chopping off the door, he would have waited for me to run up the hill, shot me and then cried out, "Lord God Almighty, they shot Elisabeth!" I wanted to laugh but I couldn't take the chance because it might just be what he needed to pull the trigger. He was capable of doing what he said. In fact he was so "smart" that if he was going to kill me he would say it before and that has played a key role in helping me whenever I had to make plans to safely getaway.

After chopping off the door; emptying the cupboards and the refrigerator; selling our only television and my wedding ring; and despite all that my husband came back for me, I was convinced that he loved me.

Maybe I just needed to be a little more patient I thought, maybe he wasn't having an affair; maybe they were just friends. Why else would he looking for me so many times? He must love me; maybe I just didn't understand him. I justified everything he ever said and did. "My marriage must work," I pledged to myself, "and I was going to make him love me even more," I thought. Now I know my senses were beaten out of me, or I had gone through so much that I couldn't think anymore.

When I asked him how he managed to find me, he said when he heard I was in a certain neighbourhood he gave the Postman one of our wedding photos to hang in the Post Office so anyone seeing me would notify him. Before long, I was spotted at a girlfriend's house. He came and got me the very night. That's what I meant when I said anything he is going to do he always mention it; just like that he spilled his guts. I can't imagine him before a Judge, but I was thankful; God had to find a way for me to outwit him since he was a bully, so he got him to disclose everything before so I could make my plans around his plans. Anyways, if I was killed that night, it would have been the Postman's fault. He delivered me into his hands. He never asked me why I ran away; he simply took it upon himself to hand me over. As far as I was concerned he was no better than the Inspector of Police who told me that marriage is so sacred only the Divorce Court can deal with it; or the Airline and the Passport Personnel who furnished him the information that I took a flight to Canada when I ran away. I'm glad I'm alive to tell the story. I hope that Postman is alive and has the opportunity to read about the friend he worked for.

TWENTY-ONE

I don't think it was gullible to believe that my husband loved me when he came back for me after I sold my wedding ring; chopped off the house door; emptied the refrigerator; and sold our television. So being convinced that he loved me, it was time to take my marriage to the next level. In keeping with a decision I had arrived at when I returned from Canada, I brought home our two children, Jillian and Colin; convinced that my family was now rooted and unshakable. The family as he knew it was now a complete unit and I was determined to have my marriage work.

The sounds of laughter and children at play in the house were like a breath of fresh air. I felt a zest for life again. My son came home, and like my children, Jillian readily called me Mommy and it felt right. I loved my step daughter, a shy soft spoken unassuming little girl. She was so very warm and gentle. I can never say enough about Jillian. If there was a word that truly describes her it would be, adorable. When I took her to school and the teacher claimed Admissions was closed, they had no more space, no benches; I offered to make the bench. Whether she accepted or declined, I don't know. All I knew was that she had to be at the same school as Dawn. Years later when she won scholarship for High school it was discovered that she had never been registered. It didn't bother me one bit my objective was achieved; she got her scholarship and moved on to High School.

Colin was accepted in an All Boys' School. From day one he wasn't a favourite of my husband's but I tried to play it down, giving them time to bond, hoping it would change. I loved being a parent, helping them at nights with their homework and then sitting down with them for warm Horlicks and Crackers at bedtime; just being a mother for the first time to all of them felt truly special. They took my mind off all my sorrows of the past. I had them to fuss over, no time to think about the past. I absolutely adored those times with my children. We all played hide and seek and tickled one another especially when dad was on duty. His temper was not a secret so any sight of him coming through the open lot, the kids would scream "Mommy, Mommy, Daddy coming," and we would studiously huddle around the TV like we were watching Little House on the Prairie, Happy Days with Fonzie or my very favourite, the Six Million Dollar Man. But again, a leopard never changes its spots and so the beatings resumed. It was so humiliating being beaten when the children were around. *"MANY YEARS LATER WHEN MY DAUGHTER TOLD ME SHE DIDN'T SEE ME AS HIS WIFE, SHE SAW ME AS HIS CHILD, THAT'S WHEN IT REALLY DAWNED ON ME THAT THEY SAW TOO MUCH."*

The beatings were so frequent and unwarranted that I can't remember all the things I was beaten for, or, the many mornings I walked out in dark glasses so no one would see my eyes. One thing was sure his behaviour was having serious consequences on me and the children and I felt sadness from Jillian for what her dad was doing to me. I could see the unspoken grief in her eyes. There was a bond that we shared with our eyes. We genuinely loved each other. I remembered her coming to me and whispering, "Mommy, Daddy took the money from where you hide it in the cabinet." He gambled the mortgage many times. The beatings while the children were around left me demoralized. It cut my power in effectively dealing with them and with the types of bonds that were forming, matters were destined to get out of control if they were not addressed with love, warmth and understanding; qualities which were hard to express when I was being battered so mercilessly all the time.

Dawn had been with us the longest and she was very attached to Daddy. Jillian became a little jealous of the both of them, understandably so. And she became friendlier with the little girl next door, leaving my two children to bond together. I'm sure they resented her for what her dad was doing to their mother and Jillian resented Dawn for the bond she had with her father. Later, the tides changed when my daughter felt she had lost her space to Jillian. Bottom line, if Mommy and Daddy were affectionate with each other, it would have spread to the children; they didn't fail us, we failed them.

I was making breakfast one morning when the two girls began chasing each other around the house. Dawn was so tiny she always ran for help. When she ran inside the house crying: "Mommy, Mommy, Mommy," Jillian still followed in hot pursuit, so I screamed at her to stop chasing her; Douglas dashed in the kitchen, grabbed the frying pan off the stove and went towards my face but I made a quick exit at the side door. Those were the types of things that tied my hands as a mother plus his dislike for Colin was destroying me. He wanted him out of the house from the very week he arrived. Every time he came home he would ask me when I'm taking Colin back to my mother in the country; I never answered him. My son was so happy to be finally home with us and not be bothered about being bitten by mosquitoes in the country. But according to him, "bumpy, bumpy pickney like him belonged in the country," that was my son's crime; the scars on his hands and feet from mosquitoes. And knowing all he had been through in his short life and what he has to live with, it wounded me.

Following a strong argument one evening, afraid of what might follow, I painfully put Colin on the bus back to Grandma with a promise to return for him soon even if I had to run away from Douglas. I still grieve over that. Years later when he told me that he was so afraid of going home that night because it was late so he stopped by his Godfather at the church, there were no words to describe my grief. It's one of those things that not even time can heal. And I will never forget the letter my mother wrote to me, but knowing my plans to leave the matrimonial home soon, in less than two months I returned for him. Strangely, Douglas never bothered him again until he brought home a school project; a little plant to study its' growth and to make notes on it. The little boy planted it underneath the dining room window outside. After a few days, the son of a bitch uprooted the little boy's project and threw it away. He got zero for his assignment. He was so afraid of him, yet at the same time I had to be careful when to run away without getting hurt.

The man hated the child so much that when the school created a new timetable for mornings and afternoons, even if his classes began at 3pm and my husband was home at 8am, the little boy had to leave with me when I left for work in the mornings and stayed at his friend's house just to be out of his sight. I hated him for what he put my child through! I never get over that. Never, never, never. For this child to be so traumatized from such an early age and then have this added when he finally got the chance to be with me, his mother, was nothing but hell for the both of us. It is my prayer that if "Sir Douglas" is still alive to read this that he would just perish; period. He was a little boy who faced hell from the age of 2 ½ when he lost his whole family in one day; father dead, mother thrown in jail, his 6 month old brother taken away. By the time the trial was over, I was pregnant. Six months after having the baby I left him again for safety. Two years later I took the baby and left him alone with my mother. Now I straightened out my life and managed to take him home with us and the little "frighten Friday country boy called husband, wrapped in Police uniform to serve and protect," traumatized my child! "If that wasn't murder in the highest degree by a member of the Constabulary Force, then so help me God, I don't know what is." "I am not going to wish it on Luke." I just want God to deal with Douglas, and He will; someday." "That's a promise, in case anyone has any doubt, read St. Matthew 26:6," *"But whomsoever shall offend one of these little ones that believe on me, it would have been better for him that a millstone(A ROCK) was hung around his neck and he be thrown in the depth of the sea."* "He might be slow but He is sure." His reward will come, if it hasn't come yet!" "The beast" didn't escape God's wrath and so help me God Douglas doesn't stand a chance of escaping it either. My only regret is I won't get the satisfaction of seeing him enjoy his misery.

A previous incident necessitated my need to be hospitalized overnight. My mother-in-law, the jezebel from hell happened to be visiting at the time (she invited herself). To ensure my family had enough to eat while I was in hospital, on my way home from work, I stopped to pick up a few items. I got off the bus, both hands loaded with groceries and I spotted Douglas coming across the open lot. I thought he was coming to assist me but I couldn't be more wrong. As I alighted from the bus, instead of helping me, the wicked wretch landed a blow in my chest. I fell backwards and crashed on a huge rock stone while the grocery bags flew in all directions. I was too late coming home again. It was as though the full weight of his body came down on me in that blow. Thank God for my neighbour across the street. His eyes must have followed Douglas from the time he saw him walking across the open field to the bus stop; they knew him. That young man dashed across the open lot like lightning and raised me up. As I shamefully walked across the open lot still weighed down with the grocery bags, I could see my next door neighbour standing by her gate. I was so ashamed, but thanks be to God by the time Jan realized it was me she turned and walked away before I got to my gate to spear me further embarrassment. She must have known how ashamed I was, I can only hope that she reads this memoir and can put two and two together. Later that night, midnight to be exact, I suffered the embarrassment of a lifetime when I wet myself in bed; the entire bed was soaked. Thank God I didn't get a beating for that too. The man simply got out of bed at midnight and allowed me to change the linens. Almost thirty years later, I still suffer from chronic pain in that area of my back that crashed on the stone.

There was no point postponing my appointment at the hospital, my body told me I needed to be admitted. A retroverted womb; not walking properly; then on top of that I was badly beaten; I couldn't wait to get to the hospital just to lie down somewhere safe and rest. The doctors and nurses instinctively knew that my case was more than a retroverted womb. My face was swollen and I was stressed and afraid. They took turns pleading with me to tell them what happened, but I wouldn't. I was in a no-win situation; I was married to a cop and I had my children left in the house. I had to return for them.

When I was due to be discharged, the wretch was right there with his big broad handsome "fake" smile as usual and I'm sure looking at him no one would have thought he was capable of such atrocities, what a mistake!

When I got home he made me a pot of fish soup trying to make up for the beating or because I wet the bed. That's how he was; he would beat me up, and then try to patch me up. Another mind game he played was a Percy Sledge song: *"If You Don't Know Me by Now"* as though he beating me stemmed from my failure to understand him. "Dear Lord!"

His mother by now was a regular guest, *"AGAIN"*, leaving only after he got paid on the 29th of the month. I was almost sure she instigated a "beat-me-up" by finding something to complain about the moment I turned my back. It had always been her hobby ever since she came by the very first time and heard that I was charged for murder; to do all she could undercover to separate us without telling him directly what she learnt. She had never invited herself and left without me getting a beating and she getting her bottle of Wray & Nephew white rum stuffed with the marijuana taken from his pockets when he went on a raid. Her asthma medicine, she called it. The woman was such a jezebel in my life that many years later when I heard she died after being knocked down by a cyclist, I had absolutely no remorse. And it never bothered my conscience because I don't expect to see her in heaven. "God wants Saints and Angels in His Kingdom, not Jezebels."

I was on my way to call my brother-in-law Malachi one night to talk to his brother, when I came upon a Convention at a street side Baptist Church. It was just what I needed but somehow I couldn't find the joy I once knew to fully appreciate what I was witnessing. I was like a lost sheep. For a while I stood there reminiscing on the good old days back in the country when I was "head cook and bottle washer" running to church from dusk to dawn; how I promised God when I was in trouble that if He delivered me I would serve Him. I felt so sorry for myself, I even thought those people in church were better than me. And it was common to feel that I was paying a heavy price for not keeping my promise with God, but the sense of security of being married to a law enforcement officer was an instant fix.

I watched for a while but with all that I had going on in my life there wasn't much of a joy in my soul. I wasn't feeling the way I used to feel when

I was excited about church from dawn to dusk so I turned and walked away. Little did I know that the "what have you" standing next to me was a scoundrel waiting for food, as soon as I turned and walked away she (yes, a she) faced me with a pair of scissors over my left breast; and with no time to think or even say Lord have mercy, I quickly handed over the choker chain from around my neck with my name 'Elisabeth" and emptied my wallet for "<u>her</u>". I was able to give a good description of the assailant to my brother-in-law. For weeks Malachi carried a lunch bag filled with stones to stone her out of the neighbourhood but she disappeared. When I told my husband; it was as good as trying to talk to the dead.

I have never had a break. It seems I was always overcoming one thing to face another. These are the reasons I could not chronicle my story in a book while my mother was alive. It would have shortened her days or it would have killed her instantly. I needed her to live and I wanted to live for her. The strain and stress, the beatings and the running up and down from place to place were taking a heavy toll on my daughter. Her lights began to dim, her grades rapidly failed; her smile was almost gone. On my way to work one morning as I strolled through the open lot, my son ran behind me with a brown paper bag as though I had forgotten something. He said, *"Mommy, Mommy, let's run away"*. My mind was already made up that we would be leaving for good soon. Timing was everything, but it hurts to know that in his eye it appeared I wasn't doing anything to get out of the situation. To save my life, I had to be strategic.

"THE DAY I COULD NOT MOVE OR SPEAK"

One Saturday morning, I was sitting in the living room couch. What no one realized was that I could not move or speak. The children passed by, looked at me and walked by as they headed outside to play. I distinctly remember my husband passing by, looked down at me, then raised his brow and went by. All along I was just praying that he wouldn't push me to get up and do something because all I could do was gaze at everyone as they passed by, I couldn't move not even a finger. I don't even remember if I had any feelings, but I could see and I could hear. It seemed the stresses of my life was about to leave me with a stroke. If my children could survive another blow, my mother most certainly could not handle another trauma. Miraculously, after a period of about 15 minutes, I was able to get up and I regained my speech. I kept everything to myself so much that it wasn't until a couple years later when I confided to a Nurse friend what happened to me that she told me it was a stroke.

Another time after Douglas learnt of my trouble with the law, I was home alone when he threw me on the floor, threw his body on top of me with his face almost pressing against mine and said, "just shift, just shift, just shift so I can shoot you and tell them that you attempted to stab me and I shot you." Whether he was armed or not I don't know, but I remember holding my breath so my chest wouldn't go up and down. I was so frightened I don't think I said a prayer, but it was fun to him because when he got up, he had a grin on his face. Those were the things that excited him it seemed; treading on the weak; for me, it was *torture in the gas chamber.* To this day, I am still afraid of the man. No human being should be allowed to demoralize and destroy another human being like that. He used my past trouble to intimidate and scare the hell out of me! If the chronicling of this saga can help one victim, then my God, my living has not been in vain.

After a beating one Sunday, I ran to Ruth's home, a Sister I had met at Bethlehem Tabernacle Church. I knew Pastor Shepherd would be in church, that's why I went to Ruth. She suggested I rested on her bed and try to take it easy until Pastor was done at church. I was lying on the bed with my eyes glued to the ceiling, lost in my thoughts when I heard a little voice within said, "first Peter five verses six and seven (1Peter 5: 6-7)". I never thought anything of it; I just figured it was my mind telling me something. I happened to mention it when Pastor arrived, and, as usual, with his big broad reassuring smile he said, "But you're getting messages man" That was the end of it. I read my Bible a lot but in those days I mostly read the Psalms, and I do get a lot of visions, but I have never been spoken to so clearly by a voice from within while I was awake. Somehow when he took me back home, I turned to the Scripture the same night just out of curiosity. This is what it says:

"Humble yourself therefore
Under the mighty hand of God
And He will exalt you in due course,
Casting all your cares upon Him
For He careth for you."

Deliverance was on the way—and that was God himself giving me hope through the Scriptures, 1ˢᵗ Peter 5:6-7. I have always had dreams, some prophetic, but up to that time, I had never had a prophetic inspiration from a voice within while I was awake. I have never forgotten that Scripture, but with so much happening at the time I never had time to ponder the words, plus, there were many times when I felt that God was using my husband to execute judgement upon me for the death of my son's father so it was hard for me to make sense of anything. All I ever prayed for was that somehow, my Brother Victor would return home from England to "beat up" my husband and get me out of the marriage. That was all I hoped for; I couldn't see a way out. Now I can say 1ˢᵗ Peter 5 verses 6&7 was a solid promise that deliverance was on the way, for little did I know that God was about to send Moses to deliver me out of Egypt from under King Pharaoh's regime.

TWENTY-TWO

I was sitting at my typewriter with the dicta-phone in my ears about to start the day's correspondence when a tall, dark, handsome man with an imposing physique wearing a hat with a cane in his hand looking like an English tycoon walked through the doors. He had his eyes fixed on me from the moment he walked through the doors right up to my desk. I didn't find anything unusual about that because as the Manager's Secretary, it was common for some of the wealthier customers to come to me directly for everything, from getting their account numbers, to getting their transactions done, or just to have a quick chat with the Manager. But this time, it was definitely not business as usual. As he approached my desk I removed the dicta-phone from my ears so I could assist him. I noticed that he glanced at my wedding ring then he leaned over in my ears with the question that would later change the course of my life. "Are you happily married?" With my heart pounding, I nervously managed to say "my husband is a very jealous man," but I don't think he heard me, either that, or, what I said meant nothing to him. He confidently leaned over my desk, looked me squarely in my eyes again and said, "You didn't answer my question, are you happily married?"

Even though I avoided a direct answer the first time, I was so desperate to love and be loved that I was sure I fell in love with him before he finished asking me the question a second time. And I am sure I didn't sleep that night. I had reached a point where my self esteem had gotten so low that I thought I was nothing but a shell of myself covered behind the mask of

195

a happy-go-lucky office smile and my hair swept up in a bun. Before long the staff saw that a new woman was emerging. There was never a doubt in my mind I was going to love him one hundred percent and he would adore me even more. Deliverance had come.

Even the beatings from my husband now felt bearable because hope was on the horizon. From a housewife who just went to work and came home just to be beaten up and kicked around in front of the kids and the helper, or be met on the street with a fist in my chest for being late; now suddenly there was light and quite possibly a way out of the nightmare I was living.

I knew if he could be so brave even with my married ring on my finger then I should be able to confide in him my desire to escape. One little thing worried me. I didn't get a chance to socialize much so I wondered if I would know how to behave or, if my conversations could be normal when my little world was so very crowded with more skeletons in my closet than a graveyard. He was only seeing the outside, not the insecure nervous wreck I was who seemed happy in the days but shivered when it was time to leave the office and go home. I strove to be as happy and as cheerful as I could to keep him interested and to find the strength I needed to break away from my husband. I had to get out and I had to act fast before the 'God sent' man heard anything about my past and walked away.

We ruled out dating while I was still at home but we talked a lot on the phone. He was a real good listener, not pushy and very compassionate. I even wondered if he was a Christian, or from a Christian home, that's why it didn't surprise me when he told me his mother, by a dream she had, could describe me to him. Just before we got off the phone once he said he didn't want to hang up, like he sensed something was going to happen to me. He was right. I was whipped that night. God knows what for; it was far too often to remember all the silly things I was beaten for. I didn't tell him because a huge part of our daily conversations were about the beatings and he would always ask me if I am going to sit down and let the man kill me, so I didn't want to load on much more in case he got discouraged and walked away. I learnt to water things down. Being so weakened mentally and emotionally from the years of beatings I had little or no self-confidence left so what seemed like a simple task to some was an insurmountable battle for me. Packing and leaving was easier said than done, I wanted to live for my mother and my children.

Eventually I found the courage to make plans to leave my husband for the last time. When I told David, being the gentleman that he was, he said, "Are you sure? Remember the final decision is yours so be careful I don't want to read about you in the papers, think about it, and if you still decide to let me know." All that was "pretty talk" to me; I needed to get out of the hole so why prolong the agony. But I understood how David felt; he knew I was a big coward so he was fearful of me getting out safely.

I waited for my husband to be on the 3 to 11 shift one Saturday evening. He drove by, as usual to do his regular spot check on me and to have dinner. By this time the window curtains were taken down; washed, folded, and boxed under the bed, ready to go. I had secured a two-bedroom apartment, but my bedroom windows faced the street and I could not afford new curtains at the time. Luckily for me when he missed the curtains and asked about them he didn't bother going to the back of the house to make sure they were hanging on the line because I probably would not have been around to pen my story. Believe it or not I must have taken leave of my senses to have hid them under the bed, and how on earth could I be running away from him and ended up getting a place in the adjoining community right by the street side where he could easily see us when he passed by on duty. It took me many years later to realize how lucky I was.

Leaving my step daughter, Jillian, behind was the most difficult task that evening. It was so unfair to her. She did nothing to deserve that. I wished to God I could have taken her. My goodness! The little girl who came to call me Mommy was so warm and lovable that even to this day I worry about the damage I might have inflicted forever by walking away with my two biological children and left her behind. That was vicious! No mother under the sun should be forced to make such a decision; one never gets over it. I had fought long and hard to get her father to own her, got his name on her Birth Certificate, brought her in from the country to live with us. I got her into the same school Dawn attended and even when the teacher declined to accept her for lack of space, I offered to make the bench for her, and now I was abandoning her. It was gut-wrenching. To ensure her safety until my husband got home from work, I left her with my next door neighbour. There was no time for chit-chat with the neighbours. They had seen and heard enough. Hanging around for too long could be fatal if for any reason he turned around and found me leaving. Everything had to be done fast and with precision. I tried to take some comfort in the thought that it was only a few mornings earlier that she witnessed her dad grabbed a frying pan off the stove to slap me because I shouted at her as she chased Dawn around the house but even that was no consolation. I had to go my body couldn't take anymore. We were a disgrace to our neighbourhood. I was either wearing dark glasses the morning after to hide a black and blue mark, or, I was getting beating from the bus stop through the open lot to the house.

A couple days after we left, Douglas met Dawn on her way home from school and squeezed everything out of her. He found out where we were living. Next came a call to me at the bank from an Officer at the Station wanting to meet with me; out of respect, I agreed to meet with him. I suspected he was calling because he was approached by my husband and I thought I would use the opportunity to let the people he worked with learn about his ugly side. It didn't take me long to realize that the meeting was to seek reconciliation. Poor thing, he had missed his punching bag.

Looking at my husband standing beside the Officer you would think he was a lamb, so pitiful, but I was uncomfortable meeting behind closed doors with two uniformed men with weapons. What if he didn't get his way and lost his temper? I didn't waste my time, I got straight to the point. "Officer, I have absolutely no intention of returning to this man who beats me up practically every week whether it be on the street from work or at home. We have been separated several times before and it's always the same thing over and over." The Officer offered no help and he didn't even reprimand him; at least not in my presence; he simply rolled his eyes, looked me squarely in the mine and said, *"Well, Mrs. Holyday, Marriage is so sacred, only the Divorce Court can deal with it."* In other words he could do nothing. Except for when I was in custody it was the loneliest I ever felt. That to me was like handing the man a gun and saying to him "kill her", and then we will charge you; literally throwing me to the wolves. I wonder if he had a daughter facing a similar situation if he would have spoken like that. I doubt it; unless he was expecting a fat insurance check after her funeral. Separation is not divorce. All the officer did was drill another hole in my casket. I could just vomit! Had my husband been a civilian I am sure it would have been handled differently. Clearly, I was on my own. No one cared. The people who were supposed to serve and protect me during my marriage failed me. In fact, that Officer in my opinion was just as dangerous as the Postman who led Douglas to the address where he had seen me. I wondered why I had even bothered to attend the meeting anyways. The man gambled, drank and was extremely abusive. We had been separated repeatedly before only for the same patterns to be repeated. The red Subaru friend told me that each time I ran away, he drove him to a Psychic. The last time they went, the moment the Psychic saw him he said to him "how many times has she left now 6 or 7 leave her alone somehow it is not meant to be." And Douglas told me personally, that everywhere he went they told him that his wife loved him. Yet I was so naive at the time, I had no idea he went to those places, I thought he meant his friends told him that I loved him. But despite all that reassurance, when it suited him I was locked out of the bedroom; allowed back in few minutes before the time I was due to start working. If he felt I was late getting home from work, I was met and beaten, whether alighting from the bus or on the street. If I took a ride from any co-worker, there was suspicion and a heated argument or a reprimand. Any gifts from customers were burnt including a pair of sandals a co-worker bought for me in Miami. I ran away to Canada and he sent Immigration Authorities for me. He harassed anyone who ran to my rescue. I couldn't visit my mother without him tagging along like a watchman. The only logical reason I can think of for this man to have gone to an officer to summons me for reconciliation was very simple; he had missed his punching bag. After the meeting with the Officer, the following morning he came by for the single wooden spoon I had taken when I left. When he TOOK it he turned to me and said, *"Let the Divorce Court decide what you can take." The Officer had freely issued him the license he needed.*

Just to see my son being able to sleep in until it was time for school instead of leaving with me early in the mornings to stay at his friend's house until his classes began in the afternoon made it all worth it. He was a very tired little boy and I'm thankful to be here to pen this story.

With a very special person now blowing the wind beneath my wings I began to feel much lighter. It was nice to have a friend I could talk to and not be afraid. I felt loved and I was falling in love, but I always had an eye over my shoulder. For a while I began to have a taste of the good life and a chance to get a feel of what it was like to be treated like a lady. I loved every minute of it. I didn't feel like I was committing adultery. It was God himself who intervened by sending Moses to deliver me. I felt good about being free, being loved and being cared for. I deserved to be; every woman deserves that. David realized how fearful I was of my husband and he made it his duty to transport me to and from work every morning and evening. Pulling up in that blue Mercedes, I felt like a lady, I was special to someone.

One Saturday morning when he found me doing the kids laundry by hand he changed that and made it possible for me to have a Helper on the weekends so I could get some well needed rest. And it was a delight to see the joy on the children's faces every Saturday morning when they got their little allowance. It was beautiful to see the simple little pleasures of life that they were finally getting; their freedom, a little pocket money, their Sunday evening ice cream, just to see them happy instead of being tense all the time was such a relief. It was moments like those that gave me a glimpse of how beautiful life could be if only I could get away far from my husband where I wouldn't have to worry about crossing paths with him. As long as there was a likelihood of us crossing paths, I couldn't predict what could happen to me. He had made me a promise that he would "mark up my face" if he couldn't have me and that really terrified me but I felt safe when David was around.

At the Banks' Annual Christmas Party that year, he confidently escorted me. I was proud and I felt pretty in a stunning off-white silk gown with broad lines of lace running diagonally from the shoulder to the hem with a low cut neckline and two spaghetti straps which began in the center of my chest, hugged around my neck and tied in the back with the strings left to dangle. My hair hung loosely down to my shoulders. I cannot put into words how lucky I felt to have had the privilege to step out with a man by my side, looking and feeling so glamorous and feeling so loved. I wished it could have lasted, but somewhere in the recesses of my mind I knew someone would someday leak my past to him; it's not who you know it's who knows you. And sadly, up to this point in my life, 33 years later, I still hope to have an occasion to look and feel the way I felt at that Annual Christmas Party with David at my side. If I don't get the chance again, then the memories will have to suffice me.

One day when David came to see me he wasn't looking too happy, and knowing what's what, I was always prepared to think the worst. When I asked him what happened he said he dreamt my husband the night before firing several shots at him, but every shot Douglas fired missed, while all his shots hit the target. We were lying across the bed just seconds after he told me the dream when my husband came peeping through the window curtains and said, *"Did you know it's my wife you're in there with?"* The brave tower of strength man lying beside me, boldly got up and said to him, *"you're talking about your wife; I'm talking about my woman."* That was my turning point! Help had finally come, finally he met his match, someone who could silence him and he couldn't beat him like the way he trampled on me every week for seven years; on some occasion twice a week. I was convinced this man was divinely sent to deliver me. I learnt that day how the rich and powerful spoke with conviction, and without fear. I couldn't believe what I was witnessing. This was exactly the type of partner I needed; one who could stand up to a bully and to not be intimidated. My husband walked away looking like a little wimp without uttering a single word. That day I grew stronger but I knew that I had to be even more vigilant knowing he could finish me off in a split second if he got his hands on me.

Many weeks following that incident I dared not venture outside of the bank for lunch; the girls brought my lunch in for me and David picked me up after work. When staffers at the bank pointed out Douglas to me lurking among the crowd in the street with marketers he was hardly recognizable. His low cut hair and clean shaven face was unkempt as a disguise as he mingled among marketers waiting for me to venture outside; but I never did. When that failed, he returned to my place before dawn one morning with threats of what he was going to do to me. I was dead scared of him because he had promised me that if he couldn't have me he would "mark up my face". We were inside but we had no phones, just huddled together behind locked doors.

I didn't wait for my ride that morning I was eager to get away instantly. Shortly after he left, we got dressed and sneaked out into a taxi. I left them at their respective schools and headed for work where I proceeded in my capacity as the Manager's Secretary to prepare myself a job letter for a visitor's visa America from the American Embassy. Without waiting for the manager to arrive, I signed the letter myself and took a taxi to the Embassy for a visa. Luckily, I was among the fortunate few whose applications were considered. As fate would have it, the computers went down (so we were told) and we were asked to pick up our visas after lunch. I was ecstatic. I called Sister Love in America, she was excited too. She promised to start dividing her clothes so I could get some of hers to wear when I arrived. We would later set a date as soon as I could get my airfare. I promised to call her back after lunch when I got my visa.

Lunch time we gathered for our visa. Everyone else got theirs except me. I was given a pink slip of paper to see the Consulate again. My heart sank. What could possibly have gone wrong? I knew I didn't wait for the Manager to arrive to sign the letter. Did they find out I wondered? When I met the officer he showed me the back of a complimentary card and asked me if I recognized the writing. I almost fainted. With a deep breath I said, "Yes sir, that's my husband's writing." I never got the visa. My husband stated that we were married but separated, that we had three (3) children; that I had a Sister in America; and I might try to get a visa to leave so they should not give it to me because I wouldn't return. I don't think anyone

202

needs an explanation of what it felt like to be in such a position and have the last open door to walk through, slammed in my face.

"Sir", I said, "my husband has been beating me for seven years now; he'll kill me if I don't get away from him. We have been separated over seven times and there was no one to help me. Are you going to let him kill me and leave my children to suffer?" Interestingly, the officer seemed very touched by my plight. He said he didn't understand why some Policemen were like that but with that kind of information in the system, he could not over-ride it so I would have to wait for four years when it was taken off the system and then I could try again. I could tell he was trying real hard to make sure I understood his position. There are no words to describe how I felt and the helplessness that accompanied the feelings. The following day when Miss. Ricketts from Personnel called me to tell me I didn't have a job because I had forged the Manager's signature it made no sense, because once I got back to the office I was the one who told my boss what I did earlier and he understood my plight; even David understood when he learnt why I left instead of waiting for him to take me to work. However, Miss Rickets was late, because I had already contacted the Tourist Board for a list of hotels with job vacancies and began setting up interviews so I could get a job as a Front Desk Clerk where I could meet a Canadian to get an Invitation Letter to return to Canada. I had my mother and three young lives to protect and my body couldn't take anymore beatings. I had to start looking ahead. A mere separation was not going to do it. I had to get away out of the country. Time was of the essence. Every 24 hours that went by was a day too long.

As the saying goes, when it rains it pours. A few days later when David came by, he wasn't looking too happy and his body language clearly told me something was very wrong. He wanted to ask me something he said, so he invited me into the bedroom. My worst nightmare came through when he asked, "What happened to you and that guy?" I stared at him without saying a word, as though I was waiting to hear more before shooting off my big mouth. Then he said, one of his employees told him I was charged for the murder of my son's father but he didn't believe him. I felt like a weight came down on me. And after a long pause, I painfully told him that I was charged and acquitted. The wonderful man whom God had used to deliver me was baffled. The lives of two people genuinely in love with each other just got ran over by a truck. I was crushed. Our lives crumbled and the lives of two children further affected again. I was so sorry for them. They didn't understand and I didn't know what to say to them. We saw each other a few more times and I could tell he was genuinely sorry to leave but he just didn't know how to handle it. He needed time and space and I gave it to him. Many years later I was shocked to learn from him that it was because my husband tried to get him in trouble why he had stopped seeing me. I had no idea. But I shuddered to think what Douglas would have done to me had I confronted the mistress he'd been dating just weeks after our marriage and ended up marrying weeks after he divorced me. The answer . . . I would have been shovelled up and dumped in the morgue.

Without my job at the bank, no financial help and no ride from David to safely get me around, weathering the storm meant tightening our belts and getting away as far as I could. It was difficult to maintain an apartment that was convenient for the three of us while I was not working. I settled for a room in a house which I shared with two male auditors from Price Waterhouse. To keep my ex off of my trail, I boarded out my daughter for two months. My son stayed with me for a couple weeks but I was scared he'd be followed so I asked Sister Bev to accommodate him for a few weeks but she only had a one-bedroom so his stay was very brief. Times got real tough, I had to find a little money for my sister to keep my son and I had to find boarding fee for my daughter plus rent for my scarcely furnished one room. I could hardly find food to eat. The guys kept a cupboard filled with canned goods and snacks which they showed me and told me I could add my own and we could all share, but I never got a chance to add anything and by the time I left, the cupboard was practically empty.

When Kerona paid me a visit she said, "Elisabeth, if I were you I would try to go back to Canada." She could see the hardship I was facing and I am sure she sensed that I was avoiding her coming into my room. When I picked up a job at a Hotel as the Manager's Secretary instead of Front Desk Clerk, my single goal was to pick up a few shifts at Front Desk where

I could meet a Canadian and get an Invitation Letter. In the meanwhile, with my new job, I could afford to get a decent place for the family.

A beautiful apartment with a lovely swimming pool provided a feeling of relief. The idea of coming home and seeing them splashing in the pool didn't sit well with me as a non-swimmer. "What if they needed help?" I couldn't save them. My son was a very good swimmer and diver, a skill he developed when he accompanied Granny to do washing at the river. No amount of talking worked. He taught his sister to swim and so getting home to see them smiling and splashing and just having fun was therapy for me. When my neighbour, a famous Radio Personality who did a show called "Man in the Street" held the microphone before me and asked me how I felt about the high cost of rent, I think I was so excited to have a one-bedroom large enough that could accommodate us and the luxury of a swimming pool that I excitedly told him, "the rent was quite reasonable, no problem." The girls at work recognized my voice and gave me hell. I had over reacted. Not used to having good times.

Despite all the precautions I took, Douglas managed to find out where I worked and just burst on the scene one Friday night; right in the Lobby with that big, broad smile . . . dangerous! I was working at the Front Desk when he walked in. We never exchanged a single word. And even though he was in his uniform, I knew he wasn't there on duty. He was there to make it very clear that he knew where I was. And he was sending a very intimidating message; loud and clear. How he managed to find me at that particular location is still a mystery. There were a number of guests around so I wasn't scared but I was shocked to see him there. Thankfully he left without creating a scene. The little job and 3 mouths to feed was all that was keeping me; I didn't want to lose it. But I knew I had to get away fast. "Trouble was brewing again." Clearly the man had not given up. Being separated from him was one thing, but being separated from one who was a cop and a wife beater with access to a weapon and a hair trigger temper was a dangerous combination. He had already threatened to "mark up my face" if I didn't return. That had me very scared; that's why, when I left the hotel after work that night, I left with the band; Oh yes, a group of people; I didn't take a taxi; he might have stopped it and dragged me out. Thanks to the wonderful TV Anchorman and his band that performed that night. After their performance, they gave me the pleasure of serenading me with Lionel Ritchie's "Three Times a Lady" then they took me straight home inside my house. I have never forgotten those *Good Samaritans.*

It was crystal clear that for my safety I had to get away, and I had to get away fast. I could never understand how he made no secret of his mistress who was almost my next door neighbour yet he wouldn't leave me alone. The only way I was going to have any peace in my soul and feel free to walk on God's green earth without looking over my shoulders was to get away as far as the east was from the west; out of the country. My body couldn't take any more blows and there was nowhere to hide that I could not be found. If I was going to be of any use to my children, I had to get away, but I wrestled with the idea. I didn't want to leave them, but from my experience 3 years earlier, I knew that even though I could hide and do private duty, without proper documentation, they wouldn't be allowed to go to school.

I couldn't call Almarine for an Invitation Letter this time; she was angry when Douglas sent Immigration Authorities for me a few years earlier and her friend was caught and deported. Soon after I managed to squeeze my way into a few Front Desk shifts, by Divine Intervention the first two guests I checked in were two Canadians, Jerry and Bob. Jerry was married to a Jamaican Police Officer. They lived in Canada. I wasted no time expressing my desire to *visit* Canada. Bob left his phone number to call him whenever I made up my mind. Little did he know I was ready for the letter but I downplayed it until he was no longer a guest and had returned to Canada; an Invitation Letter to get away was all I needed, nothing else. I was still reeling over my recent loss and I still had hopes of reigniting it. Someone so good, so special, so caring and so courageous could never say goodbye. It couldn't be. He was just scared. It would pass. It had to. I was right.

The Invitation Letter came from Bob, a date was arranged, but I didn't get on the flight, I had other plans; so while he was at the Airport in Toronto calling for me on the intercom, I was still in Jamaica hoping to find someone else who could receive me because I had no plans of just making it a vacation and he might not be in favour of an un-documented person overstaying their visit but getting the Invitation Letter first was paramount.

Through the help of a cousin I met while visiting with my mother, I was able to contact Helen; the same little girl that my sister said was given to Auntie Maggie at the Market because her mother was too poor to keep her. She was now a grown woman living in Canada and was happily married to a High School Mathematician, with two sons. Helen agreed to receive me on the understanding it was just a holiday; she had my word on it. She wasn't keen on anyone overstaying their visit but that was okay with me, she wasn't the one that sent me the Invitation Letter. I arranged for a date that allowed me the time I needed to make proper arrangements for my children's accommodation.

Bearing in mind what my husband did three years earlier when I ran away from him to Canada; part of my strategy was to make sure that the person who received me would not have been the person who sent me the Invitation Letter, so that if I needed to go underground none of the two would have had any idea of my whereabouts. If there was a slight indication that plans were under way for me to leave for Canada my husband would block me in the twinkle of an eye, just the way he did at the American Embassy. So there had to be tight security around all my plans and my every move. While my son knew my intentions, my daughter did not as my ex often met her on her way home from school and tried to squeeze everything out of her.

When I asked Colin if I should go he said, *"go on Mommy, if it's even more clothes you can buy for us."* Aside from his school uniforms, he only had one dress pants and two shirts. In my heart, I knew I had to leave the country if I was to save them and save myself, but it was a tough decision to leave them. It was like leaving two little children to take care of themselves; and I was worried too about my re-entry. What if my husband blocked me from entering Canada like he did at the American Embassy? I thought of the Pastor Cousin I met when mother took me to his Roadside Revival Meeting, so I went to see him expecting him to light a candle and be able to look at me and tell me everything would be alright; instead, he prayed with me and told me to get three mineral baths and read Psalm 21 before I went on the flight. To this day I memorize it just like Psalms 46 and 51. Later that day when I returned home, both children were splashing in the pool even though I had warned them not to when I wasn't around. This time, I couldn't even say anything to them. I could only look on with a heavy heart knowing that it may be a very long time before I had the chance to see them play again; and it was. It took nearly eight years before I'd see them play together again.

The day before I left, I fed them a big dinner. It was as though I was feeding them to last until I came back for them in the nine months I promised them. After supper that evening I had a good talk with the both of them and even though I knew they understood why I had to leave them, I just wanted to share with them again the importance of the step I was taking to save my life so I could be there for them. I couldn't guarantee my fate from one day to the next. I believe the deadliest monster a woman can face in her life is that of spousal abuse. You are in it alone. No-one wants to get involved. The Officer told me earlier that marriage was sacred only the divorce can deal with it, and by getting a Postman to paste my picture in the Post Office my husband was led to my hideout. Even the hotel where I took the job was way out of the city, like a little hide out, yet he found it. There was no place to hide where I could not be found.

Recently, a friend told me a story of a very close friend who was consistently beaten. One day after a beating, a friend just happened to pass by and found her alone in the house in excruciating pain. At the friend's insistence, she was rushed to the hospital. The husband was nowhere to be found; he had kept his promise that he would beat her and then leave her. She succumbed to her injuries and I'm told her husband was never charged. Incidentally her husband was a cop; but the goodness and mercy of some I met earlier has taught me that there is good and bad in everything. This is definitely not a case of one sheep spoiling the only flock but it was a sobering reminder of how darn lucky I was and how grateful I am to God for sending "Moses" to rescue me.

After the most difficult task of trying to tell my children why I had to leave them, I turned to the both of them again, this time after dinner, and said: "do you think I should go?" I don't remember what my daughter said, maybe because I was worried about leaving her so young and not being able to tell her of my plans long in advance. But my son reiterated, *"go on Mommy, if it's even more clothes you can buy for us."* I took them over to their Guardian, all the time trying to keep a brave face. I needed time alone that night, didn't want them to see me fall to pieces. As I walked away, my daughter in her little blue and white uniform wrapped her arms around her guardian's knees; it was as far as she could reach. My son looked on and then his eyes turned and were fixed on me as I nervously waved goodbye until I was out of sight. The two little children who were just nine and twelve years old were just beginning to enjoy the taste of freedom after years of abuse. They had seen their Mom thrown here and there and running with them all over the place, leaving them here and there for survival. Now they were being left alone with a stranger to look out for each other. It was enough to tear my heart out. I was running for my life but how different it would have been if I hadn't met my husband. The safety net I thought I needed turned out to be my worst nightmare and my children paid the price. I'll carry this guilt until the day I die. To add insult to injury their Guardian showed favouritism to my daughter. Many years later when Colin told me he was put in the laundry room to eat while the others ate at the dining-table, it felt like a sword went through my body and wounded my spirit. That's why many, many, years later when I heard that she died I could not find it in my heart to express my condolences; I was too bitter.

I returned to my apartment without my children feeling like a lost sheep. Moments after I got home, I was standing by the balcony overlooking the pool, practically hoping to see the sight and hear the sounds of my babies swimming and laughing in the pool, challenging me the non-swimmer to come in and join them. I wondered when I would hear that sound again. My son was months away from turning 13, and my daughter was only 9 years old. As I stood there on the balcony looking in the pool contemplating my uncharted journey ahead of me, in the distance away I spotted a blue Jaguar cruising in on the compound. I recognized the car very well. I had been in it on numerous occasions. My eyes followed the driver as he gently alighted and closed the door softly; then strolled past the pool, and up the stairs that led to my apartment. By the time he got to the door I swung it open and leaped into his arms. He thrust his arms around me and we embraced for a mighty long time as all my emotions came streaming down. All the times we had together, my children who I just left with their guardian, my longing just to see him, everything just gushed out. For a moment I wondered where the hell was I going, leaving this wonderful man and my children behind. And then as though we were both reminiscing, we just sat and looked at each other. There was no mistaking that if there was one person I needed that night at that very moment that it was him; the one who had led me out of darkness into light when I could not see, the one who gave me his shoulders to lean on, my lover, my friend, my deliverer; the Moses that God used to bring me out of bondage. He knew the importance of being there with me at that crucial moment. There he was again to give me the strength I needed to do the right thing, tough as it may be for me and my children. He loved me enough to want what was best for us. To stay would have been a risk. My children needed me, and he knew that. So true to the character of the man I grew to love. I could see why he was so successful; he never allowed his emotions to govern good judgment. Even at that pivotal moment when I could hardly stand, torn with so many emotions he reminded me, "When you get to Canada if you're making $100, pretend you're making $80 and save $20". It took me almost 25 years to finally implement that plan, but it was a word of advice I have never ever forgotten.

I will never forget that man! Never, never, never! The memory of his courage and bravery will forever rest on the table of my heart. He was bold and fearless. He gave me the strength to summon the courage within me to run for my life and the lives of those whom God had entrusted to me. That night when we said our goodbyes, as he walked away, I felt as though the wind beneath my wings fell. But I also had a clear sense of why God had sent him into my life; to free me from bondage. 1st Peter 5 verses 6-7 was clearer now,

"Humble yourself therefore under the mighty hand of God
And He will exalt you in due course,
Casting all your cares upon Him
For He cares for you . . ."

His mission was accomplished. The rest was solely up to me.

TWENTY-THREE

June 29, 1979, I was all set and ready to leave for Toronto Canada. My flight was booked, only to collect my ticket when I got to the airport, except; I had no money to pay for the ticket. Every Penny I could put my hands on was given to the children's Guardian to cover for three months in advance just in case I didn't get a job soon. And the only items left standing in the apartment was my luggage and the couch which I hoped to get pawned off to pay for my ticket.

As fate would have it, that very Friday morning, the same gentleman that gave me a ride from the race track when I ran away after I glimpsed my Give-away-Father, popped in to see how the kids and I were doing. He must have realized that I was desperate to have gone to the race track with no experience and two dollars ($2) hoping to learn to play, and expecting to win all in the same day to put food on our table. His timing was another divine intervention because I don't think he knew I was planning on leaving the country. I don't recall what I said to him, but I vividly remembered him looking at the couch, opening up his wallet, handing me the Seven Hundred ($700) for my airfare and said, "Here, I'm not looking body, you and your children deserve a break" then he loaded the little three-seat-worn-out red-couch onto his truck. I was sure in his heart he simply wanted to help me because that couch wasn't worth half the J$700 I needed to pay for the plane ticket. God bless him!

I took a taxi to the airport hoping to God the meter would not register more than what was set aside for the trip because the driver would have to settle for an IOU. I wasn't going to use my money for my plane ticket or the $60 Canadian which I was supposed to show as part of the requirement for a visitor when I landed in Canada. The taxi driver had the most brilliant white teeth I had ever seen and he loved the compliments. By the time we got to the airport I had sweet talked him so much that even if the fare was short a couple dollars he wouldn't have known especially when I took his address and phone number with a promise to send him a birthstone ring.

The lightest part of my departure was the ride from home to the Airport. Once I checked in and took my seat on the flight, the weight of running and leaving my babies again came down on my chest like a ton of bricks. It seemed so ruthless. We never had much but we were together, we were timid too, but we were also beginning to get a taste of what it meant to be free. Now out of fear for my ex, I had to leave them again, two little children barely 13 and 9 practically being left to raise each other. Over and over again I played the scene out in my head of my daughter's arms thrust around the hem of her guardian's dress as I walked away and the sight of my son gazing at me till I was out of his sight. It was enough to make me want to run back for them. I had no appetite for my supper on the flight. I bawled all the way from Jamaica until it was announced that the flight would be arriving at Toronto International Airport then I hastened to the washroom. I couldn't be going on a "three week vacation" and crying. I had to be ready to convince Immigration Authorities that I was just visiting for three weeks. This was no time to do anything stupid to let my children down. They held fast to the belief that they would be joining their Mommy in nine months. Of course that was a mistake.

When Helen and her husband met me it took quite an effort to keep a smiling face. The agony of walking away and leaving my babies was punishing. Little did they know when they turned into bed that night, I washed my pillow with tears. Their two sons Gary and Clement helped to put a lot of sunshine in my heart on some very gloomy days. Con, an avid tennis fan always showed appreciation for my Jamaican cuisine on the weekends. He wasn't a man of many words but when he spoke I always learnt something. When the first letter came from my mother and I told him that I shall have to get a parcel home to my mother soon because she mentioned that the church Sisters were asking for stockings he said, "Elisabeth, you cannot eliminate poverty". I don't think that's something I ever fully understood. The first thing I did before I even got a job was to send $20 from the $60 I landed with back to my mother. She couldn't be more thankful.

Emigrating from a big city to a small town in Ontario during the 70's, the difference was like night and day. It was such a slower pace than the hustle and bustle of a big city. I needed the speed and variety of a big city to keep me out of my self-imposed exile. Within a couple of months I moved to Canada's largest multicultural city. I love the energy of a big city like London and New York, something is always happening. I was back in my usual element and it felt more like home. I found a comfortable furnished basement suite at 24 Browning Avenue in the city's east end community.

As a newcomer to the city it was the ideal location, close to all amenities. A Jamaican beauty salon was less than five minutes walk away; the train station less than 10 minutes walk with only two stops to downtown; a little Caribbean grocery store with all the little specialties for a great Jamaican cuisine just a few blocks away; a strip of service stores from shoemaker to laundry mat with banks nearby made the move all worth it. Another added bonus was the yearly Summer Parade (Caribana) similar to the one in Trinidad was the highlight of my summer. I lived for that time of year. It was my occasion to de-stress, taste the various dishes and listen to Calypso Superstar, The Mighty Sparrow. One never gets enough of this very special day in Toronto's heartland.

My rent was $50 per week. Every Sunday morning when I went up to pay my landlord, that wonderful Irish soul always said, "Come on up Elisabeth come have a Guinness with us." Aside from church and those I worked for, it was my only chance to socialize with others and they really made me feel like a member of the family. And as a loner living in the basement just going to work and church with no visiting friends, she probably sensed I was un-documented so she became extremely protective of me. Not once did she ever send anyone down to me whether it was the teacher on the Avenue trying to get a date with me, or the paper delivery personnel. She was truly an angel on my shoulders.

Within days of arriving in the city I got a job. I was nervous but I had to take a chance. I had my children and my mother to take care of so I needed to get money back home. I had no idea what kind of system my employer used but Eighty Dollars ($80) per week taking care of three children seemed reasonable to expect cash for; not cheque from an Accountant. When I was asked for my Social Insurance Number, I had no idea what my employer was talking about so I avoided the subject until I got off for the weekend and got some information. The following week I was better prepared for her. I learnt that every legalized resident must have a Social Insurance number which consisted of nine numbers. Before the week had ended, she asked me again, this time I was very prepared. I made up nine numbers one through nine and gave them to her. It seems as though she passed it on to her Accountant because he called me within a day or two to confirm the number; apparently it didn't add up. This time I quoted the same numbers but I changed the last digit. He called back a second time. This time I changed the first number. I heard him say "Uh . . ." then he hung up. I believed he got the message because he never bothered me again and I had no intention of running when I had four mouths to feed and clothe, plus $50 for rent every Sunday morning.

One summer the family made plans to go to Florida. They wanted to take me along but I made up some excuse because I didn't have permanent status to travel in and out of the country. I guess her husband didn't buy my story so one night when he came home from work and was in the kitchen with me heating up his usual can of corn for supper, he casually said, "So, hmmmm . . . is something wrong with your passport?" "No sir," I said, with my lying tongue while trying to keep a brave face. "I have families coming in from England to visit me." It didn't occur to me until many years later that the man was a lawyer and maybe he could have helped me, that he was probably sending me a signal and I missed the opportunity. Being un-documented, the natural tendency was to always play it safe by not volunteering much information to anyone, but I slapped myself years later because had I opened up with him, I might have gotten my Resident Status earlier and my children would have been home much earlier too.

Living in a free society with all privileges is not the life an undocumented alien can enjoy. It was a blessing to live in a home with a family who loved and protected me; I felt secured. The one single thing that really bothered me was the movements at 4 a.m. most mornings that went on for about 15 to 20 minutes. Bob was a bus driver so he couldn't help it, but being in the basement subjected me to listening to the noise from upstairs on the non-carpeted floors. The stress of being away from my children, not being able to sleep well at nights, and the added stress of having the little sleep I got interrupted in the wee hours of the morning, often made for a miserable day; but I learnt to live with it realizing that they were the closest thing to family that I had nearby.

My $80 a week paycheque stretched to cover so much that even a mathematical genius would have difficulty deciphering how I did it. After paying $50 every Sunday morning for rent I was left with $30. First and foremost was the $40 per month I sent to my mother no matter what, then the boarding fees to the guardian for both kids plus their little pocket money. Luckily my son's High school was less than five minutes walk from home. Then even if it was a couple quarters, I always had offering for church every Sunday and in addition, I kept a barrel in the corner of my suite year round for clothes and other little goody goodies which I purchased on a weekly basis so that by the time Christmas came around my children could get something.

There were no dollar stores around in those days, only discount stores such as Woolworth, Towers, Bargain Harold's and one that still remains a corner store in Toronto from generation to generation; the very famous Honest Ed's located at the corner of Bloor and Bathurst Street in downtown Toronto. This was no time to consider the advice I got from my friend when I was leaving the island that if I'm making $100 per week to save $20 and pretend I made $80. It just could not be accommodated, at least not at that time; but I slapped myself years later because if I couldn't put away $20, I should have put away even a couple quarters.

I couldn't afford to eat properly; a balanced diet was out of the picture. A whole chicken once per month lasted a week then the bones were refrigerated and used to make soup for another week, but getting all those ingredients for soup made it too expensive; so cornmeal became my main diet. It cost less than rice, lasted longer and was much more filling. And nothing warm you up more on a cold winter morning like a steaming bowl of cornmeal porridge with sweetened milk and a dash of nutmeg. Many times when I got home from work I was so hungry that by the time the cornmeal was finished cooking, I'd be done eating. In fact I have eaten so much of it that I am convinced it's either excessively good for the bladder, or, in my rush to get something to eat, I didn't allow it enough time to cook properly.

The pressure was mounting to find a way to increase my income. I needed a winter coat, the children needed clothes and their guardian was hinting for an increase in pay. The only two things that didn't get increased were my pay and my rent. My rent remained the same throughout my tenancy. After over a year on the same $80 per week job, and paying $50 per week for rent, I simply could not survive on that anymore. Starting with my doctor's house, I began cleaning homes. Before long, I had five homes on his block and that covered me for the week. I delayed getting my coat to facilitate the children getting toiletries and clothes.

For about a year and a half, everything sounded okay with the children. I recalled a conversation with my daughter how excited she was, "Mommy, I helped Miss with the cooking, you always told me I'm too small, but Miss said let her learn". Not only was she learning to cook but she was taking piano lessons and even got baptized. There was a little grumbling from the guardian sometimes about my sons' obsession with kites, but I brushed it off. Every little bit of good news was refreshing. It was something to give me hope, and the regular communications kept us connected. Soon requests started coming in for editions of Nancy Drew and the Hardy boys. Colin got a book which I believe was published by the Seventh-day Adventists called "On Becoming A Man". I chose that book knowing that he didn't have a father and I wouldn't be around through his adolescent years.

After a while trouble began brewing in paradise as I sensed a feeling of uneasiness when they spoke in a very guarded manner as though they were afraid or weren't free to talk to me. It was so very awkward. Being so far away, every little thing was magnified because I felt so helpless. But based on the conversations, I could tell Colin had been counting the days, the weeks and the months from the day I left, so it made me wonder if they were feeling abandoned because the 9 months had long passed and I hadn't been back for them. I was worried. Colin wasn't happy I could hear it in his voice. Something was definitely wrong. Ms. Bennett was usually complaining about him. Soon I gathered that she would rather keep Dawn and send Colin back to my mother in the country. That bothered me. He was allergic to mosquitoes, his little hands and feet would be in sores all over again. Somehow when he is in the city, they don't seem to bother him. I sent David over to see both him and Ms. Bennett but he was nowhere to be found. Many, many years later he told me he was sitting in a tree when David came, that he saw him, he heard them call him and, he knew why he was there but he refused to budge because he had already made up his mind to return home to Grandma as Ms. Bennett had him eating in the laundry room while everyone else in the household ate at the dining table. I've never gotten over that.

Sometime later during a visit with Ms. Bennett's Sister in another Province, she mentioned to me that had she known I was planning to leave my children with her Sister she would have told me not to because her Sister doesn't like boys. I could only assume that she was sad because she was never married. Colin loved the city, his school and his friends. He wanted to be near his only sister but he couldn't stay, he couldn't stand eating in the laundry room while the others ate at the table and I couldn't take the chance of sending Dawn back with him because of "the beast" so they split. I could not bring myself to send a condolence card when the guardian died many years later. The pain was still raw and the very memory of Colin relaying his experiences to me puts my stomach in knots. Dawn was either too young to understand what was happening with her brother, or she wasn't free to speak.

Shortly after he left a letter arrived from Dawn, "Mommy, every time I hear the song that says ***I'm all out of love I'm so lost without you*** I think of you and my brother." To this day I hate that song; it resurrects memories that are far too painful to bear. I just could not risk sending her back to the village to live; visit yes, but not live. The thought of that monster doing to her what he did to me was too frightening.

If poverty is not a crime I don't know what else is; but this I know, I detest my husband even more for what he has put me and my children through. From the time those two children were separated until the day they landed in Canada, I don't think I was ever the same. It was always clear that I was all they had, that I'd always have to be mother and father so remaining strong was paramount, but this was a tough one to shake off and for quite a while depression took hold of me.

Even with a 20% increase in my income I couldn't adequately run three homes. With my son returning home to my mother, an additional $10 per month was barely enough so he never attended school regularly. Dawn had just won a scholarship for an All Girl's Catholic High school; the list of school supplies needed was sure to leave me in a crisis. I remember thinking that if I could just help her well enough, then she could later help her brothers. I don't know what I was thinking but back then I really thought if I spent every Penny on her and she made it, then she could turn around and school them later. She was the youngest, it didn't make sense. I must have really lost it.

When I managed to negotiate a deal with the owner of a ladies boutique to purchase the end of season summer tops at a much reduced rate, I air freighted them to a former co-worker at the bank who sold them for me to help with school and boarding expenses. It was such a success that it inspired me, so I became an Avon representative and used my commission to stock up on monthly specials. It took quite a while to fill the barrel but I had it budgeted to cover at least four months boarding which would allow me enough time to get my winter coat and possibly get my son back in school. But I was in for a rude awakening; all went well until the barrel reached Customs.

As an undocumented alien I was simply trying to make a few dollars in a way that would go undetected to help take care for my children. It never dawned on me that I should have allowed for Customs Duty. The few blouses I sent earlier went through without a hitch. This time a whopping Five Thousand Jamaican Dollars (J$5000) was levied and neither of us could afford that amount of money. At a three for one value at the time, that would have been over C$1600, the equivalent of almost four months pay for me back then. The barrel was eventually returned to me but I couldn't afford to clear it either. Every Penny I could possibly put my hand on was invested in the little business. That was a prime example of the danger in putting all your eggs in one basket. The loss was devastating to say the least. Just when I thought I had everything under control and had given myself room to breathe everything crashed. It wasn't a good time for me.

To help recover from my losses I had to cut back on something. I saw nothing that I could chop except for my food, so I reduced my portions enough to hold on a saucer. My weight plummeted. Winter was approaching and I was still without a coat. Sister Love used to help me when I was back home with some of her clothes but now I was in North America and we were both struggling plus her three children recently arrived. A niece in England could help but she would have to send me a cheque, she couldn't risk sending all that cash in the mail. I didn't have a bank account so I couldn't accept a cheque and I don't recall knowing of any Western Union in those days, and even if there were, I'd probably be afraid to go there.

Nothing could abate the pain I bore from my losses and the separation of Dawn and Colin. I was trapped in a state of mental solitude. They were some of my darkest hours. It had been almost 16 years since I was charged and acquitted. And not once in all those years did I ever reflect on that nightmare. I'd been too busy jumping over hurdles trying to survive, preoccupied with the rape and how to distance myself from the memory. Then all of a sudden, in what were some of my darkest hours, ignited by a financial catastrophe and being away from the people I love, memories since I was 14 began to surface, and I found myself looking way back. It was a nightmare.

I re-lived every moment step by step; from my first pregnancy at 14; my hunger to return to school when the baby was a few months old; the excitement of getting the Letter of Recommendation from the Justice of the Peace and returning to school. I re-lived the pride of that first morning back in uniform when the neighbours were surprised that I had a baby and was returning to school. I remembered how difficult it was coming up with the second term school fee and how Mr. Dawson paid a portion of the fee for me.

I remembered the rape by the very Justice of the Peace who gave me the back to school Letter of Recommendation. I relived everything he did and said to me during the act. I thought of the shame and the hurt that had me angry all these years and the sense of disappointment for not getting the chance to flatten his house while he slept with a little kerosene oil and the stroke of a match. I remembered when I discovered I was pregnant how ashamed I was and prayed to God it would be Mr. Dawson's child. I remembered how I almost killed myself trying to give myself an abortion. I remembered when I told Mr. Dawson I was pregnant how he looked at me disdainfully and said he felt like taking me away on his bike and kill me. I remembered how scared and ashamed I was when he visited after the baby was born, held the fingers, scrutinized them, and remarked that those fingers were not his, that all his children had a certain shaped fingers.

I recalled the horror of being charged for the death of my first son's father 6 months after giving birth to the baby that followed from the rape. I remembered running with Colin on my side down to Brother Phil's kitchen to call him for help. as he sat with the victim's stepfather smoking a cigar, I remembered the horror on his face when he looked at Samuel lying down with his arms outstretched and said Sister, what did you do?" I remembered being bare feet as the crowd descended on the family plot and how I shamefully sent my cousin to bring me my slippers from the back door.

I recalled how earlier that very morning my brother in law visited after his graveyard shift at the Sugar Estate and how I told him that I felt like something bad was going to happen to me so he should tell Mr. Dawson I needed to see him. I remembered being swarmed by a bunch of black bats around my face moments before. I remembered the sight and sound of Claire calling my name as she wailed louder and louder with a baby in one hand sitting on her side with its legs slung around her pregnant stomach shooting out as though she was ready to give birth. I remembered the sight of my precious mother as she pierced her way through the crowd wearily walking up to me gazing steadily at me, barely able to keep the tattered sandals on her feet. I vividly remembered a light complexion man walking with a slight dip on one side piercing through the crowd coming towards me and saying, "she's insane, she's insane." I remembered him resting his hand on my shoulder and kept saying over and over she's insane, she's insane. I remembered a slender young man accompanying him with what seemed like long silver and black poles that I later learnt were poles for the camera that he used to take pictures of the scene. I remembered smelling myself and wanting to take a shower before they took me away, but the officer said I'd have to wait till I got to the station because my clothes were needed "as is" for evidence. I remembered the sight of the church brethren when they gathered around the Police Land Rover as I made my way in the back. I remembered turning to face them before I sat down and said, "Pray for me."

I remembered arriving at the station with the officer that stood beside me at the scene. I remembered the crowd in front of the Guard Room looking on at us all day. I remembered the Inspector in a frantic call to another station, "get a mattress, get a mattress, we have a little girl coming down!" I remembered how "the beast" that raped me came to the station later that day and leaned over on the counter where I stood beside the Officer and asked me how I made that happen to me. My God Almighty! I remembered how I turned my head from left to right with my eyebrows lifted and just stared at him without a single word till he walked away out of my sight. I remembered the students that evening from my High school in their uniforms apprehensively walking up to the Guard Room where I was standing. I remembered one student stepping forward and in a hushed tone said, "Mi Granny (Hezekiah's Grandmother) said she want to hear directly from you what happen." I remembered the uncontrollable sobbing of Samuel's mother in Court and how helpless I felt. I remembered the initial 18-month-sentence and being taken back to the holding cell where I had stayed before bail was granted.

I remembered being visited by a Cop who brought me a Guinness stout and some toiletries and said, before I finished drinking the stout the 18 months will be finished. I remembered the loneliness I felt leaving that cell and all the people I came to consider my family, to be taken away to the Women's Prison to serve my sentence. I remembered arriving at the Women's Prison feeling scared and abandoned by the people who had been like family to me since day one and wishing I could have served out my sentence with them at the Station. I remembered getting dressed the Monday morning in an ashes colour big wasted straight dress ready to start the day's chores with the other women as we headed into what appeared to be a large concrete-based covered tent with various wash pans loaded with clothes to be washed by hand. I remembered standing over the big pail of clothes in the water contemplating which piece to start washing when a Correctional Officer briskly walked up to me, led me back to my cell, and ordered me to get on my civilian clothes because my lawyer had appealed my case. I remembered how astonished the prisoners were after work that evening to find me in civilian clothes and to learn that my lawyer had appealed the sentence. I remembered how their doubts caused me to question his decision. What if he lost? What if I got a longer sentence? What if they take away our baby? I remembered thinking that I had two boys already, what if this one is a girl and they take her away? What if I didn't have anymore?

I remembered the day I was sitting outside in my little orange and white polka dot dress a few feet away from an Officer when the Matron called out to me repeatedly "Appellant, Appellant, get dressed your lawyer won the case he is coming for you." I remembered tumbling out of the car in front of a Police Station on my way home when the door swung open and I tried to close it. I remembered getting up frighteningly, dusting off the front of my dress and saying, "let me see if I'm dead." I remembered the cops running out to my assistance and pouring a bottle of white rum on all three wounds and how much it burned. I remembered when I got home how Brother Phil said he just told mother that he dreamt the night before that I came home but I had blood all over me. I remembered how I gave birth a couple months after winning my appeal. I remembered the telegram from my daughters' father saying congratulations on your bouncing baby girl. I remembered the concern for my safety and for a change in environment that led my mother to send me away to live with Sister Love when my baby was 6 months old and her brother just approaching 4 years old.

I remembered how I met my husband and felt that it was right to fall in love, that it was right, to get married, to move, beyond my past, how he could protect me. Then I remembered all the beatings that followed that dream; in the home, on the street, off the bus when he followed it and pulled me off; I remembered how I was always on the run with my children, until it brought me to the place where I was, thousands of miles across the ocean in a little basement in Toronto feeling like a complete failure while the people that meant the most to me were left with a complete stranger to practically fend for themselves.

Whatever caused the preceding thoughts to re-surface and flood my soul so much I may never know, one thing I do know is that, it was in that place of deep despair and financial ruin that I began to feel like a 16 year old tape rewound and was slowly replaying everything that had gone on in my short life. The deeper into thought I went the gloomier it got, the more I found things that had been suppressed, things that were never dealt with. It was hell all around, falling on me like a ton of bricks. I was buried in depression for a very long time. There was just too much that hadn't been dealt with. Now, the financial loss, plus being away from my children simply magnified everything. It was as though there was a massive collision of past and present that went beyond what I was capable of handling.

It was hard finding the strength to get up when life had knocked me down so many times. Without my children and my mother I most probably would have lost the will to keep fighting. It was for them that I found strength to go on, but even in the depths of my despair, I struggled with the fears of what impact my dilemma could have on them and future generation. I crumbled to my knees, but I didn't have the luxury of staying there. Though my soul was crying out for help, I had to suppress it because my children still needed to eat and the people I trusted with their care still needed to be paid. So, after the financial whipping, I never did bother with the business again. I resigned myself to be contented with my portion size. Furthermore, I had lost my appetite. Anything more would have been wasted. And in a mysterious way, Angella, a young lady from Toronto, was visiting England, met my niece Val and was given £300 to assist me with a winter coat. It was the largest sum of money I held since my days in banking, and boy oh boy was I ever grateful, but most of all, I am thankful for the blessing of friendship that Angella has brought me and her sister Kim who I met later.

TWENTY-FOUR

Just as I was slowly beginning to accept my losses and move on, came another blow; the news of my divorce. I wasn't ready for anything more. And I certainly wasn't prepared to hear that my husband divorced me, instead of me divorcing him. For sure I didn't want to live with him, I was afraid of him, but I wanted to fix him and as weird as this may sound, there was something there for my husband that hadn't quite died, not yet. The divorce drained the life out of it.

But for him to be successful in divorcing me on the grounds of mental cruelty after all the beatings I endured at his hands; be successful at getting our house sold without my signature as the Joint Tenancy Agreement necessitated; get a divorce so soon after our separation; and then marrying his mistress so he could join her in America; it finally sunk in that she won and I lost. It was the final blow. And it was all one-stop shopping. The same lawyer took care of all the transactions—Real Estate and Divorce.

Out of curiosity, and maybe, to hear Douglas personally say that he got to divorce me on the grounds of mental cruelty; and to learn how he did it; I telephoned him. When I asked him how he managed to get it, he laughed and said, "I'm a Police Officer; all I had to do was go down to the Ministry of Home Affairs and cooked up a thing." I wondered if he really wanted to divorce me, or he was only out to get a little "quickie" divorce so he could marry his mistress and go to America, because that was really what it sounded like. And considering how soon afterwards he had his third marriage, I was right.

He wouldn't give me the name of the lawyer and at the time I had no idea that he had forged my signature and sold our home, which incidentally, was purchased for pennies by a member of staff at the very Building Society that carried the mortgage. And by a Divine Intervention, many years later when I was called upon to provide a Defence Counsel for a friend, the very same Lawyer my husband had used in the Sale of our home and his "quickie divorce" was recommended to me after I was unable to get hold of the one I knew, but at the time neither of us knew each other.

When the lawyer learnt that I would be bearing the financial responsibility for the client's defence he wanted to know me. "You're not Mother Theresa, you're not the Prime Minister of Jamaica, I need to know who this person is," he said. And that's when I told him what had happened to me and how one of his "Learned Friend" defended me. He travelled to America to meet me. It was on that occasion that I learnt that the "Learned Friend" I spoke of, my daughter's father had passed away years earlier from cardiac arrest but I didn't tell him that he was my daughter's father. I had premonition it many years earlier and mentioned it to Dawn. Initially, we had no idea of the duplicity, and we did not allow that information to spoil our relationship. He did what he had to do for his client based upon what was presented to him; getting him a little "quickie divorce" and selling the house so he could marry his mistress to get a Green Card go to America. I met a very likeable professional who I was delighted to do business with and was thankful we had the opportunity to meet. I'm sure he was left with a different opinion of me than the one he learnt about in a bid for a little quickie divorce.

Months following the news of my divorce I was still tormented. The separation of my children, the financial predicament, the divorce and being away from my children went beyond what I was capable of handling. I found myself one night lying in bed with the lights off looking up at the densely black ceiling when I heard a little voice within said, Jeremiah chapter 3. I scanned the darkness expectantly as though to see or feel someone. I was sure I was alone in my apartment. After a long pause I turned to switch the lights on, but it felt like I was rolled back on to my back. I paused for a while again, making every effort to stay calm, then I turned on my other side to switch the other light on, but again, I found myself rolling over again on to my back. The only little window in the basement was in the bathroom, so without lights in the suite, it's extremely dark. I mustered all the courage I could and just laid there pensively for a few minutes longer. In the meanwhile, the little voice inside my head kept saying Jeremiah chapter 3 repeatedly. I was anxious to turn and get the lights on but I felt restricted. Eventually after a long period of just lying there gazing in the dark, I managed to roll on my sides, switched the lights on, and opened the Bible at Jeremiah Chapter 3.

Walking through the chapter shocked me because I was in bed agonizing over my divorce and the audacity of my husband to divorce me on the grounds of mental cruelty, when I should be the one divorcing him for adultery and the every week beatings he inflicted on me. The very first verse of the Chapter states: "They say if a man put away his wife and she goes from him and become another man's shall he return unto her again, shall not that land be greatly polluted, but thou hast played the harlot with many lovers yet returned again to me said the Lord?" I was so stunned that I began to scan my suite as though God was lurking around. For a while I just sat there staring at the words and scanning my bedroom almost expecting to see the Lord God himself. To add fire to fury, the verse closed with the words *"said the Lord"* which meant that it was the Lord himself speaking to me through His prophet Jeremiah. I felt like God was a bit too harsh with me. Suddenly I remembered some folks when I was a child who always said that they are not going to church because *"Pastor liked to pick on them"*. And the very moment I remembered that remark, it occurred to me that it wasn't the Pastor that picked on them, it was the Word of God that had the power to convict an individual. Feeling like a convict after reading the 1st verse, I began to dissect and read the rest of the chapter defensively. When I got to verses 2 and 3, I felt like the one and only Person who I was supposed to lean on had turned his back on me . . . *"I have polluted the land, therefore, the showers have been withheld from me; I have a whore's forehead and I refused to be ashamed."* There was no leniency, just sheer hammering by the "Only One" I had to call upon. Verse 4 gave me a glimmer of hope: "He guided me as a child; now I need to cry out to Him as a Father." Verses 8 and 9 convicted me of adultery: *"Backsliding Israel defiled the land with whoredom and adultery"*. This time I had to stand up for myself. I felt the right to challenge God on this one. Was I supposed to sit back and let my husband kill me? I thought, how could God revealed 1Peter 5:6 & 7 to me then provided me with David to deliver me and now he was accusing me of adultery. What was wrong in dating him? Verse 11 replied with a slap in my face: *"Backsliding Israel justified herself."* In other words, I was trying to justify everything I did. Oh please! The convictions were like bones in my throat. Verses 12 and 13 gave me another glimmer of hope: *"If I returned to Him, His anger would cease and He'd be merciful to me."* Verses 14 & 15 extended invitation to return to Him. He wanted me back: *"I will give you Pastors according to mine own heart who will feed you with knowledge and understanding."* Verse 20 puts it all in perspective: *"As a wife treacherously departs from her husband so have I dealt treacherously with you."* In other words, as I understood it, God was dealing with me like an enraged husband, whose wife had deserted him. And that's how I learnt that His relationship with me is similar to that of a husband and wife or God and the Church. But I had slipped away from Him and He was enraged so He withheld His Blessings.

For all I had been through in my short life and was still facing, I really wondered at the time how a loving God could see my relationship with Him more important than all the grief I bore. I was very disappointed. I didn't feel like God was putting me first, it didn't seem like He was sympathetic towards my plight. It was all about Him. And for all I had gone through and was still going through, I didn't think it was time to neither judge, nor condemn me when what I needed was an arm around me. I had a hard time accepting the chastisement, I found it unjustifiably harsh, and given my situation, it was far too much to expect of me but amidst all the harshness, there was hope in the promise of Pastors He would assign to me to nurture my growth.

I never considered myself to be anything less than a Believer, but clearly none of that mattered. I had turned away from Him with my lifestyle, nowhere close to what He considered acceptable. I had ceased to grow spiritually so the Windows of Heaven were closed and my Showers of Blessings were being withheld. I didn't want to think that God was getting me because I covenanted with Him when I was incarcerated that if He set me free I would serve Him. But it occurred to me that I really hadn't kept my promise, and I had gone away from the dusk to dawn church person He was grooming for His purpose. In my own troubled world I only expected Him to see, understand and share my pain and suffering. Jeremiah chapter 3 bore no resemblance of that. It seemed to just add more pressure to drop everything I was going through and returned to Him. It wasn't humanly possible for me at the time. I was far too broken. I was more concerned about the plight of my children; who I am; where I was; and trying to make sense of Douglas getting away with divorcing me on the grounds of mental cruelty. Ironically, the very last verse of the chapter said, *"We lie down in our shame and our confusion cover us because we have sinned against the Lord our God."* It made me want to cringe in a corner. Each time I remember the experience, I shun it and plead "not guilty." Since that night I have not given another thought to the divorce or my husband and I have no explanation for it. It's as though it was ripped from me, and the only words to describe that, is divine intervention.

It has been the story of my life, one obstacle down, another up, always something that's waiting to be dealt with. And that letter from my daughter had been plaguing me: *"Dear Mommy, I'm all out of love I'm so lost without you.* I wrestled with those words. They practically strangled me. No matter how hard I tried, I could never erase them from my mind. I heard it when I went to bed; I heard it when I turned at nights; and I heard it when I woke up. I had to do something. It has been the story of my life. The moment I think I've gotten through one hurdle and can take a break, there comes another. Even though I was undocumented and couldn't personally sponsor her on a vacation, I had to find someone who could but I also had to secure the airfare. A Manager friend with the bank of Montréal was looking for someone to clean her apartment on Sundays so to secure the airfare, I made that commitment for nearly 3½ months, from noon to 2pm so I could get back home on time to be ready to get on the church bus for the 6pm Service.

Angella's sister, Kim, helped with the invitation letter. I didn't have permanent status. Out of my senseless fear of deportation, I accompanied Kim to the airport but I stayed out of sight. I was shocked at how stoic my daughter looked when the Flight Attendant brought her to Kim. I remembered hovering over her and saying, "where is your smile, where is your smile?" The little girl I left with the round baby face looked stressed like a person who cried a lot or who didn't know how to laugh anymore. Then in a cracked voice with teary eyes she said, "Mommy, why can't I live with you?" Sometimes I wish I could forget some things just so I could have a normal life, but I can't. They literally chew away at any little happiness I may try to forge, and this is one of them. Even if I try to brush them aside, it doesn't take much to resurrect them because as a parent I only had one chance and it was plucked out of my hands.

Within days of her arrival, a letter came from Colin, *"Mommy I am begging you, is the one sister me have, send for me too, please."* News travels fast. I thought I was careful in keeping her visit from him since I couldn't afford to do both of them and he was a little more comfortable back home with Granny. His letter shred my heart to pieces so much so that throughout her vacation every bite I took was difficult to swallow. I couldn't afford to do the both of them. And to have packed Dawn's bags and sent her back to her Guardian without even a Work Permit at the time, much less the prospect of becoming a permanent resident so I could sponsor them was crucifying.

She needed to be in school, but I wonder as a child how she interpreted what I did. I don't think I want to know. All I know it's not worth it to put children through such suffering, because in the long run, mother and child lose more than they gain. If a parent must leave, take your child with you, save yourself the heartache. No amount of making up can ever recover what was lost, and sometimes you don't even get time to make up before a spouse takes over and leaves you with a pain that not even time can heal. It is not worth it. Period!

One Sunday when I stopped from church to attend a get together Kim and Angella were hosting at their apartment Angella said, "Elisabeth, you better try to see what you can do now while Uncle Pierre (Prime Minister Pierre Trudeau) is in power because he and Michael Manley went to school together, they are buddies, so anything you can do to get through now, you better hurry up because anyhow you wait until the other Party come into power that's it you're doomed because them not for the little people." From time to time, there were some false alarms about amnesty for Illegal Immigrants but it was more like playing politics, nothing concrete. And being illegal, every idea I conceived of was always accompanied with a measure of uncertainty.

In the midst of trying to figure out what to try, I got a letter from my daughter's High School classmate, she was uncomfortable with some gestures from the maid's husband. I knew I had to go, and, and I also knew that I had to return to sponsor them. To cover my tracks in case there was an amnesty and the authorities needed to prove I had been living in the country, I hid my passport under the carpet and under the pretence it was lost, obtained a one-way Emergency Passport; got Angella to prepare me an Invitation Letter which I would need to re-enter as a visitor. Within days of receiving that letter from Dawn's friend I was in the Island. No one knew I was coming. From a distance she glimpsed me and came running, "Mommy, Mommy, did you come for me?" After a meeting with her guardian I was anxious to meet with her teachers. One teacher took me aside and said, "Mrs Holyday, all the money you are spending on Dawn will amount to nothing if you don't get her beside you because she misses you, all she talks about is her Mommy." I could only sigh.

I was anxious to see my mother and Colin. Without a phone, we only communicated by letters since he went back home to Grandma. On my way up to mother I was anxious to see the little boy that had been with the Dawson's since he was 6 months. The last time I saw him was the day I got bailed, during my trial. But ever since I opened the Bible and came across the passage of Scripture that says, Can *a woman's tender care cease towards the child she bears* I had been thinking of him. Of course I had mixed emotions because I had no intention of staying in touch with him; that way no one would know I was raped and I could just pretend I had two children. I was pleasantly surprised by the warm reception I received.

And even though I hadn't seen him since he was a baby, there was no mistaking who was who, even with his head hung low, the shy little boy bore no resemblance to the other kids. And he must have instinctively sensed that I was his mom because from the moment I got there he never took his eyes off me. I was convinced the Dawson's family knew all along something was very wrong, even though it was never confirmed. I wasn't about to say anything that would open a whole can of worms. I had more pressing issues to deal with. Dawn's safety and my re-entry to Canada was enough on my brain. But my visit that day eventually led to him reuniting with the family that very day.

The moment my mother saw me she knew something was wrong. She knew I wasn't just there for a visit; that something brought me home; but as usual, I never burdened her, always tried to shield her from more pain, but it broke my heart to see my innocent little boy who I left boarding with his sister in the city; who eagerly finished his homework so he and his sister could jump in the pool, played marbles or flew his kite; my little boy had now dropped out of school and was smoking. He was so happy to see me, but the pain of disappointment underlined every word he uttered. "Mommy, I thought you said you were sending for us in nine months?" It didn't help his confidence that I kept writing year after year and saying next year, next year. He believed in his heart that I would send for him eventually, but his confidence was shaken from years of being told that he'd be coming soon. Sadly, it was all l could think of saying to keep their hopes alive. Guilt, sorrow, doubts and confusion left me perishing inside. What a price to pay for freedom! Back in the city while I made plans to relocate Dawn, the life shattering experience of seeing us all scattered in the four corners of the world made for a very sombre mood and a determination to return to Canada and "just do it". I was going to have to take the bull by the horns.

One never makes the right decisions when the mind is in turmoil. Ms. Bennett did her best to convince me she would keep a closer watch on Dawn but I was afraid of taking another chance. *At the back of my mind I kept thinking what if he made another attempt and no one was around so I followed my heart and transferred her to someone I trusted. It would later prove to be the biggest mistake of my life. On many occasion Dawn said she slept with a knife under her pillow, and to cover for her son-in-law, the mother in law who slept beside Dawn said my daughter talked in her sleep. That witch! If God was like mankind, after my daughter came away, He would seal the pedophile's mother-in-law's mouth with dumbness till eternity.* And as for the culprit, who loves to behave like a Mercenary, I hope for the day when he will slip up and gets nationally disgraced. And if the God I serve has anything to do with it, it's only a matter of time.

In less than two weeks I had a new passport to return to Canada but it was hardly enough to reassure me of the outcome when I returned to Canada. Undocumented, living in Canada, left for a vacation to another country and hoping to return undetected as a visitor again with a new passport sounded a little unheard of and beyond brave; desperate times calls for desperate measures.

Days before I was due to leave the island, my ex was on my trail again. All the way from America with his mistress (correction—now wife) he got word I was in the island and managed to get a hold of me right where I was staying at a girlfriend's house. He wanted to meet me he said and he could leave at once. I was so fearful you would think he was right there at the door. I was afraid of saying the wrong thing so I told him to call me back in an hour. In the meanwhile I asked my girl friend what to say, she suggested that since he forged my signature and sold our house, if he wanted to see me let him pay me five thousand dollars $5000(the equivalent of US$60 at the time of writing) I should have requested a half of what the house was sold (given away) for, I would have gotten around 6½ times that. He quickly agreed and sent me to the same lawyer who "cooked up" the divorce for him. Of course the lawyer had to find a reason not to give it to me the same day. I hoped it wasn't a trap for him to meet me there the following day. The next day when I picked up the money I headed straight for the airport. While he was landing, I was taking off.

The man was now married to the mistress. One would have thought he got what he wanted and he would be so very happy that he would leave me alone. "What the hell did he want to fly from America to see me for?"

I didn't want to find out. For all I knew he was probably coming to block me from entering Canada like he did earlier at the American Embassy. But at the same a part of me felt like I wanted to see him, maybe to get the love and attention I never had from him. Could this be the moment? Had traveling changed him? Could I take a chance? I was bombarded with a multitude of thoughts.

Another part of me felt like there was something wrong with him and I was the only one who could help him. That was always my problem, wanting to fix everyone and everything. It was as though if I fixed them, I would be okay, but there was something bigger eating at me. I couldn't forgive him for the way he hated my son especially for having me send him off on a bus back to my mother alone one night just to save my skin. I despised him for that. I felt like I threw out my child to save my skin. And I could never get past the day he told Dawn while they were playing that whenever her breasts begins to grow he would beat her on them because it would mean she was dating. I knew I had to block him out of my mind.

I believe I became so confused and frightened after the phone call that in my anxiety to get on my flight and leave the country, I left without returning to the country to say bye to my Mom and my sons. And despite all my efforts to have a straight face, I guess chaos and uncertainty was registered on it because when I landed the Immigration Officer didn't buy into my story that I was just coming for a visit. I was so stressed out with so much from every angle that she sensed something and she intuitively began to dig for clues. One thing I was sure about: I would not be denied entry. I must bring my children home to Canada. She questioned me on and off for about five hours; at times leaving me and coming back. "Where is your Staff ID from the bank?" she asked at one point. Usually bank staff had an ID but little did she know I left banking a while ago; had been living in the country illegally; and had just gone home to see to my daughter's welfare. I was confident I would make it through but seeing that it was taking so long, I worried a bit about Angella. I had an Invitation Letter from her and if she got cold feet and went home, there would be no one to receive me, especially, if they decided to release me on a bond. Deliverance came around 2 a.m., nearly six hours after my flight landed when the officer brought in a Senior Officer. God bless his soul. He didn't waste another minute. He released me to Angella on a bond which she quickly signed. As soon as we got out of the building we burst out in laughter; but I believe the experience was partially responsible for me to be even more determined to take quick and decisive action to bring my children home. I didn't want to face that again if any of them had an emergency.

After my experience at the Airport, everything inside of me was hungry for a change in my status. I needed my freedom and I wanted my children home. A nephew from America came for me to try to get me across the border but I was afraid of getting caught and then be blocked from re-entering both countries. I wouldn't know what to tell my children. At one point I was thinking of asking someone I hardly knew to do a business marriage for me to help me get my permanent papers, but the night before I approached the person, an Angel stood before me in my dream with the Bible opened at Deuteronomy chapter 6, paused for a little bit, then flipped the pages to Deuteronomy chapter 11, and held it up again in full view; so I took that as a warning not to proceed. It seemed like God likes to quote from his Old Testament Prophets.

I was sick and tired of all the "what if's". "What if the Immigration found me and deported me?" "What if someone reported me?" "What if I tried to apply and they rejected my application?" What if there's no amnesty for illegal immigrants?" Well I just got so darn tired of all the "what if's" that it became better to do something than to do nothing. So I quickly liquidated the bond indebtedness and kept a copy of the money order. I knew I was going to do something drastic but up to that point I had no idea what it would be. And deep down in my heart at the time, I never felt that I wanted to be sponsored through marriage. I didn't like the idea of a second marriage, or, someone wanting to hold on when I wanted out, there had to be a way out.

Good thing I kept my cleaning assignments and just told everyone I was going on a 3-week vacation and would be back with a taste of Blue Mountain coffee. Sometime after I returned, I was on an assignment when the vacuum hit against an object under the bed. I sprawled out on my stomach, lifted the bed skirt and was pleasantly surprised at the sight of an old IBM typewriter. With the vacuum still running, I stopped and began to reminisce on my days in banking before I emigrated—sitting at my desk five days a week before a typewriter with a dicta-phone in my ears; my beautiful home, cuddling up with my children watching Little House on the Prairie or Fonzie, rushing to the country with Sunday dinner for mother and watching her share her carrot juice until just the nutmeg was left in the glass bottom; the sight and sounds of my children in the pool. Discovering the typewriter was an eye opener, it was turning point just like when God called Abraham to do the unthinkable and at the very last minute his eyes caught the sight of a lamb stuck by its' horns in the bushes. Now over 2000 years later the vacuum brought the typewriter to my attention; another divine intervention. I found some typing sheets and when I was done typing I had an eleven page petition addressed to the Immigration Authorities which I hand delivered the following morning. There were no stones left unturned.

The following morning I woke up early; placed an under wear in my bag in case they decide to deport me and I needed to freshen up; and I headed straight for the Immigration Office. I did not say one word to Angella or Kim in case I got talked out of the approach I was taking. It was so early I believe I was third in line. For the occasion I wore a hunter green pinstripe pants suit with a silk ivory blouse on the inside, accessorized with a shoulder strap brown leather bag and matching shoes with my hair resting just below my shoulders. The outfit was designed to boost my confidence but I must admit, as the final moments approached to meet with the Officer, my knees wobbled.

As soon as the Officer called me and guided me through the appropriate doors, I anxiously waited for the moment to shake his hand when he introduced himself, in the hopes of calming my nerves. He appeared so shy and spoke so softly, I was confident I had met someone with a heart and a soul. That was very clear. I don't remember what I said to him, I was eager to present to him the letter. He read what seemed like part of it then he excused himself within a few minutes leaving with every sheet I presented. Then he returned, read a portion again, left and then came back again. It seemed something puzzled him or maybe he read the part about my being in trouble and was checking to see if there was a warrant out for my arrest. That was just my guess. When he finally settled down, he looked me squarely in the eyes and said, "We do check you out thoroughly, so make sure you are telling the truth because we can't help you if we find out that you are lying". Assuming he was referring to the outcome of the trial, I quickly interjected, "Oh yes sir, I remember everything." The Judge had given me eighteen months but my lawyer appealed and I was set free so there is no conviction. I didn't get into details pertaining to the charge that was laid against me as I do in this Memoir, but they were made aware. Then there was the question about my children. "Are you sure you only have three?" And again he reminded me of his obligation to thoroughly investigate to ensure every applicant is truthful and honest. That was a wake-up call for me because I had wrestled with the idea of naming just two children in my effort to distance myself from the shame and pain associated with the rape. Had I done that, we probably wouldn't be in Canada today.

I doubt I mentioned anything about the rape and I am sure I didn't say anything that could jeopardize my lawyer. I always try to protect him. His final question was, "Did you see a lawyer?" "No sir," I replied. I guess he thought it was professionally prepared, but it wasn't. That wonderful soft-spoken gentleman looked me in my eyes and said, "You have done it better than I could, probably better than any lawyer could, you should be commended." That was exactly what I needed to hear from someone the evening before when I typed the letter. I was feeling so good about what I had done, I wanted a pat on my shoulders, so on my way home from work that evening I stopped by one of those so called "Consultants" and asked him to look it over for me as I'd be going in the following morning to see Immigration Authorities. When he read the part where I mentioned that I was placed under a bond and I liquidated the indebtedness, he handed my papers back to me and swore to God that if I ever put my foot in that office, the authorities would deport me immediately. I collected my papers and turned away. As I walked away he called me back and said those old familiar words often told to illegal immigrants when they solicit the services of some of those unscrupulous Immigration Consultants: *"Bring your bank book and I'll see what I can do for you."*

The next morning while I waited in line for my name to be called at the Immigration Office, I saw the very same Consultant passed by looking like a High Court Judge and his client looking like a condemned prisoner. I could only assume his client had a fat bank account. At the end of my interview, I left with a Work Permit and a clear understanding that the process for permanent status had begun for my children and I simultaneously. The Government of Canada rescued me. Mr. Buchanan sent out the lifeboat. God bless him.

TWENTY-FIVE

M y Work Permit was like a life saver. It was the first time in many years that I began to feel like a real person, someone who existed, not just an illegal alien trying to survive underground. Relief and a little freedom completely changed my thinking and my attitude. Just to be able to write to my children and confidently say to them that the process had begun, that soon we will all be together, was one major stepping stone. It made me feel like a responsible mother again and it was the first glimmer of hope since my losses.

Since all my clients were willing to supply me with job letters which was a requirement for obtaining a Work Permit, I faithfully stayed with them. At my next appointment with an Immigration Officer, I learnt that one of the requirements to have my children join me was to satisfy them that I had suitable accommodations for them. It was tough saying goodbye to the folks I regarded as my family for over 4 years, and even though I should have at least had a two-bedroom, I found a huge one bedroom apartment capable of holding two Queen Size beds in the bedroom. For $650 per month, more than 200% my previous rent, I had to make the oversize one bedroom apartment accommodate all four of us, I still had mouths to feed and boarding fees to meet.

In the meanwhile, the Work Permit allowed me to get a little part-time job at a five-star Hotel, famous for its Dining Room. Just to walk through the lobby made me look forward to going to work, but leaving my house on Saturdays for work was spiritually gruesome. It was the day I spent with WDCX Radio Host Doug Riley listening to some of the best Gospel songs ever played on radio between 2 to 6pm on Saturdays. Just about every song he played I recorded as part of my Retirement Investment, however, with the children coming and higher rent, some sacrifices had to be made.

As a Room Service Cashier working the 3 to 11 shift, when the house was full and the Dining Room busy, I had a busy night. A slow night in the Dining Room or low hotel occupancy could make for a boring night so I always had my pocket Bible ready to read between breaks. Weekends were always expected to be busier than midweek, so three Waiters were assigned to Room Service on the weekends. Every Waiter liked a big order. The bigger the order, the more likely it is to get a bigger tip; though not necessarily so.

Saeed, the youngest of the three, and the newest kid on the block, was a new immigrant with a family struggling to make ends meet like I was, so when he asked me to help him with a big order if any came in I understood his plight plus, I had a tender spot for him because of his gentle demeanour. When Saul and Zachariah were behaving like "*Lords of the Ring,*" he went about his job in a humble and respectable manner. He made me want to protect him like a big Sister. Zachariah always boasted that he bought his wife a refrigerator one Christmas from his nickel and dime tips, and the coins that fell between the seats of his living room couch. Saul, the Romanian, always looked rich in those gorgeous European cardigans and heavyweight gold jewellery that I often wondered why he bothered to work.

Later that evening I caught a big fish and discreetly handed Saeed the order to fill and take up to the Guests' room, but Saul used his seniority to bully him and confiscated the order when he realized it was a big catch. I was so angry that when Saul passed by my station with the tray I burst in tears and told him that I wish to God that the tray would fall out of his hands and shatter everything! I meant every word that I said; everyone. I was that angry. As the saying goes "be careful what you wish for." Moments later he returned with everything on the tray shattered. When a

Chef ran to meet him and asked him what happened, he said as he entered the room and was handing the tray to the guest, the chandelier fell out of the ceiling, landed on the tray, and shattered everything between him and the Guest. Saeed's family must have been hungry.

Even though I missed my 4 hours of non-stop Gospel Singing on Saturdays I loved my job, but an auditor made it his full time job to be a thorn in my side. As a Room Service/Dining Room Cashier, with my station positioned to facilitate waiters servicing both Room Service and the Dining Room it could get very chaotic. Reading my Bible before my shift began and in between breaks prepared me to handle the chaos. At the end of my shift I was supposed to balance all transactions, and along with the cash, forward everything to the Night Auditors at the Front Desk. I was never allowed that privilege when a certain auditor was on duty. He would arrive early as well, passed by my station, pushed his long arm in the cage, ripped the Bible out of my hand or thump his fist on the desk.

On several occasions, instead of allowing me to balance and then forward the work to him at the front desk for auditing, he would be right at my station standing over my shoulders while I was balancing eleven o'clock at nights. The man intimidated me so much that I became afraid of him. The moment I heard that "six footer" coming in those thunderous heavy boots, I began to tremble. Any sign of arrogance was a strong reminder of my ex and all my past woes so he really scared the daylights out of me. It got to the point where I didn't look forward to going to work anymore. Instead of feeling excited at the thought of getting dressed up and going to my posh job at this big hotel, I was reduced to just worrying about him and what he might do next.

After getting home from work one night, I called the Manager on Duty, couldn't take anymore I was too afraid of the bully. My little pocket Bible was my only refuge but the man scared me so much that I wondered if God was using him to make me quit so I could return to my Gospel Recording on Saturdays. Whatever it was, I was too scared to continue. Moments after I lodged my complaint and fell asleep an angel handed me a purple candle twisted like a rope. Those days, I wasn't into burning candles and I only remember my church using white candles. But I guess the angel must have lit it for me because a few weeks after I left I heard that the bully became a Dining Room Waiter and then left to work with a company that went to the same hotel at nights to spray cockroach repellent, so in a sense he was still with the hotel at nights except he wasn't auditing, he was spraying cockroaches.

Luckily for me, less than a year after I received my Work Permit, I got my Permanent Resident Status which allowed me to go out and broadly search for a job rather than trying to find a Company that was willing to accept me with just a Permit. And as an added bonus, one year after becoming a Permanent Resident I became a Citizen. The standard three year wait to apply for citizenship was waived apparently because I had been in the country for so many years. It was the icing on my cake. I am still enjoying it. And many others, as a result!

I picked up a job in the banking sector since that's where I was most experienced. But faced with a substantial rent increase and three children arriving in a few months, the nine dollars per hour at the bank would sparsely prepare me for three airfares much less food, clothes and shelter. I decided to do some hustling in America. The airfare and a single bed for each son, to put on either side of my Queen Size Bed which I intended to share with my daughter was my biggest challenge.

Since Angella and Kim lived some distance away, I asked "The People's Cop" a friendly young officer named Glen who frequently patrolled the neighbourhood mall, to oversee my apartment while I was in America. Glen laughed hysterically when I laid down one strict rule, that my stereo remain at the same dial, WDCX, so that the Gospel Songs could continue to administer grace upon my apartment while I was away. Six months later, my little windfall from America allowed me to meet my commitments and I had enough left to allow me to be home with them for a full two weeks. Dawn and I shared the Queen Size bed in the middle of the bedroom along with the dresser. And my sons shared a chest of drawers. Their Single beds went on either side of the Queen Size bed just as I had planned and there was still adequate space to freely move around. And by divine intervention,

244

when I returned home from America, as soon as I began turning the key in the door, I heard the Host of the Radio Program said, "The more you praise Him, the more He'll give you something to praise Him for." That's what I meant when I requested Glen to keep the dial set at the same place. There was always something each day to treasure; whether it was an inspirational thought, a Scripture passage, a special song that might address an issue, a word or a thought from the Program Host. Whatever it was, I could always count on getting something, so to have gone away and turned the stereo off would not only have made the place lifeless, it would in my opinion be an insult to the Holy Spirit. And while I was in America, Family Radio's Nightly Bible Readings and Dr. Gabriel Otero were my constant companions keeping me nurtured and focused on what matters most.

Glen offered to help with a ride to the airport when the children came. I didn't know what I was thinking, whether I thought they'd be lost or frightened if they came and didn't see me, or it was just my nerves, but we got there 2 hours ahead of schedule and I wore the same navy blue strapless jumpsuit that I wore earlier when Dawn came on vacation, in case they had forgotten my features. As I waited, a myriad of thoughts went through my mind: "Did they all get on the flight?' "What were they thinking?" "Did they think I abandoned them seeing they had to wait almost 8 years instead of the nine months I had promised them?" "Will they be too excited to eat?" "Did they still love me?" "Will they like the meals I prepared?" The amount and variety of dishes I prepared was nothing short of an all you can eat buffet. I believe I was trying to make up for all the meals I couldn't prepare them in the last eight years.

Finally, the moment we all waited for arrived. As each one made their entrance on Canadian soil, my daughter being the city girl and the fabric of one of Jamaica's most prestigious All Girl's Catholic High School, dressed and walked like a model but my sons appeared so tiny and underfed they broke my heart. They more looked like 10 and 12 year old boys rather than 17 and 19. My pay couldn't stretch to sufficiently do all that I needed to do. Rent and Boarding Fees drained me. It was the price I paid for not keeping Dawn in the country with my mother because of "the beast".

With all the joys and excitement of finally being home, I don't remember what we talked about and I don't remember how well they ate that first evening. For Colin and Dawn, the 9 months took 8 years. For Chase, it had almost been a lifetime since he was taken away at six months, the very day I was incarcerated; so in all fairness we hardly knew each other except for the occasion when I returned home to relocate Dawn and I popped in to see him briefly. Deep down in my heart I just didn't know what to expect, because there was a measure of rage and anger in the letters he sent to me after he left the Dawson's and began spending time with the Hannikim's family; especially, when he enquired, "how comes the father business is like that?" And it didn't help when his close friend sent words ahead of his arrival to warn me that I have three children coming and the one I am to watch out for is Chase, so I didn't feel his presence was going to make it any easier for me. But the following day after they arrived, that little boy did something so profound; it struck at the very heart of my soul and practically eradicated my fears. From his $20 pocket money that I gave him, he walked across the street to Woolworth's store and bought me the most beautiful "Thank You Card." I thought, this little boy who only met me in his teens, who was practically just acquainting with me for the first time in his life, was so very appreciative. It was just the most wonderful thing to do, he really touched my heart. I don't think that any mother would ever forget such gesture. Colin clearly wasn't a shopper, he shyly followed with one of those usually picked up by visitors on a vacation, the one that requires postage: *"Greetings from Toronto, Canada, To Miss Elisabeth Holyday telling her thanks for what she have done bringing me here one love and it's forever, Love, Colin."* The innocence it conveyed, the imperfect words of a simple child, makes it a favourite among my collection.

It seems that absence really does make the heart grows fonder. Shortly after they arrived, Dawn got a call from her guardian, Winsome. No idea what they talked about. All that she said was, "Mrs Lawrence is crying." Nothing more, end of story.

They arrived just two weeks prior to the biggest holiday Festival of the summer, but first there were things to see, places to go and a whole lot of shopping to be done for them all. They needed to learn some things like how to use Pedestrian Crossings, how to use the Transit System, east, west, north and south. In a matter of days I sent them off in one direction and waited for them to find their way and meet me at a certain point. It was refreshing to watch them hopped and skipped their way; and even telling me of places I didn't even know how to get to. The clothes shopping excited them. They were like kids in a candy store, but it was a delight to see them home and happy. The biggest excitement though was the Caribana Parade two weeks after they came; a yearly event of cultural festivities parading the various Islands of the Caribbean usually held on the last Saturday in July. The Parade travelled through the streets of Toronto with drums blaring, and folks in bright costumes dancing to the rhythm of island sounds. A real midsummer treat culminating with boat rides from Toronto's Harbour front across to the Islands where weary participants after a long day in the parade can enjoy a variety of dishes, calypso and reggae music and a chance to see Calypso King, The Mighty Sparrow in action. The opening of the Canadian National Exhibition or CNE two weeks prior to the re-opening of school in September was another summer treat with every kind of ride imaginable for kids and adults. And by Christmas they were well on their way to settling in and had established friendships of their own to make for a great Christmas. Everyone pitched in to make the first Christmas cake.

When I took them for a Medical Examination, Doctor said, "Elisabeth, Dawn impress me as being very intelligent, I am sure she'll do well, send these boys to trade and they could earn forty dollars per hour or they could hang around and learn nothing and end up lifting boxes for ten per hour." The boys had long dropped out of school; I couldn't stretch my meagre resources much more so I focused the little I had on Dawn in the hopes of saving her from falling into a similar fate as mine. I tried getting the guys into a trade but they never seemed interested and I don't think at the time they realized the importance of a trade. They were excited about their new homeland and the glitz and glamour of getting dressed up and meeting young ladies.

Chase had one intention, "Mom, I must be independent by the time I'm 21." I don't want to work for anyone beyond age 21." When I took them on a visit to the Scenic Centre, he got a part-time job in the restaurant. Whether rain, sleet or snow, he bundled up and went to work, and he always had a copy of the Sun Newspaper curled up in his back pocket, constantly searching for new opportunities. Several years later he went on to become a Chef and is still in the business after several failed attempts at business ventures. There's no doubt in my mind this young man would have done exceptionally well in business had he gone back to school. He is very ambitious, so even if his ship doesn't come in he WILL go out to meet it.

Initially, Colin had difficulty adjusting to the cold and snow, partially I think because he was skin and bones looking more like a thirteen year old instead of twenty-one. For a while I thought he would be in the printing business, but he changed to painting. His fear of heights puts limitations on him but his dream of becoming a Pilot and his passion for making kites never left him. He has been making and flying kites all his life and children always surround him when he's hoisting it. He once told me that often times when he is hoisting a kite in the air or spending time alone by the riverside, he's usually working out a problem. It seems it's a form of therapy that he learnt much earlier on. I can only guess when that all started. Some kite paper and bamboo from Dollar Rama or J Michael's for Christmas is like therapy in a box.

Dawn never understood why their departure date from the island was just weeks before her graduation from High School, but I deliberately planned it that way since she would be living in Canada; to have her graduate from High school in the country as part of her Canadian experience and to bond with friends. She found many at Notre Dame High and books still remain her passion. I have never seen a person who could stay up all night reading, then start a new day as though she was just waking up. It's a stark reminder of a statement she made many years earlier after surveying all the manuals in the doctor's office: "Mommy, if I had money I would invest in books." Now with added family responsibilities, she gets them on CD's so she can "listen and ride".

TWENTY-SIX

After a while it became a bit claustrophobic with the four of us stuck in a one bedroom suite. The only recreation was a swimming pool nearby and our little 14 inch TV in the living room which seemed to have had the guys name written on it. Dawn had her own preferences but she could barely squeeze in and the constant noise from the Television hindered my taping from the stereo.

An extended family member suggested I try to get help from the Government before taking on the responsibility of a house, but at the time I felt the Government had done enough for us already, and the rest was up to us. When I realized that I'd be depending to a large extent on the help of my sons if we moved into a house, I called for a Social Worker.

While the Social Worker and I were having our discussions at the Dining table, Dawn passed by. I didn't want to disturb the interview and I was thirsty so I asked Dawn to hand me a drink of water. The Social Worker became upset because I asked my daughter for a drink of water. "Oh, you use your daughter as your maid?" I was so injured I don't remember what else was said but it was the end of the interview. She got up and left and I never heard a word from her, neither did I bother them again.

Dawn was completing her final year in High School. She held a part-time job at the very hotel I had worked at but she needed to save her Pennies to get her Graduation gown. Colin held a temporary job at Canadian

Company and Chase worked at a Restaurant. If we moved Dawn would need to find a job closer to home. My salary at the bank could only pay the rent, so before we moved into the house, it was agreed that everyone would need to pitch in a little bit to help out. I can see now that it wasn't proper timing, there would be nothing left over if one didn't pitch in or if I lost my job. We should have stayed where we were for at least 3 years till everyone was financially stronger. But for three young people who had their lives growing up in the outdoors to suddenly be in a living room chair before a little 14 inch TV was somewhat punishing. It was a tough decision. As usual, I called on my friends Kim and Angella. Kim helped us to get a lovely home to rent from a co-worker.

Within months of leaving our one-bedroom apartment for a three-bedroom house, I resigned from the bank for a Data Entry position at an Oil Company that paid $2 more per hour. With no second opinion to lean on I jumped for the opportunity thinking it could help to accommodate the growing expenses. Big deal! I don't know what I was thinking but that's what happens when you don't have someone to share your thoughts with. The only difference that $2 more per hour made in my life was to help develop my geography of Canada as most of my time was spent screening Credit Card Applications from cities and Provinces across Canada. And to make things worse, within a couple years, the Oil Company began downsizing. Anyways, Dawn finally got her own room, Colin and Chase shared a room and I purposely chose the middle room so I could get a feel of what went on either side of me. At times I heard what sounded like toes tipping towards the boys' room but by the time I tip-toed out of my bedroom they would all be sitting in the living room couch like kids in Sunday school class. Once when I confronted them, Chase reminded me that they were paying rent. It was a grim reminder that if I wanted to be in charge, I should have found a place that I could pay for by myself.

Eventually, the guys became huge wrestling fans and the "banquet hall" living room was like license to blast the little 14 inch TV higher every Saturday. It wasn't possible to hear anything else in the living room on Saturdays when wrestling started, except their voices, and the fans at the ringside. And there was no point asking them to be quiet. It would be as good as talking to the four walls. Saturdays had been a very special day for me for many, many years. It was the day I tuned in to a Radio Station then known as WDCX with host Doug Reilly from 2 to 6pm listening and recording some of my favourite Gospel Singers: Dotty Rambo, Rusty Goodman, Jimmy Swaggart, Henry Slaughter, The Speers, The Hemphills, The Calvary Echoes, Squire Parsons and countless others. I didn't miss a beat with them, but with the single TV in the living room sitting beside the stereo unit, some concessions had to be made for peace sake, because just as I was passionate about my Gospel Music, they were just as passionate about their wrestling, and it was clear I wasn't going to win without resentment and animosity.

I decided to record from the stereo with the volume as low as I could and replay them later to keep everyone happy. It worked. They could watch their wrestling and scream to their hearts content. Through them I came to know names such as Hulk Hogan; Macho Man Randy Savage; The Million Dollar Man; Koko Bird; The Ultimate Warrior; Sting; The Rockers and the Bush Whackers who marched their way straight into the ring. I loved The Rockers, they were clean wrestlers. Randy Savage looked like he could intimidate the Red Sea to part in two and make way for him. Didn't think Koko Bird was much of a wrestler, but I found him and his bird very entertaining.

Eventually I took a big liking to wrestling, I couldn't let my sons know or else Dawn and I might not have been able to watch anything else on TV. I was attracted to their prowess, but I shivered when they got violent; couldn't stand to see blood. Many times I locked myself in my bedroom and chuckled, especially when the Bushwhackers came marching in. But the high point for me on Saturdays was to see Miss Elisabeth climbing the ropes. I wonder who designed her dresses. It didn't matter what she wore, she was always able to climb and stretch her way straight over the ropes into the ring. I'm sure that was part of the fun. I loved her. She had nerves of steel. I can see why Wrestling has so many fans; it's comedy, drama, power and passion. It was a vehicle that removed every fibre of stress from my body for those few hours on Saturdays and Miss Elisabeth's drama had me hooked. When I stopped watching, I lost interest in the sport, but I have never forgotten the excitement and the passion. It could be easily aroused if I were among fans. By the way, I hope my Christian friends don't see it as a sin. A very famous Wrestler who I was a huge fan of became a Preacher, which in my opinion is a marvellous idea, because a lot of us *"holier than thou Christians"* would never go to the ringside to save a soul, Oh no, too holy, so God chose one of their own to help redeem them. Wise move.

One Sunday morning when I was replaying the previous day's recordings, Dawn must have been touched by a special song. When I stopped the tape, she cried out from her bedroom, "Mommy, Mommy, play that song again." It felt very rewarding; the Holy Spirit was at work in her, something was happening on the inside. I wonder what their lives would be like today if the circumstances were different; if they had the opportunity to be with me from birth, the impact Gospel Music might have had on their lives. I wanted so much for us to be a family band of Gospel Singers travelling the globe singing in every language. I look at The Isaacs and I see a mother who faced unspeakable woe as one of two sisters to survive holocaust atrocities; now her children are giving thanks to God through the power of music. For all that God has brought us through, the correct thing for us, would have been to do exactly what the Isaacs are doing. It's no wonder sometimes I feel like heaven has closed its doors. We have not expressed gratitude for the privilege we've been given. I have to believe that somewhere down through the line of my offspring a great Gospel Singer will arise and shine. And it will happen.

Except for weekends, getting the family together for supper was a challenge; particularly with Dawn in school, a part time job and after school activities; but it was always a blessing to sit with them at the table. It was one of those things that I waited years to do; to sit together and eat as a family. She always had friends over from school and the neighbourhood so there always seem to be a teenage party in the works. The guys loved that, according to them it was time to go fishing. I indulged in those moments and I missed them. We were barely making ends meet but we were happy and we were all together. There was only one little itch, Dawn was usually late getting home when she worked and no amount of talking worked; but as a High School dropout with a baby at 14, I had my eyes wide open. I was planning to spank her behind once but I got the urge to call Glen; he said, "Elisabeth if you do, I may be the one to come and charge you". Years later when I told Dawn she said to me, "So Mom how did you feel when Glen said that, welcome to foreign." But I often wonder if she would have gotten pregnant a month after graduation if Glen hadn't stopped me from slapping her backside.

Chase was a hard worker from day one, but Colin was either the direct opposite or he was afraid of winter. He was just skin and bones and there wasn't much cash going around for vitamins. On my way to Supermarket one Saturday morning with $20 for a family of four, Chase shouted, "Mom, lend me $10." I turned around and smiled at him. Little did he know I took a peep at his bankbook the evening before and realized that he had deposited $600, but I was happy for him, he had a plan and the process had began. But I was a bit concerned about a distant cousin that he always sending Post Cards to because he didn't grow up with my mother to be familiar with those people. When I asked him, he said they were good to him when he left the Dawson's and reunited with the family, and that the lady told him that Dawson was not his father; that the man I referred to herein as the rapist/beast was his father. Up to that time I hadn't talked about my ordeal with anyone, except briefing a sister who felt that I should not say anything to him; so my guess is, "cousin whatever" saw the Hannikim's family resemblance and made the decision to tell him even though it was not in her place to do that. I didn't deny or confirm; still couldn't talk about it; couldn't go there; far too deep. I knew he went through a lot but he never said much to me except that Mr. Dawson drank a lot and was always angry, and he was always afraid to go anywhere with him because friends teased him that Mr. Dawson was not his father even though he tried to cover his forehead. And several years later I learnt from Sister Ilene too that the Dawson's neighbours sent several messages to members of my family to come and get him because he was being abused; also while I was penning the story Dawn said he told her that his stepmother once put him in a pan and rolled him down a hill. I believe now that I should have sat down with him and have a talk and we would have learnt a lot from each other, but I had difficulty talking about the rape verbally and somehow I really believed it would all go away and

I'd never have to say anything. But based on what that "cousin whatever" told him, he formed his own opinion, the wrong one; and maybe out of sheer confusion, a feeling of abandonment, or simply not feeling like a part of us, he kept insisting on getting his passport and I insisted on keeping them all. I thought, children move around; documents get lost or stolen; they were safer with me; but he insisted and I eventually gave it to him. The following day when I came home, his bed and all his personal belongings were gone. I had no idea where he went. He visited periodically only to pressure me to give up the house and let everyone go on their own. Honestly, I understood how he must have felt why he decided to leave. He probably asked himself, "Who is this woman called Mom, who left since he was a babe and never even bothered to see him again till some 14-15 years later?" "Why should he care now?" While I was afraid to face my demons all those years, thinking if I never had to deal with that part of my life no one would ever know I was raped and he would just grow up believing they were his family; didn't work. I can only guess that it was too much for him to bear and in his struggle to adjust to his "new" family he became overwhelmed. His leaving left a hole in the family and a devastating financial blow on the budget. I considered it "payback" time. And the rent became a big struggle.

With Dawn in school and doing a part time job to help with her graduation gown and Colin's on again off again assignments things weren't looking good. My nephew stayed with us for a while but when I asked him to help with the toiletries he floored me with his response; soon he was gone too. I picked up a part-time job. When I did my Tax Return, they took back every cent and more. I did a crash course in Word Processing but I felt insecure leaving the Oil Company to pursue a career based on a few hours crash course that I didn't fully grasp. I was falling behind in rent and the Oil Company began downsizing. All credits card were maxed out.

At the apartment, one cheque covered everything but at the house there was a bill for everything under the sun. Out of frustration they decorated the refrigerator like a toddler's drawings, hoping my children would help to save on utility. When my nephew introduced me to a friend, the first $100 from him was like winning the lottery. Before long he was sharing our home to help keep the roof over our heads. It went against everything I stood for. I had a big crush on someone at work; my father died when I was nine months and I never ever saw my mother living with a man in the house around us; and I totally resented the fact that for over seven years while I waited for my children to come home I had wrapped myself up with church and doing my Gospel Recording on Saturdays and now to keep a roof over our head and food on the table I was sharing my house with someone I didn't like and would never grow to like much less love in a million years. It made me want to throw up. I knew I had to get out of the mess, I had to. My little world the way I knew it and the way I envisioned it wasn't coming together. One day I was so frustrated with life that I locked myself in my bedroom and sobbed; all I could hear in my head was the voice of Gospel Singer, Rusty Goodman, singing, *"When life has stung you, remember He loves you, He really loves you, He understands, so give Him your hand."*

The family was increasing rapidly. Dawn became pregnant one month after graduating from High school. Colin's girlfriend gave birth to a son a few weeks earlier and Chase was long gone. I couldn't help my son, my daughter or my grandchild and I still had an obligation to help my mother. I knew if I could just work out my children's well being I could return to the States and be able to help my family. More than anything else, I wanted a home so my grandson could have a backyard to play in by the time he turned four years old. That was my long term goal. My short term goal was to leave fast so I could get preparation underway for Dawn. I didn't wait for the axe to reach me at the Oil Company. I was working for them through an Agency and I knew we would be the first batch to let go. I left everyone in the house and head for greener pastures in the States for deliverance.

TWENTY-SEVEN

For every financial crisis I faced, I saw the United States of America as my Deliverer. After all, it helped me before; good old USA will have to help get me out of this dilemma again. As it turned out, this trip was one of mixed blessings, it lasted much longer than expected; took so many twists and turns that this period had to be broken down into 3 chapters. There was some laughter, friendship, a praying partner, a break from all the stress, some conning too; and I lost two of the greatest people I have ever known in my life, my precious mother, and Brother Phil.

When I got to Sister Love in America it was close to my birthday but with all the responsibilities confronting me and the disappointment with Dawn's pregnancy, birthday was the last thing on my mind. I was just thankful that I had her home to stay at for a while and not to be bothered about rent at once. When she came home with a bottle of champagne for the occasion and found me making a pot of cornmeal porridge; she looked at me and said, "You want to go and tell people that you spend your birthday at my house and I gave you cornmeal porridge, you drink that porridge another day, not today." I truly believed in my heart that my children and I were going to be forming a Gospel Band when they arrived, not planning for babies. Plans were underway for Dawn to attend School of Journalism in the fall. My dreams were shattered again. I was forced to face the reality that the babies I left behind were no longer babies. I couldn't impose my desires upon them. Less than two years after they arrived, Colin became a father before acquiring any form of skill much less

257

a permanent job. The mother of the child, a brilliant French and Music major; still living in her parents' house; became a High School drop-out. None could help the other. For several years the greater portion of the responsibility was shared between the two grandmothers. The $16.00 per month baby bonus that I was receiving for Dawn monthly expired a few months before her graduation.

Being away from the situation, I could think a little clearer. I decided that the best thing was to relinquish the house and divide the contents between Colin and Dawn. I knew that once I got a place of my own, it would have been impossible to carry rent in Canada and America; and still be able to assist with the additional family expenses. There was no time to procrastinate. Within three months I was back. The moment I walked into the house and turned the stereo on, Susan came upstairs. She had heard "The Jesus music," she knew I was home. It was family time again with the sad realization that it could only be a few days.

Looking at my baby with her little pumpkin sticking out and having to do what I must, so I could help children, grandchildren, and my mother was overwhelming. I was happy to see them but I hated everything that I was faced with. My daughter was sobbing, my son tried to stifle his emotions while trying to get a piece of furniture onto a truck which he couldn't even drive properly at the time. It was sheer hell but I did not want that man in my house even if he could fill the gap. It was taking me against my wishes for the sake of making ends meet. I hated it. And now with the family rapidly increasing, quick and decisive action had to be taken to avoid any dependence on him.

When a neighbour heard the bawling and came over I could barely contain myself to talk to her. I remembered her arms around me but I don't remember a single word she said. For almost eight years, we were separated, now they were here I wanted to feed them well; take care of them; have quality time together; laugh and play together; instead they were forming families of their own before we ourselves were able to stand on our own two feet. It was frighteningly difficult and very discouraging after waiting almost 8 years to bring them home. All I could think is that they got too excited.

I couldn't make it back for the birth of the child. As a non-resident of the USA I wasn't comfortable running in and out so frequently even though I was a Canadian Citizen but her classmates in the delivery room put my mind at ease. I don't think my brother was happy with the way I dealt with the situation but I was just trying to do the best I could. And I think too that I was stressed out from the years of waiting and all that had gone on in my life prior. It was a lot for me to carry over such long period of time and to be faced with more. What was even worse was many years later when my daughter told me that when the baby cried, she cried too because she didn't know what to do. There are no words to describe that feeling. I groan in my spirit each time I think of the times I have had to leave them for greener pastures; I'll never be able to repay them and no amount of making up will do, never.

Five months after Dawn gave birth, and fifteen months after the birth of my first grandchild; I became a grandmother for the third time: for a total of three grandchildren within 37 months of their arrival. It seems like the chain of poverty was now destined to extend to the next generation. For many years, I learnt to keep the receipts when I made a purchase, and I learnt from early not to try on clothes in the store with lipstick on in case I needed to return them to get my money back to help with a financial crisis. It was common to buy a gorgeous dress for a special occasion from the finest store, wear it and then carefully return it so I could get the money to do more important things. I had my mother to help too. Whenever I couldn't be with the children, I would arrange for the family to spend Christmas with me in America. I didn't want to deny them anymore.

When a letter came from Dawn, I grew suspicious, she was up to something. We were close enough for me to read between the lines and when she mentioned going to Jamaica, I instinctively knew she was going on a mission but I didn't know what the mission was about. She deliberately put it in writing in case I tried to talk her out of not going. I read the letter about three times then I said to Clive I have to go to Canada immediately,

Dawn is up to something she's leaving for Jamaica. I showed him the letter but he didn't see anything to worry about. I knew my daughter. Without saying a word to her, I head for Canada within days. No doubt she knew I'd be on my way so by the time I got there, she was gone; typical of Dawn, always silent about her next move.

I knew it wasn't easy on her financially but I was doing the best I could to make sure the Pennies stretched so everyone got something. Three weeks later on her return she called, "Mom, I have something to tell you, please don't be mad with me." Frankly I was too relieved to hear from her and to know my grandchild was okay, nothing else mattered. After a long pause, she broke the news that she got married. Somehow I couldn't find it in my heart to blame her; they had been through enough, they had suffered enough. I blamed myself and I blamed God even more for always finding ways to punish me. But honestly, I wondered about the parents of the groom how they would feel if their only son did that to them. Thankfully 20 years later, with a daughter in University, a son aspiring to be a Building Engineer, another who is sure to be a Scientist and a seven year old who reads like an adult; their marriage seems solid while I still pine for the loss of my baby.

It's nice to have two heads together when making important decisions. I never had such luxury and looking back now I made some bad judgements. I strongly believe or maybe out of guilt, I feel that by leaving my children so very early after they came has weakened the family bond. I weaned them before the time and the effects are still being felt and somehow it seems it has extended even to the next generation. But I saw myself as their rock; I was just trying to help keep food on the tables. I have had to keep reminding myself at all times that my desire to be parents and grandparents, to be all things to everyone, and to want to fix everything; have probably cost me well needed time with my family. I was always on the run for opportunities to make life better and sometimes those runs took me away for years. It's a crime for which I'll pay for the rest of my life, and sometimes, children conveniently forget sacrifices. I had no one to ask for advice. I simply did everything as I saw fit and in the long run, may have caused some damage even though my intentions were well intended.

Looking back now, I realize too that I was also trying to escape more pain and stress, I just couldn't take anymore. I never had a break since I was in my teens. For seven years I didn't enjoy a Christmas; didn't think I deserved to without them being around to enjoy it with me; the only smile I had, came from a bus driver when I rode his bus; each time I saw a mother with her children, especially during Christmas season, I cried. All that kept me going was the day when they would come home and everything would be sweet and dandy, I lived for that, and it was not. I was thrown into a world of one baby after another before they had a chance to complete their education. And before I could begin to enjoy them they were making families of their own when we ourselves were struggling to keep a roof over our heads. Enough was enough, I needed a break. I couldn't go anymore. I ran, and the search for greener pastures for all took many turns and much longer than expected. I've always had my plate full and at the same time I had to find a way to live and give myself some well needed respite.

Within a couple of years of returning to the USA, I liquidated all my credit cards indebtedness that had been used like a second pay cheque. I was determined that my grandchildren were going to have a backyard to play in. I've always felt that I had a responsibility to my children out of guilt I suppose, to do for them what they couldn't do for themselves; always playing the role of both parents and grandparents. I might not have had the strength to stick around in the midst of the family as it increased, but using the power of the "almighty dollar" to fix everything from a distance made me feel I was still parenting; but looking back now I realize that I was overwhelmed, had no room to accommodate anything more so it was an escape. Luckily, my job wasn't very demanding and I was in a community of Christians.

Two years after arriving in the U.S, the prospect of greener pastures led me to New York City where I hoped to realize my dreams faster. I loved everything about New York. Its fast, it's exciting, full of energy. Even a train-ride into Manhattan is exciting; whether it's the passing out of so-called fresh sandwiches for a little tip, someone claiming to be seeking a few quarters to start a business, or even an early morning sermon, but there was never a dull moment. There was one peddler who changed his clothes just before getting on the train at the very first stop, then rode all the way to the end of the line with a paper bag pan handling. Once when he got off the train I followed him straight to the bank. He told me that was the only way he could pay his mortgage. Another told me he had a wife and six children. The hard luck stories seemed to have been a way of life for a few but I also found it entertaining and I always look forward to hearing the next story. My train ride would not be complete without them.

In Manhattan I was always on the lookout to spot a famous person. One day when I went into a Christedes Supermarket on Lexington Avenue, the Cashier excitedly told me I just missed seeing one of America's favourite First Ladies, but I did get a glimpse of her leaving Central Park wearing white pants with yellow top and those Sophia Lauren looking sunshades.

Whether it's the beauty of Central Park; a stroll down to the famous Rockefeller Centre during the Christmas seasons; a night at Shaw Stadium watching Tennis Star Monica Seles grunt and slam; a "comedian" on the train; or a sumptuous dish of fried green plantain at the Cuban Restaurant in Queens, once you have lived in New York there will be nowhere else quite like it.

Within days of my arrival in New York, I picked up a job in Great Neck, Long Island. And what a job it was! It was my first experience working with a person with *alzheimers*. She was such a beautiful person with an infectious smile and an enviable waistline from years of golfing; yet one of the deadliest diseases known to mankind was destroying her mind. The very stove had to be unplugged at nights and getting a good night's sleep was only a wish because for whatever the reasons, they tend to get restless from sundown. I was in bed one night when I heard the doorbell rang, it was the cops; they had found her wandering some distance away. I would have sworn she was in bed. Luckily, she was wearing her identification bracelet.

Another pleasantry for her was going to the "bank"(the garage) except, in her mind the closed garage door meant her "bank" was closed. One rainy day she was standing by the "bank" in a thunderstorm waiting for the "bank" to open. It never did. And I couldn't just stand by and watched her soak in the rain. The key to getting her to respond to me depended on how calm and diligent I was with her. I thought I was, but maybe she misinterpreted my actions, so when I tried to lead her inside she grabbed my hair at the root like she was drowning, and there was no way out than to be extremely sweet and kind. I had to think fast, there was no one else around and the houses were far apart. I remembered that she loved food, so I said to her, Okay sweetheart, let's go have some food. Once I said that she let go of my hair with a smile and said, "Oh, you're a darling." Her relationship with food probably saved my life that day. Caring for a person with *alzheimers* is probably the most challenging task an individual will ever face. It requires a lot of warmth, compassion, patience and tolerance. And yes, having lots of food around helps. They have a healthy appetite. Zero tolerance for noise or loud music. Families need to be aware that it's much harder on the person extending the care. Support is crucial. Healing could take years, and the memory, a lifetime.

TWENTY-EIGHT

One Saturday afternoon, a few blocks from the famous Shaw Stadium where I watched some of my favourite tennis players; Steffi, Pete and Andre, to name a few, I came across two to three Sales Representatives from a cable company. One handed me a flyer regarding cable installation which I barely glanced at, but I held on to it since I had just gotten an apartment and was considering getting cable in the future.

A few months later, I called the Representative for cable installation. When he wrote up the order, it seemed he had difficulty getting up and leaving. It was going to be more than just a cable sale. I sensed it. About three months later, I had a call from him inviting me to a movie. At age forty one, I believe it was either the second or third time that I went to the movies, and I am sure one of them was the not so long ago, Mel Gibson's, Passion of the Christ. I dressed like I was going to see a Pavarotti Concert on Broadway.

While my eyes were glued to the screen like I was attentively watching a Sunday Morning Church Sermon, he was feverishly trying to hold my hand, while pretending to find the movie funny. It had been ten years since I was divorced and the only social occasions I had were some earlier times when I attended a Baptist church and couldn't wait for service to finish so I could get to Coffee Time next door for my Cornmeal muffin and hot chocolate. That's exactly how I treated the bag of popcorn I was given at the movies. Instead of nibbling on it throughout the movie, I treated it like it was hot chocolate and muffin. Years later I was still agonizing how I lost my civility.

I guess I was so excited about being taken out after so many years that something else very important slipped by me from the very first date: he had been separated for thirteen years and was in the process of getting a divorce, bad sign. Normally, with my keen sense and eagle eyes, that would not have passed me. I would have certainly questioned that, *in the process* line after 13 long years. I don't remember what we talked about on our first date nor do I recall what the movie was about. With so much in my past to hide, I'm sure I rattled off the evening impressing him with my love for Gospel Music, naming the various artists, everything about church and the way how I loved to sing. I made sure that for every song I mentioned, I named the artist just to impress him and to stretch the conversation; that way, there'd be no room for many personal questions. I even recited a few of my favourite Psalms from the Bible while he tried to keep up with me by rattling off the last line of each one.

After the movies, he took me home then continued on to his Long Island apartment. On a couple occasions, he invited me to his apartment. I can never forget the appearance of his desk. It was either a genius at work or, it was organized chaos. And he was always quick to talk of the Past Students' Association and his position as Chairman, but it was his cooking that really made an impression on me. Finger licking good!

Within a few months, we were seriously talking about settling down together. Bearing in mind the hell I went through with my husband, I was sure at the time I wasn't ready for marriage and I never thought I was capable of loving with such intensity again. However, I wanted to start with a clean slate since there was a part of me telling me things could get far. I told him a little and covered up the rest. While he listened, the tears streamed down his cheeks. I wasn't sure whether that meant he was leaving or they were tears of sympathy, but I felt strongly that he was overcome with emotions. He never said a word. We saw each other once after that conversation and then he took a long break some eight to ten weeks.

He called after returning from one of his Past Students' trips to the Island;
his rent was short a few bucks. Another call came one Sunday morning wanting
to come over for breakfast with a few friends from the Association he said,
who were in town for one of their Sunday Meetings. It didn't take me long
to realize that the Past Students' Association Meetings was as important as
the Federal Reserve Chairman meeting with The International Monetary
Fund Committee. Later that evening he returned, and there was plenty to
talk about: He felt that there was something there worth exploring. Starved
for love and affection I guess, the feeling was mutual.

Months later, when his friend was helping him move into my apartment,
I felt a deliberate squeeze on my big toe at the door like he was trying to get
my attention. When my eyes made contact with Rowland, he leaned over
into my ears and said "Did he tell you he wasn't working?" I pretended I
didn't hear, totally dismissed it. After all only a couple of weeks ago he was
with Cable & Wireless and he impressed me as a good and decent man;
so thoughtful that he wasn't bothered by my past. In addition he was so
generous to my grandsons when they came down from Canada for a visit
I saw that as a good sign. This gentle handsome man with his glistening
white teeth and a horse shoe bald head practically lit up a room when he
walked in. There was no way anyone was going to talk me out of what
looked like a very promising future. Not to mention how impressed I was
when he took a trip back home and paid a surprise visit to my mother and
brought pictures back for me. I thought that was so nice of him. According
to him, he had to meet the mother I talked about so much.

The first few months we lived together something bothered me a bit,
but I felt it was right to make concession seeing I was divorced and alone
for ten years and according to him he had been alone thirteen years. But
those books, papers, folders and all sorts of Past Students junk scattered
all over his desk in the corner of the living room reminded me of what
I earlier referred to as organized chaos when I visited his apartment. In
addition, he was always up until late at nights but his snoring could keep
the entire building awake all night so that didn't bother me. Not yet. But
a book he liked to read, "How to Live On Other People's Money," caused

me to question the title. I didn't read the book, but the title aroused my suspicion because I was the one footing all the responsibilities.

It didn't take me long to confirm what his friend hinted. The unemployment cheques started rolling in, but it seemed he never thought he got enough to share in the expenses of the apartment even though he liked to cook. When he suggested that we move to a larger apartment, a two bedroom equipped with a dishwasher. That didn't make sense since he wasn't working at the time. When I shared his proposal with my Jewish landlord, a very shrewd businessman who could more than afford one of those gorgeous homes in Kew Gardens or Great Neck but chose to live in one of his apartments on the same building; he suggested that if Clive needed to move into a two bedroom apartment, get him to pay three months rent first. I never did get a Penny but he did give me Three Thousand Dollars when he got his settlement from a Wall Street firm he had sued. According to him he was a passed up for a promotion while working with them and attending York University. I misread the $3000 gesture. I thought it was a sign of things to come. I even remember thinking that since he hadn't been very generous, he must have gotten about $50,000 but he never discussed it and I never asked.

When he got a job as a Realtor where his friend worked, I was confident things were moving ahead, so he convinced me to sign the new lease for the more spacious two bedroom apartment that could help to accommodate Past Students coming from out of town for Sunday meetings. His desk went straight to the guest room and the volume of "stuff" on the desk increased even though there was a newer more modern roll top desk in the foyer. Anyway, since it was out of my way, there was no point picking on him and his snoring could keep the entire building awake all night so it was better for me if he stayed at his desk all night.

Ever since I was little I've always wanted to give my father a headstone. Unlike other tombs on the family plot, the only thing marking the spot where he was laid to rest was a tree mother planted, just what she could lovingly afford. As soon as I mentioned it to Clive, he "jumped on the bandwagon" like it was top priority. It's only now when I remember now that he said when he was in Jamaica he felt like he was home, but when he was in America it felt like he was on vacation, that I begin to put two and two together.

Just two weeks after returning from one of his Annual Past Students' Reunion on the island, he went back with me to have my life-long dream fulfilled, giving my father a headstone. When we arrived, a past student commented on his quick return and wondered why he didn't take me with him when the group met just two weeks earlier, instead of returning to America then flying back just to do my dad's headstone. But those were not things that bothered me; I thought if he was man enough to look beyond my faults and see the goodness in me, then certainly I could do the same. And getting my father a headstone almost 43 years after his death was a major milestone for me.

The day in question, as I watched the workers prepare the site where my dad's headstone would be placed, Clive walked over to me and whispered, "Honey, I think you should be with your mother feeding her and taking photographs of the occasion." It turned out to be the single most important advice he ever gave me. They were the last photos taken of me and my mother surrounded by two of my brothers. I treasure that photo. Just before I left, my mother's last words to me were, "Elisabeth, remember to stop at the church, remember the church." Little did I know those would be the last words I heard from my beloved mother.

After getting my father's headstone done, I decided that I needed something that would wash away the memories of my last 14 years on the Island. The rape, the trial, the years of beatings and the running away from place to place with my daughter was all that occupied my mind.

We visited 12 of the 14 parishes. The places I was discovering for the first time made me wonder if I was still in Jamaica, and question myself as to how we could leave the warmth and beauty of such a glorious place to live in an ice box abroad six months per year. The parish of St. Ann, the garden parish, is truly what it's nicknamed, "The Miami of Jamaica." Spotlessly clean with more historical sites and gardens than any other parish; even the roads are like highways. I tried swimming in the famous Porto Seiko Beach near Discovery Bay, and even took the challenge of climbing Dunn's River Falls near Ocho Rios. The Green Grotto Cave near Discovery Bay was where the James Bond Movie "Live and Let Die" was filmed. Tour Guides at the site narrating the story of the Cave stated that the site was part of the ocean but the waters receded and the creatures of the ocean were left at surface level. Some 36m below the surface visitors can go on a boat ride, but it is so densely black that the fishes are blind, and when the lights were dimmed to give visitors a sense of how dark it is, the screams were horrifying. It should be an interesting visit for students of Oceanology.

Another historical site nearby is the famous Rose Hall Inn that receives thousands of visitors yearly hoping to get a glimpse of the ghost referred to as "The White Witch of Rose Hall" And not so far away is the birthplace of Reggae Superstar, the late Bob Marley.

Hidden in the eastern part of the island is a Healing Resort where steaming hot water flows between the rocks. It has been said that it was discovered by a pedestrian with a wounded foot which was healed after walking in the water. Even though a hotel nearby enjoy the same water, guests mostly retreat to the rocky hills nearby to enjoy the experience but caution is required, the water is very hot. The site remains a popular destination for churches especially, on New Year's Day. In my opinion, this Mineral Bath is the Island's best kept secret. With a little publicity it could be a major tourist attraction.

About half an hour away from the fountain, is the statue of one of Jamaica's National Heroes, Paul Bogle, who on October 11, 1865 led hundreds of men and women in a march which started the Morant Bay Rebellion. He led the Rebellion and was later hung in the very courtroom where he was tried. A friend recalled going on a school trip many, many decades after the hanging to see history unfold at the back of the courthouse where thousands gathered to witness the unearthing of mass graves, some were apparently buried alive during the rebellion. Mouths were opened wide, bones scattered and skeletons huddled beside each other. Not very far from this historical site is a little market selling everything to quench your thirst after a day in the sun. I have no idea why they named the little market "Jack Ass Behind."

There wasn't enough time to visit Blue Mountain, home of the world renowned coffee, or sail the Rio Grande, but the chance to see my mother and to feed her, seeing the only sister who was left on the island, my brothers, extended family members, the satisfaction of giving my father a headstone, and the opportunity to discover most of the island was gratifying. Even the idea to just sit back, relax, and to feel like I was sightseeing was therapeutic. It was my first opportunity to put everything behind me and had fun. I would love to do it again.

Back in America, Clive started driving taxi after leaving "the office" in the evenings to help purchase a new car. Keeping a car was a constant struggle. He battled with that because to keep one running takes money and being responsible towards financial obligations. He wasn't good at those things. Except for $40 on two occasions, up to that time he never assisted with the bills; yet he never missed the New Year's Eve Family Reunion and Past Student Association Reunion even if it meant working temporarily with a Travel Agency to secure a complimentary ticket.

Every holiday was an occasion for celebration and birthdays were no exception. I can still see him coming with a bunch of roses and a balloon marked "You're Special" in one hand and his attaché in the other hand, quite likely loaded with Students' Association "stuff" or some Real Estate deals that never closed.

Since I wasn't much of a socialite, birthdays and special moments were spent dining his home cooked meals on a blanket on the living room rug watching favourites like—Scent of A Woman, with Al Pachino, Driving Miss Daisy, Mrs. Doubtfire or watching my favourite Morgan Freeman in the unforgettable character of New Jersey School Principal, Joe Clark. Clive's passion for basketball drew me to the game just the way my sons' passion for wrestling got me hooked to it. But I was mostly interested in seeing Kobe jump and spin with the ball as he dunked it in the net. And it was equally interesting to watch Clive root for the New York Knicks and screamed at Patrick for not getting a ring as though he could hear him from our living room. A boat ride on Maryland's "Spirit of Baltimore" eating crab and lobster all day was an experience I'll never forget but it was odd seeing Hezekiah on the boat, very odd, it didn't make me comfortable at all and Clive picked up on something. On the bus back home he made sure we sat in the seat before Hezekiah. I don't think Hezekiah will ever forgive me for that. Those twenty-odd hours ride from New York to Miami on two occasions for Aunt Sybil's sumptuous Thanksgiving Dinner added to a few of the simple pleasures I really enjoyed.

My fondest moments though, were those Sunday mornings devotion. They were moments when I felt like nothing else mattered. To listen to Clive take a line or two from the Daily Devotional and develop what sounded like a sermon was awe inspiring. He became so absorbed in Scriptures that even his countenance glowed. And he was so fervent in his prayers that I missed hearing him pray. Equally, there was a peace that flowed from him which practically blocked me from confronting him about his financial responsibilities. It's like it was something negative. Had he been a Provider, it would have been a good match. That was disturbing.

A couple of times I hinted to one of his nieces how cheap he was, she always made the same comment, "No Aunt, that's not how I saw my father (Clive's brother) treated my mother." Poor me, I was just enjoying my freedom, finally having some laughter and forgetting about the past that I didn't even see it for what it was. When the children commented how happy I was, it's like they were sharing my happiness too. Occasionally when Chase would ask him what he did to make me so happy, he would say that he waited many years to find someone he could share himself with. Like a darn fool that made me feel even more special. Oh boy.

When he came home from the office and said, "Honey, I love being home," it was as though something on the outside intimidated him, and he felt safe being home. And he always had plenty of jokes to share; like the day he said he was walking down the street during his lunch hour when he looked up in the sky and said, "Life is beautiful." I chuckled because I could just picture him in the heat with water beading out of his horse-shoe bald head; but in my heart I thought "what a con artist, of course life is beautiful, you don't even know how the rent is paid." And when I talked to him about my growing uneasiness of living a life of fornication and I had grandchildren who were advancing in age and will be asking questions soon, he always said he had every intention of making me his wife when we moved to Jamaica. To me his answer meant "next never." No point reminding him that my immediate family was in Canada, he would always be quick to point out that everyone loves a winter get away in the sun.

Twice per year he visited the Island for the Annual Family Reunion and Past Student's Reunion. A master at fundraising and getting people together for a cause he chose to believe in. The Students' Association was his passion. Whatever it took, from boat rides, to solicitation by mail, he was capable of getting the job done without a Penny from his pockets. It was all about raising the funds needed to get the job done. Letters went out by the hundreds and I learnt that for every hundred letters that were sent out, one can expect no more than ten replies. It seemed the kids for whom the funds were raised fared better than me since his job as a Realtor brought in zero. He was always closing a "dead deal" or one had just failed. I had gone to quite a few of those pep talk sales pitch meetings and they all sounded good at the meetings; but none of them converted to hard cash.

My patience was running thin. On the surface I remained very calm even though I was drying up inside and I began to experience menopausal changes which I believe was brought on by stress. Ironically, he practically journeyed with me through the process, if I was warm, he was warm too, and if I was cold, he'd be cold too. And he found it humorous when I sat at the dining table topless because of the heat so it made the experience both laughable and tolerable. But humour couldn't pay the bills, yet on the other hand I dread being left alone, I wanted to hold on to him for dear life but the weight was strangling me.

Six months after giving my father a headstone, the news of mother's death came. Clive was in the UK on his second vacation for the year. He had just returned from Family Reunion in mid-January and was scheduled to leave again mid-summer for the Past Student's Reunion. Luckily for me, that same evening, I got a settlement cheque for Clive from a motor car collision in the amount of $1500. After telephoning him in the UK for his permission to cash the cheque, I left a couple days later. I didn't leave him a cent. There I was in America hustling to get a home in Canada so my grandchildren can have their backyard to play, and I was wasting time with one who didn't even bear his weight. Then at this pivotal point in my life, the third month in the year, he was on his second vacation with a third one set for the summer. Fortunately, Val and Shirley were visiting from England. To lose a parent is devastating, but to lose the only parent you ever knew, I don't think anyone can truly put into words the emptiness one feels from such loss.

I went straight to mother's bedroom when I got home. Her life was a living testimony and in death she left a testimony on her bed. Her hymn book, her Bible and her Daily Bread Devotional were left opened at the day's reading. Just as she had done on a daily basis, she talked to God the very last day and according to Brother Phil, "she sung her way to eternity until she took her last breath. My brother was a visibly broken man. He looked so defeated. Every ounce of energy was zapped from him. Not only had he lost his mother, he lost his best friend. With his head hung low and his eyes fixed to the hardwood floors in her bedroom, fighting to control his emotions; he rubbed his thumb against his fingers and said "and she wanted to live you know, she wanted to live."

My beloved brother who had given up his life since he was a young man, to stand by his mother when their father deserted them and following the death of my father when she was left with an additional two children; the one who was like a father to his siblings: best friend and confidant to his mother: and finally her caregiver; faced the worst day of his life. And so it was, we all came together to mourn the one single thread that bound us together; the one who encouraged peace, love and unity; and the only person we had to pray for us daily. We were left like sheep without a shepherd and Brother Phil was too broken to lead the flock.

After my Mom's funeral, I began to re-examine my own life. I never knew my father, now the only parent I had ever known was gone. There will never be another mother to pray for me every morning and every night. No more letters to cheer me on with a word of encouragement. I will never open another letter that reads, "Dear Daughter, Greetings in the Precious Name of Jesus Our Soon Coming King" or a memory verse to lift my broken spirit, or that special Psalm to guide me along life's road. The wind beneath my wings was taken away and I was left with a burning desire for some form of change.

Even with the wind taken out of my sail I needed to be strong for myself and my children. Seeing them two or three times a year and having them rent a van at Christmas time to bring the family down to visit me wasn't part of the plan when I left Canada. I began to miss them more and more, and I began to see my time in America as a complete waste of time. I was growing increasingly uncomfortable living with Clive. My grandchildren were getting older and I didn't want them to find us living together unmarried especially because I professed to be a Christian, plus the death of my mother and financial stress was strangling me.

On one occasion when I mentioned a past due furniture bill, he said, "Honey, tear up the bill; tear it up, the Company made their profit on the first 100 pieces that were sold, tear up the bill, tear it up." I have to admit that I got a good laugh out of that. If there is any truth to it I don't know but I really wondered. A lot of my grumbling happened on the weekends when I was in the kitchen and he was at the computer writing letters soliciting funds for getting computers in school, or on someone's tax return while the financial burden of the house was left on me.

At times I felt guilty because most of my grumbling was on a Sunday after a lengthy devotion, but it was my way of crying out for help and it was the time when we'd normally be home together. But being the good natured person he was, the moment I started grumbling, he would walk in the kitchen, rest his palms on my shoulders and said, "Honey, the Good Lord wouldn't be pleased with you behaving like that." It always seemed to melt my heart and I would just smile at him or complained to him about other things instead of the real issues because there was a measure of truth in his comments. His very presence had the power to deflate any preconceived ideas that I often found myself powerless when I considered talking to him about financial stress. I saw it as making him feel unworthy. I don't know how to explain it but there was a level of angelic peace about the man that I felt compelled to reverence and there was a tendency to be patient with him. So every time he used those words on me "Honey, the good Lord wouldn't be please with you" it melted everything because there was a measure of truth in his remark. I even wondered if the death of my mother was destroying me so much that it was driving a wedge between me and the one person I should be leaning on.

When I mentioned to my niece Val how disgruntled I had become because of financial stress, she said, "Aunt from the man isn't hitting you, there's no reason to leave him." It was exactly what I wanted to hear, I clutched to those words like the Bible and felt I was being foolish to entertain the thought of ending the relationship knowing full well I would probably never meet another man who would see beyond my past but deep down inside I was still discontented.

I decided to do a Memorial Service for my Mother a year after her death. I was hurting so much that I just wanted to get back to the place where she was laid to rest. Clive patiently managed my nightly rehearsals of *"Thank you Mamma for praying for me."* He taught me when to bring the mike close and when to extend it and I was sure he recognized that it wasn't just a rehearsal it was therapy, real therapy. My mother's death was tearing me up inside. I remembered bawling all the way from Hartford, Connecticut to New York City, Penn Station after a visit with families. From the moment I got on that train and sat down all I heard in my head was Dionne Warwick singing, *"How can I forget you when there's always something there to remind me."* It tortured me like hell. I don't think I ever stopped missing my mother.

Incidentally, when I went home for the Memorial Service, the church was having Prayer Meeting. And believe it or not, some 14 years later after that Jeremiah 3 experience; the very spot I stood to make a few announcements pertaining to the Memorial, as soon as I moved away the Pastor went and stood at the very spot, opened the Bible, and read *Jeremiah Chapter 3*. I got goose bumps immediately. I still haven't been able to figure out what God was trying to tell me this time, or maybe I do but I am afraid to acknowledge it.

After the Memorial, I suggested to Clive we take things to another level that we shouldn't continue living the way we were. It was the usual comment, "We will get married when we move back to Jamaica" as though he expected me to leave my family in North America to go live with him on the Islands. When he inherited a piece of land from his aunt in exchange for assuming her financial responsibilities; he engaged his brother's architectural skill and an impressive plan for a four bedroom home sitting on a hill overlooking the ocean was drafted . . . When I asked him why a four bedroom, he said I have three children with no mention of his two; but when he suggested that he should do the building and I do the furnishing I didn't like the smell. Especially when I suggested that my name be put on the Title because we both had children who need to be protected and he said the land belonged to Father Abraham we are only here to live, pay taxes, and be buried on the land. Something didn't add up.

I can only assume that my mother had seen my plight and decided to lend a helping hand from below. A little over a year after the Memorial Service, I got the break I had been hoping for that could help me realize my dream of a home in Canada with a backyard so the grandkids could have a place to play. How I managed before I got the break to pay a sister to help care for mother, help children and grand children, assist my little nephews back home, keep a roof over my head, and be home in Canada periodically, is a question I cannot answer.

TWENTY-NINE

To help hold on to my Pennies, I kept a lid on my plans while still bearing full responsibility of our two bedroom apartment. Six months into the little "God sent job", barely two years after the death of my mother, Brother Phil was laid to rest beside her. The years of stress, hunger and doing without so the family could have, took its toll on his little 5ft 105 pound body. He was so loved by his siblings that if love could keep him alive he would still be with us, and he was the only one who could keep us glued together.

"Growing up apart from each other as poverty dictated didn't help us. There is not enough expression of love, joy, harmony and laughter amongst us. There is always a sense of distrust because some of us barely know each other. I'd love to see more brotherly love amongst siblings during my lifetime even if it's lukewarm. We are all from the same womb. We all have families of our own, but we are burning inside for the kind of love that siblings share. We are drying up from a lack of love and warm embraces necessary to sustain each other. The only thing we do together is to rise to an occasion when a situation demands it; usually funerals.

As we grew, so have we lived, separated without much feeling for each other. Now that we are older and our children are having children of their own, maybe we can make up for the lost times by seeing each other a little bit more; not just at funerals. There are injustices some of us have experienced because of poverty. If we could all be just a little open and honest with each other, step out of our shell and share our experiences, I'm convinced healing could begin; probably we could get to know each other and maybe we could grow to trust one another while on earth . . ."

As for Clive, I had reached my limit. Time for action, enough was enough. In mid January, 10 months after my mother's memorial, when Clive returned from his Annual Family Reunion, I had a quiet talk with him in the bedroom, brief but concise. "Honey, if I eat, it's my pocket; if I drink, it's my pocket; if I wear clothes, it's my pocket; if the rent gets paid it's my pocket while you travel twice per year." With that being said, I threw his pillows in the guest room. On three different occasions he brought them back inside but I threw them back and he eventually settled there. But I got a kick out of seeing him coming into my bedroom with a towel wrapped around his lower half every morning to get his undergarment out of my armoire. Big deal, I thought it would be so simple, if he really had something to hide to just keep his undergarment in his bedroom, but I'm sure he got a kick out of tormenting me.

It was such an effort to live that way, like the time he came home, reached out for a hug and I distanced myself to show him I was serious. There was no fault I could find in him, except he wasn't a provider. I didn't remember in the dating stages when I asked why he had been alone for thirteen years that he had said, *"women love to go the supermarket and I don't have it to give them."* That was a clue, but I didn't pay attention. As long as I could get a good laugh, it was a big dressing to all my wounds. By the time I found out I was nothing but a "provider" and began to rewind the tape in my head I had given away a part of my life; smitten by one who was ready to accept me for who I was. But the truth is I didn't expect him to remain under the same roof with me after being thrown out of the bedroom so it was a bit painful for me, almost regrettable. When I asked him if he was leaving, he said there was no point in leaving me in a two bedroom apartment by myself when he could just remain in the guest room and be company to me. But looking back now, I think he was very clever. He realized I didn't hold out much hope of meeting anyone else because of all the baggage I had, so he played the game: either that or he had a plan.

A few months after I got my break, he got a job working for a reputable company at the World Trade Centre. He always looked so well tailored, there wasn't a resident on the building who never felt he was an attorney and we didn't make them any wiser. About 6 months later he still hadn't offered to help shoulder the responsibilities of the apartment until I found one of his paystubs and demanded half of the rent. It really disturbed me to see the distance I had to go to get help from him. I never understood how he was such a perfect gentleman yet so irresponsible towards financial obligations? I guess only Financial Expert, Suze Orman, could answer that.

Because things had changed between us, when he boarded the train while I was on my way home from work one evening I wasn't sure whether I should walk over and greet him as a friend, so I tried to keep out of sight. When we got off the train, the moment he spotted me, he walked over, took my hand and held it all the way home. Starved for affection and not having any idea how a man should treat a woman, I felt so lucky and so proud to be seen walking hand in hand with him. As we got to the gate, a resident looked at us and said, "What a beautiful couple". I still have the dress hanging in my closet. Glancing at it reminds me of the day, the time, the place, the comment from the resident and the pride I felt with him holding my hand from the train station all the way home. What a pity! It's all I ever wanted, to love and be loved unconditionally by the one I was in love with and so far I was only lucky enough to get that from David, no one else so far.

That innocent remark "what a beautiful couple" and Clive holding my hand from the train station all the way home for "the world" to see, had the devil playing tricks with my mind. Either that, or my heart was about to govern my head again. Then one night I heard him going through the doors. I jumped out of bed deliberately wearing the same little skimpy lingerie that I wore in bed. He was going down the staircase with a large empty suitcase.

"What are you doing?" I screamed. He turned around, looked me squarely in my eyes, without a word and came back inside, and then he gently dropped the bomb: "Honey, we need to talk,

who started this?" As far as I was concerned I didn't hear a word he said, I was as mad as hell. Then as though I was begging him or out of the fear of loneliness and rejection I said, "You're still living in my apartment, I still wash your clothes, cook your food and clean for you; you can't do this to me." Then in a very hushed tone he said, "Honey, if you cook I will eat, and I will probably eat more." "And I may even enjoy it more; but the truth is I don't love you anymore." "Maybe I should leave, but I haven't decided yet; I am taking the suitcase to lend a friend who works with the airline." I thought, right, a friend at 3:30 in the morning, give me a break . . . For a long while I just stood there and stared at him, I could tell he was waiting for me to respond but I just kept staring at him; pitifully. I don't think I heard one word he said, or maybe I didn't want to believe him. All I was thinking to myself was, "what a Dummy you can't get anyone better than me." "Who else would put up with a man who can't even help his woman with money for groceries?" My stare and silence must have worn him out; he left without hearing a word from me but it seemed he never had far to go.

The following evening, he came home from work, set up a little tray table in his bedroom, spread out his Chinese food, was about to eat when I walked straight into that room and stood in front of him and the tray and declared, "we're still under the same roof, I still pay the major portion of the bills and there's no way on God's green earth you are going to walk in with your Chinese food and eat it off without me." He raised his eyelids; looked at me, and never took another bite. But I think he ate when I went to bed because it wasn't in the garbage the following morning.

The moments became less laughable as it became clear we were headed in different directions but we still remained respectful to each other. The notes we exchanged—"honey I'll soon be back", "you were asleep when I left, call you later" or "I went here or there" were no more. A part of me was still agonizing over the decision I had taken. He was a praying man and I loved that plus there were many qualities in him that attracted me to him. I also knew that my chances of finding someone who would accept me in spite of my flaws was slim and for that I still wanted to hold on to him; plus, a part of me still cared deeply for him even though he said he didn't love me anymore, and frankly, I didn't believe him one bit. I blamed myself because I threw him out of the bedroom.

When my assignment ended I went on two week's vacation to the Island. It didn't make my burden any lighter. I found myself sitting between the tombs of my parents remembering how he had helped to get my father a proper headstone; the many times he visited my mother; the many photographs he took of her; how he sent me to feed her when they were laying the headstone for my father; how he read from the Daily Devotional on Sundays and prayed fervently, his hands on my shoulders in the kitchen when I grumbled telling me the good Lord wouldn't like that; the crab fest on the boat ride in Maryland, the time spent touring the island; the laughs we shared when he came home from work and made fun with some of the days' events; how he guided me when we climbed the Falls, my thrills of a lifetime with him at his famous beach, and now it was all over. Had my mother been alive, I am sure she would have blamed me. She always said that if a person did one good and ninety-nine bad, we should use the one good to cover the ninety-nine bad. Understandably so, she was always around Christian people, not around con artists. Her husband was unfaithful and my father died of pneumonia.

I was still undecided when I returned even though my things were packed. I undid everything then went to see my children and grandchildren in Canada. One look at my family and I knew I was on the right track. I was doing the right thing. It was time to return with my few Pennies and get the house with the backyard I promised them. The decision was made.

A phone in his bedroom rang when I returned and he grabbed it at the first ring. I thought it was strange since I only had one phone installed. According to him, it was a call from the island, his dad was seriously ill and he'd be leaving in a couple of weeks. That statement was a "cop out." It didn't add up and I didn't believe him. When he told me the date he was leaving to see his dad, I arranged with my family in Canada to pick me up the same day. I wasn't about to leave him my bedroom set and the few valuable pieces I had acquired.

When I called the phone company to cancel the phone service and put the number in his name he had already done that months ago and even added an additional line in the guest room, but true to his character he never had the lease for the apartment transferred to his name; that was too large an expense. I made sure the owner had my name released from the lease immediately. Incidentally, the landlord told me only one month's rent got paid after I left even though he got a tenant soon after I left and spent approximately one year there before leaving to live with a family member in another state.

The night before I left for Canada, while I was packing some odds and ends he was packing to visit his dad too who was "sick" according to him but I was more interested to see what he was packing. If his dad was really "sick" and he was going to see him, I had an idea what he should be taking. He didn't say a word to me when I tried to watch him from the corner of my eyes. According to him, he knew I always loved to have my nose in the ground; and he was right. While he was packing, he would periodically glance around to see if I was watching him. Our eyes always meet each other. I had never seen him pack ladies underwear before or any men's sneakers and it bothered me to know who could have been so fortunate when he had never bought me one. Normally when he was travelling, he ran to the Dollar Stores the night before to pick up some toiletries and maybe a perfume for his son. Once I saw him packing a Dollar Store perfume for Andrew, I asked him if he couldn't get his son something a little more "pricey" he said, *"Honey, as long as behind Andrew's ears smell sweet it's all that matters to the young ladies; by the time they realize he has no money he'll be gone about his business."* Sounds familiar?

Those men's sneakers were definitely not Andrew's. He would only get one and it would be a cheap brand. And those undergarments were definitely not for Andrew's girlfriend! For the first time, I was convinced he had someone on the island and she probably had some sons. Neither of us slept that night and even though I didn't tell him, he instinctively knew he would not be seeing me when he returned. Regardless of everything, I do believe we were torn to pieces by what was happening. Either that or I didn't want to believe it was the end. Infidelity had never been a problem before, at least not to my knowledge.

At the break of dawn I was in my best lingerie and strategically stood between the organ desk in the foyer and the bedroom door. When he was ready to leave, he reached out and we hugged passionately. We knew it was the last hug. As we let go of each other, he walked to the door and without looking around he said, "Remember, we're still friends and I'll be broke when I get back so if you can, leave me a $100" Typical of him, very typical. As he strolled down the corridor to the elevator with his luggage, I offered to help but he refused my help. Truthfully, all I wanted was just for him to turn around so I could see him again, knowing I would be leaving in a few hours. And something else, I wanted him to turn around and beg me to stay, to promise me the financial support I needed, just to get the chance to say to him, "I can't now, it's too late" but he didn't give me that privilege. Very much the man I knew, an old soldier, once a decision was taken it was final! No turning back.

A couple hours later my son, my son-in-law and a friend arrived. They packed the contents of my bedroom, and a few pieces from the living room deliberately leaving behind the couch he liked to recline in. Colin asked for the tools but I refused. "He is used to having all these things around the house", I said. He then asked for the vacuum. I declined, leaving it opened with the bag partially intact so he could know how to change the bag and beside it, I left him $50. When Colin saw that I was leaving the apartment practically furnished, he said, "Mom, if I had a woman walk away and left me like that with all her belongings, I would have to wonder what I did". Truth is, his only fault was not accepting financial responsibility so it didn't make feel good about myself to leave him stranded. Even though we were splitting, I still felt connected to him; it's like I was deserting my home. I even left my housedress hanging behind the door in my attempt to pierce his soul and I recorded some love songs on three cassette tapes. At the end of each tape, I recorded my voice saying goodbye three times. Why I did that I will never know but I came to regret it months later.

As usual, the home was left in an immaculate condition. No one could have known one party had moved out in case he walked in with a "client". He was always expecting one. I have never regretted that, it was the decent thing to do. And sadly, less than a year later I was thankful that I didn't leave him stranded. It would have tortured me.

Once we drove off, I was convinced I was finally doing the right thing. I was returning home and it felt good. I didn't know his phone number so it took me a few weeks after he returned to talk to him and when we did there was no animosity. I promised to return for the Piano desk but I never did. I just couldn't do it. Our times together were nothing but fun and laughter. For all the troubles and heartaches I faced in my life, my years with him were like the vacation of a lifetime. He made me forget my troubles, he made me laugh. When he wrote a letter and asked me to edit it, it reminded me that I was of some value, that I had a brain, that there was a measure of intelligence which he trusted. He awakened my sense of self. In spite of his shortcomings, and God knows we all have them, I'm grateful for that period of my life. I can look back and say I had rest for my soul for the most part from all the stresses of my past. He never gave much but I felt free. It was as though I was on a new path, away from all the stress. I needed that, whatever the cost.

A few months later, when Colin and I visited New York to shop, we went to see him. He had a roommate. I thought that was quick but he said he was very helpful to him with his knowledge of computers. On our second visit, I was very concerned about his stomach, it was far too big. When I expressed concern, he clapped both sides of his stomach with the palm of his hands and said, "What happen honey, don't you like a man with guts?" When I saw the pile of beer cans (those favourite of his in the red and white can), I associated the size of his stomach with his drinking and even felt guilty that I brought that on by leaving him.

Within a few weeks he called me teasingly, "I am going to get married," he said. I said to him, "Are you crazy, how could you live with me for seven years, separated for less than a year, and was now talking about marrying someone else?" "If you expect the family to give you high marks for that, you are dead wrong." Only then did I entertain the thought that all those twice a year trip for those so called Family Reunion and Past Students Reunion was a hoax. He laughed it off as my being jealous. Then in a conversation months later, he said he wanted to tell me something because he knew I love to have my nose in the ground. I said to him, "Yes, anything to do with you I want to know so my nose will always be in the ground." And just like that, he casually said he got engaged to someone he knew on the island. A ton of bricks fell on me. He never told me when he got married but I heard. Truth is, I never thought anyone would put up with him unless they're willing to support him so it didn't bother me. I knew it couldn't last and whatever the case, we shared an eternal bond, that's how I felt. Shortly afterwards, he called to say he wasn't feeling well, tests were being done, he had advised his family and there was no need for me to rush down now, he would keep me posted. There was no mention of the marriage. Since I was still considered a friend, one of his brothers asked me to see firsthand how he was before the family made a decision to fly to the USA.

A couple blocks away from the apartment complex, I stopped at the little fruits and vegetable store. The moment the Korean owner spotted me she screamed out in her broken English, "very sick, he told me he missed you very much." It's like she was almost questioning me, how could I do that now. I gathered three bunches of flowers along with three cards I had professionally framed; his favourite vinyl record "Love and Happiness", which inadvertently left with my things when I moved to Canada and some tape recordings of with what I called "healing hymns" from my Jimmy Swaggart's collection.

When I got to the apartment and he opened the door, I don't know what was more shocking, what I saw, or what he did. I believe now it was what I saw. He was nothing like the man I knew, not even close, clearly he was a very sick man. He didn't allow me inside. He slammed the door in my face; never got the chance to bask in those healing hymns I took with me from Brother Swaggart's collection. He had been diagnosed with stomach cancer and was rapidly declining.

After driving all night from Toronto to NYC, I wanted to get in and freshen up but I could only leave the things by the door and take a cab back to Penn Station bathroom in Manhattan. I had taken my name off the lease. The apartment was no longer mine.

The moment I returned to Canada, I ran to see my doctor, I needed answers, I needed help, I needed advice and I needed everything fast. I had to save him. I didn't care about what he did. That was my initial reaction. By the time my name was called I was a nervous wreck. My doctor fixed his eyes on me as though he sensed I was there with the worst fear and he was eager to help. When I told him why I was there, he brushed his nose and repositioned his glasses. "I've been in the business thirty years now Elisabeth, anything you have to say to him say it now because I have never seen anyone with that type of cancer last more than 18 months." My God, I was so frightened I don't think I heard or believed a word he said; it couldn't be for real. Jasmine's brother died from cancer she ought to know more, but the news wasn't good either.

A few days later, I called him and he sounded like he was anxiously awaiting my call. He didn't apologize but I read between the lines when he remarked that he wasn't perfect. I knew him enough to understand it was his way of saying he made a mistake. And even if he didn't; I would still have forgiven him. He was a very sick man. But it wasn't the end of the story, because when I returned so quickly to Canada, my children wondered, but I was ashamed, so I told them I got a ride from his niece to Buffalo, New York, so I spun around fast, but they knew better, for while I was gone, since it was so soon after the 9/11 tragedy, they were worried about me. When Colin called to make sure I had arrived safely, he said he was told, "Mom was not welcome here so she is on her way back." I was floored with shame. I couldn't comment. At that very moment Colin said to me, "Mom, are you sure Uncle Clive would want you at his funeral?" "You'd better ask him." My children have never asked me about him since that day but I kept the lines of communication opened. He was a very sick man. But when one of his sisters asked me to go and stay with him, I told her I was doing a course in school. I was too embarrassed to tell her that a brother had sent me before to report on his progress before the family flew in from Jamaica and he closed the doors in my face.

I searched myself for any possible signs I might have missed. I couldn't find anything and he was never one to complain so there were no clues. I could only recall him on a couple occasions using both hands to lift his lower abdomen; maybe that was a hint of a medical problem. It was difficult to accept what my doctor or Jasmine told me, it's like I was still searching for answers so I turned to God to show me a sign, and what a sign it was! A couple nights later I had a dream, not the one I expected, but from the One I dared not question. In my dream I was playing the organ. While I was playing the organ, an angel appeared to me with a huge white wreath, shaped like the heart and embellished with stones of gold. After holding it in full view for about five minutes, the angel walked away and hung it on a tree some distance away then she disappeared. I read it to mean that the wreath was for a future occasion. After the angel disappeared, I continued playing the organ but I noticed that I was playing from a vinyl record that was left beside me. The record was labelled with Clive's last name as well as the first name of the artist. Underneath his name were the words, *"FOR GOD AND GOD ALONE."*

For over twenty five years I have collected some fine gospel records, mostly Jimmy Swaggart's; so when I awoke, I searched my collection and to my surprise I found the identical Record I was playing from in my dream, "Steve Green: For God and God Alone." After reflecting on the dream and on what my doctor and Jasmine said to me I drew my own conclusion. It was another prophetic dream. A decision had been made by God, soon he would be gone. I didn't tell him the dream. He knew I had prophetic dreams from time to time and I didn't want to scare him. A few days later, I sent him a very fine card but looking back now, I wonder if the words of the card I sent him were influenced by the dream I had. I just don't know. He returned the card to me enclosed in a new envelope, addressed by him, and, mailed directly from the Post Office. I knew him, he was angry and he was sending me a message.

To have seen him so sick and not be able to help him because he turned me away was mind boggling. To learn from Colin that he called when I left to see him and he was told that I wasn't welcome was cold. And to finally have the cards I painstakingly selected for him, sent back to me, I severed communications. Months later when he lost his battle to the cancer and I wanted to attend his funeral I was warned by a brother not to attend because he had led the family to believe I caused him to have cancer because he married someone else. I pity those who believed such necromancy, but to avoid any hostility I did not attend. It is my sincere belief that had it not been for his lack of financial support, we would have made it. He wasn't perfect but he had some very fine qualities. He was a praying man and that meant a lot to me.

I hold dear some very precious memories of times we shared. They far exceeded those with my ex-husband and they were quality time. He was a very sick man when he did what he did; I forgave him. What we had was special while it lasted. When we moved in different directions, we still talked and we still cared for each other. As he said earlier, I liked to have my nose in the ground so I wasn't surprised to hear from a brother at his bedside that I was on his mind in his final hours. There's got to be a reason for that, which is why I must pity those who could remotely think I was capable of giving him cancer. Rubbish.

Regardless of his shortcomings and God knows we all have them, it is impossible to remember him and not have something to smile about. To say otherwise is to incur the wrath of anyone who has ever met him. There was warmth in his handshake, a sense of peace in his presence, his zest for life was contagious, his love for family and friends was undeniable; his dedication to a cause stirred others to want to make a difference. His adorable smile and gentle mannerism is unforgettable. His faithfulness in taking the time to visit with my mother each time he went home even though she was at the other end of the island is a testament to his character. The times he took to do all the pots and pans for me just so he didn't have to look at chipped nails and for all the laughter and the fun, he was therapy for me when I needed it most. He gave me a chance to escape and forget my pain for a very long time, to help prepare me to pen my story and add life to it. And maybe that's why God sent me to America. Fate brought us together and fate took us apart. He was not for me. He was *For God and God Alone.* He was placed in my life for a purpose; I had done what I was supposed to do for him. It wasn't a part of the Master's plan for me to go through another dilemma, so a plan I believe, was divinely orchestrated to pull us apart and left me with a song which I learnt from a passenger in the wee hours of that October 4th morning in 2002, as the bus rolled into New York City where I'd see him for the last time. Just minutes before the bus came to a stop, I heard a passenger softly humming. I pulled closer, the closer I got the more beautiful it sounded. I had to get the words so I tapped on her shoulders and this is what she wrote:

> *"Jesus you are my bread when I'm hungry.*
> *You are my shelter from life's storm.*
> *You are my ship upon the ocean.*
> *But most of all you are my best friend."*

Indeed, he was my best friend, even for a while. He gave me almost seven years of laughter that allowed me to roll my troubles away for that period of my life. So even though he closed the door in my face the last time I saw him, could it be that God had pre-destined our coming together to give me some laughter and a little vacation from all the stress I had carried all the years, and then used the occasion to New York City to write the final chapter of our lives with a song? "You may not agree with me, but I think so." "How else would I have learnt that song?"

I will always love New York City. I encountered a few rough patches, but it also added a breath of fresh air to my life story.

Adios amigo! Adios!

THIRTY

No brother or sister knew the depths of all I had experienced. I have never had the stamina to open a dialogue regarding anything that happened. The little that one or two might have heard from me was a thin layer from what I felt like sharing. I have found it very painful to be the only half sister and the youngest of the sisters wearing the label that I have. It's like I have smeared what would have otherwise been the perfect family had I not been around. And there have been times in the past when I felt like I was diplomatically shunned from events that I wanted to be a part of; that I can't help thinking that my name or my presence could still bring discomfort, because unfortunately, when a member of a family makes a mistake the whole family pays. So everything has been pretty much "*hush hush*" until now to protect everyone. Now I am sick and tired of the "hush hush" it has me living in a pit.

Sister Lynn who always found a way to get humour out of everything, has said that each time a sister comes to visit, the neighbours always asked "*is that the one?*" My sister with her sense of humour always had the same answer "No, not that one." Over forty years later they're still not able to figure who did what. But I was very shocked when she mentioned that of my three children only one of them got their father's name. She knew more than I thought she did. Whether I was too shock or what I don't know, I just tightened my lips and stared at her without a word. When I got over the shock I hinted her about the rape, but she didn't think it would be a good idea to tell Chase; in her opinion I should convince him that he is who he is and that people are lying. At the time I thought it was a good idea, but once he came to live with me I knew I would blurt out the truth eventually; either that, or the weight would kill me. Many, many, years later when I shared a few bits and pieces with her she could only fold her arms and listen. And really, it was all I needed. I didn't need to hear one sound.

Sister Love, because of our closeness in age, and all the times we spent together, is capable of seeing through me like a book and might have learnt a little more but I was always on guard. She never got much out of me for fear she might share it with mother; and because of how she cried when she visited me in custody, I always did everything to shield her from reaching that point again. Even years later when she suspected my husband was beating me, I denied it. There have been times when she has marvelled at my strength because of all I had been through and still managed to hold my head high, but she would just scratch the surface because she really didn't want to see me in anymore pain.

From my best recollection, the most I have said (openly) happened at the Church's 75th anniversary when I saw a spear and it reminded of the night in church before I was charged; and during a visit with a sister in England when I hinted her and she said, *"but what you need is understanding,"* and really that's all I think I need. That's why it disturbed me when I learnt that one Sister was referred to as "the sister of such and such a one." It is comments like those that leave me feeling so much more scarred that I could never find the courage to talk about anything. And frankly, no one has ever asked. Then again, I never talked about the rape or the circumstances surrounding my child with my lawyer or the beatings from my husband so they really don't know much. Even my children will be learning a lot now. I would rather they read and then ask me if they need to have something clarified, that's why I have written to them. I have never been able to sit and share anything in full detail with them. It's the reason why Dawn was able to give birth to the Title of the Book after typing three (3) chapters; she was shocked by what she discovered and from the depths of what she felt, she recommended the Title.

As for my mother, the only time we ever talked about anything, was on the morning of the incident when she pierced through the crowd to ask me what happened. Up until her death 26 years later I never had the strength nor the courage to raise the subject with her; and I never felt she had the constitution to go there either; far too painful and much too deep; but thankfully, she found the strength to make it a little easier for Colin who spent most of his first 21 years of life with her. In fact he told me that both grandmothers were quite candid with him.

On the other hand my Godmother was openly forthright when I went to share the news of our marriage. I distinctly remember her pulling me aside in her bedroom and saying "Did you tell him?" "Did you tell him?" "Don't let him find out from other people." Even though I said yes, I wasn't being truthful. I buried everything inside of me out of fear, as though nothing would ever surface. It didn't even dawn on me that Douglas was a cop and anyone from the station where I was detained could easily have exchanged information with him; much less to consider that we were living in a city just 55 miles away where villagers from the community often commute. Looking back now, it doesn't make sense, but at the time I was much younger, I didn't understand, and I just felt that opening up one thing could lead to everything and I couldn't risk so much. I simply guarded my privacy the best way I could.

It is through this medium that I am speaking for the first time, thanks to all those who helped to make it possible. It actually began when I packed a suitcase, got on a plane, and went to see my childhood friend Jasmine in the United Kingdom. There was a lot that I had not known. The man that raped me had been her dad's best friend.

Jasmine had been gone for so many years that we had lost touch with each other. With the help of the Salvation Army I got a letter to her. A reply came much sooner than expected but I was worried even before I opened the letter. Did she hear about my troubles? How much does she know? Would she still consider me a friend? Would she want to have anything to do with me? Was she the same person? Paragraph by paragraph, I combed through expecting to find, "is it true that . . . ?" I studiously looked at her penmanship; how the letter was structured; quotation and spelling errors as though to measure the letter against her scholastic achievement. After a long pause, following more than quarter century of waiting for the moment, I made the call. So much had been pent up for so long, but I had to be sure that the chemistry was right before I started blabbing. She was excited about being married and expecting her first baby. It was just how I perceived her, very proper, getting everything in order, quite possibly even being a virgin when she got married. I was so embarrassed when she asked me the ages of my children. There I was talking to my friend, my school mate, only a few months older, who got it right; education, a profession, marriage, and then family. I was preparing to be a Grandmother with two adult sons and a teenage daughter about to graduate from High School. In my attempt to feel like I "measured up" I tried to impress her with my stellar banking career but it was artificial. The weight of what I would soon have to share with her created a feeling of uneasiness, but I couldn't spoil our first conversation in almost quarter century. Those things on my chest would have to wait.

After a couple years of steady correspondences I decided it was time for us to see each other. Pen and paper could not do it; nor could I talk about it on the phone, and I wanted to tell someone how the rape had ruined me. She wasn't one of my sisters, she was a friend practically the same age, someone I grew up with; I could confide a little, mask a little and cover up the rest until I could muster the courage, but at least I could share a little with someone and not be embarrassed as I would have been sharing with a sister; so I packed a suitcase and headed to England. Entering into the gates of her London home, two words readily came to mind, peace and tranquility. The fragrance from a beautiful dome shaped lemon tree that so tastefully graced the veranda was like a breath of fresh air Inside, an organ graced the living room, both children were doing music lessons and everything around, from drapes to tea towels Jasmine made them herself. The landscape with its therapeutic waterfall and weed free green lawn punctuated with England's finest English roses in full bloom of pink was breathtaking.

When I sat down for dinner, I felt the need to be so proper that I barely ate. Seconds after closing my silverware, I had to reopen them because I was still hungry and the variety of food was mouth-watering. Everything I thought and pictured of Jasmine when we were growing up came alive. I couldn't put it into words or in perspective as a child, but I knew even then that there was something very special about her and I wanted to emulate her. Here she was a wife and mother with a profession and could sew and bake just about anything. She was all that I saw in her when we were little that drew me to her and made me want to be like her but I never told her. That's why when she left, I felt like that part of me that was aspiring to be like her dried up. When we were little, she would pretend to be a nurse and I would play the role of a teacher. After she left, my sole ambition was to be able to heal people like my Church Mother and be a Gospel Singer travelling the world singing in different languages.

When I saw the way Jasmine lived and all she had accomplished I didn't feel like me and my bag-of-luggage had any place in her life. I didn't feel like she deserved to hear my failures; she was too far ahead; couldn't identify with me, but I had to get one thing off my chest; the rape. Apart from Sister Lyn, only Dawn and Chase knew after I had seen a similar story on the Oprah Winfrey Show. And even then it took a lot of coaxing from Dawn to tell Chase. And I strongly believe that I only told him out of fear Dawn would if I didn't. Surprisingly, when I told Jasmine she didn't appear shocked at all; at least not on the surface; she just glanced at me with her eyelids raised. That's when I heard from her own mouth why she had left for England so suddenly. It was her dad's idea. She had no idea whether she was going to Paradise or not. Her daddy knew something that we didn't; the "beast" was his old pal and he was well aware of his behaviour. And that's why he kept her in Boarding school until he could get her away to the UK. As she said, *"Daddy said he sent me away to Boarding School until He could send for me in England because he knew it would only be a matter of time before Hannikim got his hands on me, and he didn't want to leave England to come and kill him."* All I remembered saying to her after she said that was, "You didn't tell me, you didn't tell me, you didn't tell me."

Too poor; I didn't stand a chance! Months later when I returned to Canada, she wrote in a letter that "if I had killed Mr. Hannikim she would have visited me in prison," and since then she has pleaded with me to put my story in a book. She even wondered why I didn't write a song about it. I thought to myself, if all she knew about was the rape and she's telling me to write a book, what if she knew everything? I had no such interest and I made that very clear; just as I had told Dawn some 20 years earlier when she first suggested it to me. No interest. End of story. I did not want to relive that moment, that minute, that hour or that night. None of it! Full stop! As it turned out though, my meeting with her in London would later become the beginning of my journey in penning this Memoir, because for 33 years I never thought anyone would believe me; not even when Oprah Winfrey Show aired a similar story I wasn't convinced any one would believe me. But when she told me that her dad was aware of Hannikim's behaviour and that was what led him to board her at school until he could get her to England; it opened the way. And even then it still took a lot more to get me to pick up the pen and the paper, a lot more; and a few more years.

I took full responsibility for having a baby at 14, but when I picked up the pieces, brushed myself off, returned to school, and someone I trusted and looked up to hauled me in the bushes and dumped himself in me like that and then told me, "that's a boy", it seemed like that vindictive act was set aside for those who weren't as fortunate as Jasmine with a father who could pull her away. I have to admit it's a struggle not to be bitter. I was treated like an animal.

Sometimes I am in awe of everything I have lived through, but I don't waste time on myself; to avoid pain I simply take on another's needs and wants; reaching every cry for help to shield me from my own pain, and once again I have successfully completed another day without having to face myself. Truth is I have probably spent my whole life helping everyone else while unintentionally suppressing my own ambitions. It was always such a nice little hideout, no wonder I shared my life with Clive for seven years even though he was not a provider, without realizing that that indeed was also abuse. I learnt to be satisfied with what I had, so long as I had my peace and quiet. And maybe that's the reason why penning my story was out of the question when Dawn mentioned it some 20 years earlier; I saw what I carried as something that should be closely guarded for life. That's why I could never soar or focused on myself, I had sandbags on my wings. For the same reason crowds for prolonged period exasperate me. It robs me of time alone. The more I was alone, the less anyone would know, the more secured I felt.

In my Probationary Report at the first bank I worked Mrs. Adams said, I was brilliant and industrious, but I resent being spoken to. She was right on target. I was hiding behind an invisible wall. She had no idea of the weight I was under and that keeping aloof was my way of guarding my privacy. I was very moody; no one could understand me; not even me. Coming out of the closet and embarrassing my family was never a consideration. My only desire was to live a quiet Christian life, playing my Gospel music; going to church when I can; watching mass on TV; fasting and praying in the privacy of my own home; playing my $100 organ which I bought from the Thrift shop, observing the Sabbath and paying a visit to my spiritual church in the island periodically. Pious as everything sound, at times even a simple task seems very difficult because I struggle between who I am, and who I should be. But it became clearer when I visited Jasmine that my story should be told. And I have never forgotten the look in her eyes when she said my growth was stunted and that I should titled the book "Little Girl Lost". My Lord! Even though I understood what she meant I felt like I still wanted to cry out for the little girl. That meeting with her broke the camel's back; but it would take much more to get me started. "Everything seems easier said than done."

A couple years after my visit with Jasmine, I was lying in bed one night watching a Presidential State of the Union Address when a statement the President made, left me feeling so worthless; I felt like I wanted to cringe in a corner and hide from the world—*"When the gates of prison open, the path ahead should lead to a better life."* To this day I don't remember anything else that he said in the speech that night; whether before, or after that statement. But since then the statement has played like a continuous tape in my head with a picture of Mr. Mandela from Prison garb to Presidential suite after 25 years of imprisonment, while I was still living in bondage chained by the shame and pain of my past, unable to shake myself off and pick up the pieces. So in addition to Jasmine prodding me to tell my story, I had the President's remark pounding in my head. And then like a twist of fate, sometime following that remark, I ran into Barnes and Noble in New York City eager to get my hands on a newly released Autobiography; then called my daughter Dawn to make sure she picked up a copy too. When I told her she said to me, *"Mom, of all the books you have read, there's a book that has not been written and that's your book."* I was struck by the comment but I brushed it off. I knew I could never go there; never, never, never, just too deep.

A few pages into the Autobiography I came upon an article on *Secrets* that stopped me in my tracks. It was as though the Author was directly addressing me. I probably read the article about 10 times that day. Each time I opened the book with every desire to move forward, all I ended up doing was turning to the article on *"Secrets,"* read it, and then closed the book. At times I found myself staring into space with the book before me opened at the very page. I could never get beyond that article. I love the Author, huge fan, I eagerly purchased his biography to read it but I couldn't get pass that point no matter how hard I tried. To this day, almost seven years later I still struggle with it. In summary the Author said: *"We all have secrets but they can be an awful burden to bear especially if a sense of shame is attached to them, even if the secret holder is not the source of the shame."* *"The place where they are kept can be a haven of rest or retreat from the rest of the world where one's identity could be shaped, but if we share them our relationships could become more meaningful."* It pricked me.

There was something very soul-searching about the statement. I didn't know if the secrets I harboured injured my relationships, but I was sure they kept me aloof. I remember wondering if what the Author said could really help me seeing that my wounds were so wide and deep. A side of me felt like I needed to do something, but another part of me felt confused because I never thought what I carried was something that should be shared with anyone much less share with the world. I agonized over the article on *"Secrets"* so much that it almost felt like it was either torturing me or unshackling me. But trying to unshackle from a life filled with pain and shame of such magnitude was like trying to pull myself from the bottom of the ocean when I didn't even know how to swim. At the same time I wondered if a revelation could bring an end to the agony I experience every father's day for my children and the grandchildren who will someday ask about their grandfathers. And I wondered too if sharing it would cause me more pain and embarrassment. I struggled to find answers; but I just couldn't picture myself doing it, not even for the family. It would be a long way to go before I could pick up a pen and paper. I just wasn't ready, not ready to go there; far too deep, and much too painful.

Then December 2006, I was on a special assignment for a week with a lot of free time on hand so I spent the time reading the book of Judges and then transcribing it in my own words. As soon as I put the pen down, I heard a little voice within said, *"An In Depth Look At A Woman Call Elisabeth Holyday."* I made a note of the date and stuck it in the Bible, December 12, 2006. Two weeks later at our Family Christmas Dinner, Jordanna blurted out: "Oh Grandma, aren't you supposed to be writing a book, what's taking you so long, even if you were raped it's okay to talk about it." I was shocked but I didn't comment. She had no idea of the shame I had been living with for years; I simply raised my eyebrows and looked at her with the weight of a shame so heavy, I had no spoken words. It was beginning to appear that at every juncture I was being reminded that there was a book to be written, but I believed that by this time the process had begun in my head; still, it would be over a year before I scribbled anything on paper.

On one occasion while I was overlooking the article on *"Secrets"* I took a block of sticky pad and started jotting down little bits and pieces that I remembered; placed them in a transparent zipper lock freezer bag and kept it inside my purse. Later I copied some of them in a journal Jasmine had sent me and threw the rest away because I didn't think the world needed to know about my dirty laundry. Jasmine was relentless. Always calling me to find out if I had begun writing, so the few I kept, I read them to her whenever she called, just to keep her happy. Little did she know, I still wasn't convinced that a book was the way to go; that all the pens and one journal was still resting on my night-table.

Months later into my scribbling, I asked Jasmine if she knew or heard I had faced the capital charge. "Yes, she said but according to her, when she saw me she couldn't ask me because I didn't look like a person with problems. "It didn't add up" she said, so she ruled it out as gossip. A couple months passed then I fed her a little bit more. She suggested that not only should I write a book, but I should address a letter to each child individually and she followed up that with a barrage of pens and another journal. When I got that letter I quit writing. The few little jottings I had saved, I got rid of them in my attempt to forget the whole thing. Too much was expected of me. Already I lacked the capacity to handle anymore and now she was telling me to write a letter to each child individually. "What the hell was I going to do individual letters to my children for, to tell them I had been running and hiding from all the secrets and the shame; that I was afraid to talk about my past; afraid of being asked any questions?"

Couple weeks later another journal and more pens, she wasn't just suggesting that I begin putting things on paper, she was handing me the tools to work with. That got me so mad. I couldn't stand the pressure of being driven to delve into something that was so painful. It looked more like God was ganging up every one on me: my daughter; my grand-daughter; a Biographer; A President in his State of the Union address who almost knocked me off my bed with his remark as though I hadn't done anything with my freedom, and now Jasmine with a barrage of pens, journals and every week phone calls to find out if I had started. She almost drove me over the edge. I lied to her so much that out of frustration one day I just picked up a sticky note pad and resumed my little jottings here and there. And somehow, inside of that struggle within to put my story on paper was a side of me that was getting stout headed with her opinion of me that I have a flair for words and should probably try writing, so I wanted to impress her. That was my sole ambition when I started; if Jasmine believed I could, I had to do it to impress her.

I began writing, but something was bothering me, something I hadn't addressed in 40 years; I still hadn't told Mr. Dawson that I was raped even though I had mentioned it to Chase many, many, years earlier when the Oprah Winfrey Show aired a similar story. I didn't expect him to be surprised, because he has had his doubts from day one and I was sure Chase mentioned it the same day he heard to both sides of the paternity. But I was still embarrassed to talk about it. What I had to tell him was bad, but what he had to say made me wonder if it was for real or, I was watching a daytime soap opera. Mr. Dawson commented,

> *"Hannikim always boasted that any woman he got his hands on*
> *Would be left with a baby to prove that he had been with her*
> *And he penalized me on my job because he wanted*
> *One of my daughters and I wouldn't allow it*
> *Then he took away my girlfriend and fathered 3 children with her*
> *That's why when he died and I was asked to do the eulogy*
> *I refused to do it."*

I was stunned, could not believe what I heard, and to this day I cannot remember anything else that was said either before or after he made that statement. But he was talking about his boss of over quarter century. And that's when it dawned on me why he had made that comment some forty years earlier when I told him I was pregnant; he knew it couldn't be, so he thought I was one of Hannikim's many "skirts." That really hurts. I was a child, like a lamb to be slaughtered, no idea who Hannikim was at the time or how he lived, except that he had several children. It wasn't until many years later when I heard he was living with one of his son's ex that I realized how far he had sunk. It's for the same reason that I am afraid when I passed by his house one of his many kids could say, that's my brother's mother. But I have to let it go because un-forgiveness, hurt and shame has destroyed me for so long that I want to salvage the little I have left. I want to live now. I'm tired of hiding behind the mask. And furthermore the Dawson's have cared for Chase since he was 6 months old, so in a sense they're his parents. Hannikim drawing me in the bush like a dog on a leash and forcefully dumping himself into me doesn't earn him the right to fatherhood.

When I confided in Mr. Dawson that the Lawyer that represented me was Dawn's father, he said, "We knew all along, we thought you sold yourself to win the case." Dear God Almighty, I didn't need to get in details with him, but that was a slap in my face, and another reason not to break my silence. Yet when I told him that I am thinking of writing a book about my life, he said, *"you should, and you'll get money for it, nothing is wrong with your family, it's a good decent family, it's only that you were poor."*

My road has been plagued with sand and gravel; unpaved even now, I couldn't have charted this journey for myself; I wouldn't have wished it on my worst enemy, and I am still not sure what happened to me or how it could be possible for one person to go through so much. But, Bishop Jakes in a sermon during the penning of this memoir said *"Your trouble will stop when it has accomplished what God sent it to do."* If that is so, then My God Almighty, will someone please help me to understand what it was used to accomplish, or what will all this hurt and suffering be used to accomplish, and if so, "why me Lord, and why so much?" I am neither Job nor Jesus, I'm Elisabeth.

I wanted to be the Champion of the family; the one with the big house; the one who would accommodate the entire family; those who had been sent to live with relatives would have a home to return to; dreams that by age 24, I would've had it all—career, home of my own, happily married, finished having children and aspiring to be numbered among some of the greatest Gospel Singers, another Dottie Rambo maybe. It wasn't in my plans to have 3 children by the time I was 18. I didn't count on being raped and then abandoning the child for 15 years. I didn't plan on being charged for murder. I didn't expect the man defending me to get intimate with me and then left me alone to raise our daughter. And who would have thought that the man who was supposed to love me in sickness and in health for better or worst would turn around and scald the little skin that was left to cover my scars.

There is nothing normal about being raped and left with a child to show from it. There are times when it is Chase's birthday and I chose not to call, or I call much later and I expect it to be understood which I now realize is very unfair to him because he is a victim too. But to feel like I am being reprimanded or chastised is sometimes more than I can bear as it feels like I am being forced to relive the worst moment of my life. As tough as it may sound, I can deal with everything else that's been thrown at me except for the rape. I was treated like an animal and I could do nothing about it except wiggle my head and beat my palms on the dirt and I feel like it has led to every hell that I have passed through since then and within the context of all that, I must love and nurture him and constantly remind myself that he is a victim too. That is tough. No matter how you try to put it, bottom line. It is tough.

A lot happened and was over by the time I was eighteen years old but they created a life time of havoc for me. The prescription for failure was written all over my chart and I hid a lot from my mother to shield her from any more pain. I look back at times and wonder if the story of my life would have been different if I had gone to her, but it doesn't even make sense wondering now because I am sure it wouldn't have happened then or now, I wouldn't put her through an ounce more.

My feelings are not of hate, but grave disappointment, discontentment and hurt from being deprived of my dreams and the chance to be all I could and desired to be; literally stunted and stained for life. It hurt so much that at times I feel suffocated. The additional blows my husband inflicted on me with a cop sharing our home and another living directly across from us, yet none of them got involved, in itself is another blow that goes beyond painful.

There are acquaintances who think of me as the "life of the party," but it's a blanket I use to cover my sorrows. Sometimes it works, sometimes it doesn't. In one instance, during the writing of my story, I found myself at the library reading a few newspapers from around the world when I came upon the story of a rape victim. The victim states, *"I feel so violated and struggle with a myriad of emotions every day." "Just yesterday morning I sat at my desk and just burst into tears." "I feel so violated and angry that someone would approach me in that manner." "I wonder if I am being laughed at." "I feel dirty, I feel used and that is why I can understand why some women don't report rapes because you don't know if people are laughing at you." "You don't know if people are saying things about you." "You don't know, you really don't know."* The victim was a cop. She echoed my feelings then, and now. Just to think that when I passed by the animal's house, his children could very well be saying, "That's my brother's mother" is a huge embarrassment for me. That's why I could never confide in anyone what had happened to me; I was ashamed. And if my mother was alive, rest assured my silence would not have been broken; I would never see her go through any more heartaches.

Sometimes I wonder if God allowed me to face these trials and then write a book about them to show the world the power of His redeeming love so we can glorify Him, or He has a bunch of people somewhere out there, who have faced similar experiences and He needs a book of this nature to bring healing. I just don't know what to make of it. Every emotion I feel has left me so drained, it's like it has zapped all my energy out of me. That is why it felt so much safer to remain, silent behind closed doors. I cannot recall feeling anymore pain that has come even remotely close, except when I read the story of little Adam Walsh and the Sharansky's story in "The Journey Home" a Jewish dissident held prisoner in Russia and the battle his wife Avital fought to win his release. But interestingly, it was in the moments of brokenness and despair, when I felt that it was easier to just drop everything, than to punishingly recount the horrors, that a surge of memories are released and words begin to form, so maybe there is a measure of strength that comes from being broken. I don't understand that, I really don't, unless I relate it to *The Crucified One.*

I have always believed beyond the shadow of a doubt that I was born for greatness; to do and achieve great things. I never stood a chance; chopped down so early I have carried a baggage that has practically crippled me. It's as though I bear in my forehead the mark of being raped and left with the proof to walk around with for life. I can defend myself against an accident; I can't defend myself against that. It wasn't an accident. That's why I found it so difficult when a Pastor who knew me from I was a little girl in church, told me 35 years later that I shouldn't go where anyone knows me. Dear God in Heaven, the very Pastor whose church I stopped at the night before I was charged in the death of Samuel. He knew the type of home I came from and the life my mother lead; I wonder if he realized how much more he damaged me even though he told me in the privacy of his church office.

All I was looking for was to be a part of a body of believers who shared my faith and could help to heal me. He literally threw me out of his church and out of Toronto for over 5 years. And for a long while, I made up for church attendance with Bishop TD Jakes, Amazing Facts, Joyce Meyers and of course Daily Mass and my constant companion *Our Daily Bread*,

It is my prayer that my lifting the lid off all this disaster doesn't cause me or my children more pain because I have no more room and they don't deserve one more ounce of pain and suffering, period. Anyways, as I journey through the process I realize that part of purging demand that I do address them individually as Jasmine suggested.

THIRTY-ONE

Dawn,

In the midst of what should have been the darkest period of my teenage years, God planted a seed of hope, and you my dear became that promise, a rainbow after three years of flooding, the dawn of a new day. You, my dear are my miracle baby. And as an additional bonus, he answered my prayers since I had two boys already. I love you more than you will ever know.

By now, you realize that I walked a very rough road so Grandma decided before you were born that a change of environment was necessary for me. Nothing was easy in arriving at that decision. I was very sad to leave you at 6 months old and equally sad for Colin, but I always return home to see you both regularly. And I am grateful that I had a mother who I could confidently leave the both of you with. Admittedly, the time you spent with Grandma seems to be most stable years of your early childhood.

At around 3 years old when I took you from my mother you were very brilliant. Syllable by syllable, you spelled and pronounced everything in sight. Even at times when you waited on me at the bank after leaving school, the staff often took you on a spelling contest and you never cease to amaze them, and within weeks of your first semester at the Kindergarten Preparatory, you were voted Form Captain. You had the sharpest intuition of any child I have ever known and a passion for ballet. Even though I couldn't afford the cost of ballet, nothing stopped you from dancing and stretching your little petite frame like a pro across the living room.

In a waiting room at the doctor's office when you were about 7 years old, you looked around on all the manuals and astounded everyone when you looked at me and said, "Mommy, if I had money, I would invest in books" and if left alone you'd be up all night reading and still ready to go out to school the morning after. I remember learning from you that my elbows shouldn't rest on the table at dinner. I guessed you learnt that at Alpha.

I am deeply saddened to see that leaving a doting grandmother and your brother to join me didn't provide you with a kinder atmosphere. It must have been confusing to see how much "daddy" laughed and played with you and yet so abusive to me. I never understood his behaviour, and running from place to place with you for refuge didn't help. I saw how the horror of what happened around you caused your grades to decline when you transferred from Alpha to St. Richards. I hope you understand now that we were both victims. You were the youngest of three children I had by the time I was 18 while living at home and before I earned my first pay cheque. And along the way things happened in my attempt to forge ahead to create a future for us. You've all paid dearly for the tremendous hardships that resulted from that. I am deeply sorry. And I'll spend my life trying to make up for it. Remarkable, where so many would have fallen through the cracks you hung in there to graduate from High School and college. With a little more nurturing and the presence of a mother close by the sky would have been your limit. You were well on your way.

I probably panicked when you called. My initial reaction was not well thought of. I am sorry. Whether out of a sense of helplessness being away in another country and not being able to leave at the time or trying to keep matters from escalating, I slipped up. As for the lady who slept beside you but claimed that you spoke in your sleep in order to protect her son-in-law, while you slept with a knife under your pillow, she will get her reward. And rest assured all the pedophiles camouflaged as CEO's walking around with attaché have their reward coming. It's only a matter of time. The higher they climb, the harder they fall.

I got to tell you I have never harboured any animosity towards your father, after all he saved my life, he won me my freedom, I wouldn't dare, but after that call from you, I thought darn him! A high profile Barrister-at-law, just minutes away from you his flesh and blood, without any contact with you because he fears losing his license to practice law. That was tough to bear. But because of his position I was afraid to say or do anything.

No amount of pen and paper can convey the pain I must live with for leaving you during the tender years, nine to sixteen. There are so many things I didn't get to share with you that will haunt me for life. To have walked away and watched as you thrust your little arms around the hem of your guardian's dress is a picture that will forever be lodged in my memory. It seemed you were trying desperately to take all the love and security that you would be lacking for the next seven years. I don't want to imagine how frightened and insecure you both were, but the years of waiting were completely out of my hands. I couldn't beat the system and I didn't want to get marry again. But when I look at the grandchildren now and see the opportunities they have I'm glad I stayed the course.

Sorry Colin had to leave you alone and return to Granny, I'm sure you understand by now how torn he was, but he had no choice. What she did to him was unforgiveable. And I have to take responsibility for some of the childhood hardships, if I didn't get married a lot could have been avoided. It was all part of paving the way for all of us. I had no one to help me, and because of "the beast" I really could not take the chance of sending you back to live with Granny. We know now too that my instincts were right. If there was a time when you thought that I had abandoned you to the wolves, this letter should change that. My judgement may not always be perfect but my intentions were good.

Nine to sixteen were delicate years but leaving was a decision I had to make for all of us. I am the only parent the three of you will ever know and I didn't want to make you orphans. I look at you sometimes and I worry. Silently. You don't have a sister that you know of, yet. You have one daughter and me. I wish I could have given you a sister, but immediately after you were born my mother told me that she saw the number 3. I have no explanation for

*that but you are my third and last child. You need a sister and I hope you do
everything in your power to find your father's children. The last time I heard,
there is a daughter in America who is a lawyer. And you have other brothers
too. Don't give up trying. Use all the available resources.*

*Remember the good times growing up with Grandma when you and Colin
jumped up and down on the bed and played hide and seek, the three of us
together when both of you would challenge me to jump in the swimming pool
with you, the time when I whipped him on his feet when he skipped classes to
fly kite and you pulled the whip away and said, "he's my brother I have to feel
it for him" then you hugged him and cried with him. Remember.*

*I have come to realize that your vision of a book many years ago was the
right thing but fear crippled me. I was held captive by my past, could never
dream of opening up. And I'm sure you had no idea there were so many
worms in the can. The sacrifices you made day and night typing even during
your lunch hour is a testimony of your desire to have the story told. You know
who you are there is nothing to be ashamed of. You didn't get here by chance.
You're part of a divine plan. And I don't want you to see your father as a bad
person because he wasn't. I'm sure he was scared as hell and probably that's
all he could think of doing at the time to protect his license. Pick up yourself,
shake off the dust, step out in confidence and reach for the stars. You have the
DNA of greatness in you. And, I hope you realize your dreams of acting beside
Denzel.*

I'm glad you you're my daughter.
Mom

Colin,

*I am so very sorry about the death of your father. Simply walking away
that morning would have prevented an argument and a struggle. To see you
deprived of a father and now your children who will never know him is a
daily reminder that will haunt me for life. I don't want to try to imagine the
challenges of being a father without ever having a father figure to model. No*

amount of words can express my sorrow. And I am very aware of how extremely difficult it must be for you on Father's Day. But as you make your way through these pages I hope you will have a deeper understanding. I have been candid as I possibly can to help you have an open dialogue with your children. I know that has been a huge concern for you. Remember, they too will read for themselves and draw their own conclusion.

As a baby, you came into the world on a weeknight weighing 6½ pounds just 5 days after your cousin Trevor was born. It was a very busy week for Granny trying to assist two daughters. At around eighteen months old you showed sign of allergic reaction to mosquitoes. No amount of home remedy Granny tried worked, and your most comfortable moments seemed to have been when you sat and splashed water in your bathtub. Outside of the water they seemed to itch so much, you often scratch until they bled.

Your cousin Brandon was like your male nurse. He was always willing to help with you when I needed to go to church and when I returned to school. The close bond between you two developed from those early years in the crib. I don't want you to ever forget that. Sister Love and Granny helped too, but Brandon was like a big brother.

At 2 years old when Chase was born, you never left my side, anxious to hold him in your lap and wanting to help bathe him. Later when he was bottle fed, you stood by patiently to get his leftovers. In order for me to get a nap sometimes I had to get you to fall asleep too because you always wanted to play with Chase, even when he was asleep you tickled him saying, "chucky chucky, chucky chucky." Then in the twinkle of an eye one fateful Monday morning when he was 6 months old our lives shattered, and life as we knew it then would never be the same again. What followed, left us standing in the middle of a crowd of mourners, with two sobbing grandmothers in shock mourning the fate of a daughter and the loss of a son.

There was nothing to warrant such tragedy. I was shocked. Looking back now, I knew that I was very bitter and angry since the rape, trying desperately to get the opportunity to flatten the house of "the beast" while he slept with the stroke of a match and a bottle torch. I lived for that moment. And that's how

I can agree now with the Investigating Officer at the scene that morning when he said I was insane, because there is no comparison between the person that was charged and the person I am. I can only assume that the stain of being raped was destroying me. I crumbled under a weight that was too much for me to bear and I was too ashamed to share.

There were so many times when I want to ask you what you remember of that dreadful day, what it was like for you after I was taken away, when you woke up the following day and realize "Chucky Chucky" was not back beside you in bed, no more leftovers and I wasn't home. And I wonder too if you have any memories of your dad sitting under a tree with you. My attempts to engage you in any such conversations always seemed to fall on deaf ears, leaving me with the impression that you are trapped in shock, unable to put into words the meaning of the bawling and the crowd that descended on the yard that morning or you just don't want to go there with me. I will never know for sure. It wasn't until I began this memoir and you asked me to detail everything because it might be easier for you to read than to ask me, that I realize you wanted to know but were afraid to ask me.

It was heart warming to learn from you that both of your Grandmothers remained friends despite everything that happened and give you the kind of nurturing only they could give. It has eased my burden and left me feeling even better knowing that I had met with her and we too made peace with each other. But for you I feel like it's a lifetime of worry, because every sorrow you bear, every crisis you face, I feel responsible, and at times it seems more than I can bear. It's the reason why my husband's repulsive attitude towards you and the guardian's motherless act burns me to this day. And I felt bad when I took Dawn from Granny a couple years before I could afford to take you. You two were too close for that to have happened but I was backed in a corner as you've probably read by now.

Recently, when you asked me, "How does a child learn when he is afraid of going to school?" I was shocked. Because you had spent so much of the growing up years with Granny and the constant stress I was under I missed a lot. I had no idea of the additional blows you endured in school, but it was refreshing to hear how nurturing and supportive the church and your Godparents were. And

I'll be eternally grateful for your cousin Veronica Chamberlin and my good friend, Basic School Teacher, Mr. Chisolm who you said was always there in school for you to defend you when others picked on you and called you names. Most likely had it not been for them you would have to settle for Granny's home schooling out of fear. I guess they never knew that children grow up and children don't forget.

May all those who mocked and ridiculed you, scorned you and called you names because of a few scars on your body; may them and their children never experience such humiliation and isolation. Anyways, shake it off.

There is still a smile that emanates from you when you get bamboo and kite paper that I love to see. May the child in you with the passion for making and flying kites continue to smile, and may your dream of a kite store for kids be realized even in your retirement years. I know how much you thrive on their adoration. And make sure you teach the skill to your 3 sons.

Listen to me son, you are loved by your 4 children, idolized by your brother and sister, adored by your mother and cherished by your friends. And with cousins Brandon, Veronica, and Ingaird in your corner, you're sheltered. You have Granny's prayer behind your back. Find your way back in church, you'll get a lot of support there, enjoy your passion for hockey, learn to take a phone call in between too and continue to laugh with your comedian friend, Misses Bucket (pronounced Misses Bukay). Make as many kites as you want, watch as many UFO's as you want to. God has blessed you with four gifted children, they are His gift to you, how you love and care for them is your gift to Him. And take the challenge of using my life story to un-shackle yourself, awake the giant within, rise up with wings like an eagle, pursue your dreams and begin to live life to the fullest. You deserve it. And Granny would be proud.

Mom

. . . .

Chase,

You are a gift from God, He doesn't make mistakes. Remember that.

I was very concerned about what your reactions would be of me penning my life story, so first I want to applaud you for your courage. You have made it much easier for me. Secondly, I want you to understand that I have bottled up everything inside for over 40 years and this venue is my chance to destroy the monster within once and for all. I don't have another chance so I have to be candid if I am going to get the release I need to help me heal.

First of all I gave birth to three children. You are one of them and that can never be changed. I am your mother. Secondly, even though we may not understand it, God doesn't make a mistake. As you can see it has practically taken a life time for me to acknowledge. And third, I really am sorry for all the years you have missed with your immediate family, growing up with a family you weren't biologically connected to; met your mother at 15, only to learn a few years after meeting her that you were the product of rape; "It almost sound like a movie plot." I can't imagine how difficult it must have been for you.

The circumstances under which you were conceived left me so stained that it destroyed my life and left me with such unspeakable rage that separating myself from you was all I could do to help kill the pain. And in the process an innocent life was left to carry what I could not bear for some 15 years. I am very sorry.

Make no mistake you were one chubby little adorable baby who was loved and cared for. Your brother doted on you from the day you were born. And there were some adorable moments when he sat and held you in his lap, or stood by patiently to get your leftovers from your nipple bottle. Nothing made him happier. Then in the twinkle of an eye all hell broke loose one Monday morning when you were just six months old, and life as we knew it would never be the same again. That is extensively covered in the story. Mr. Dawson took you from my mother after I left but it is the sight of you cradled in his arm as he passed the Police Station with you on his bike that morning that can never be forgotten. It was a feeling that I still can't find words to describe. I don't remember how long it took for me to be granted bail, but the very day it was granted, I remember being very anxious to see you, but with the uncertainty of my future and having so much on my plate, leaving you with the Dawson's was the best thing for the both of us at the time.

After my acquittal and another baby at age 18, it was more than I could handle. And it didn't help me months later when I passed by Hannikim's house and his friend butchering meat shouted at me if I'm not going to get you because the moment he saw you, he knew that you were Hannikim's. No one at the time knew I was raped, so for him to have seen you at Mr. Dawson and drew that conclusion meant it was quite clear, and from that moment I took matters into my hand to separate myself from the hurt and the embarrassment that could follow me a lifetime, in the only way I could think of at the time. And that was to leave you right where you were with the Dawson's, and pretend it never happened, just to kill the pain and the memory without even thinking of the long term consequences. I empathize with you for your feelings of abandonment, but we're both victims. And I faced a life with more on my plate than most people ever will in a lifetime. Your brother is a victim too when we think of what must have went through his little mind when suddenly the little brother he so loved to hold in his lap and waited on for his leftovers was no longer around. That was cold.

What the beast did to me was vicious, what he said can never be forgotten, and for his friend to see the resemblance and tease me, was the final straw in making my decision to separate myself as far as I could from the whole matter. Mr. Dawson, you might have heard, had the same experience with me when he came to see me at the bank; he was intentionally ignored for so long until he walked up to me quietly and said all he was there for was to get a copy of your birth certificate as he was in the process of changing his family name because of issues he himself faced as a child. My attitude towards him was the extent I went to in order to disassociate myself from the shame that could follow me a lifetime.

You might wonder how it is that I was charged in the death of Colin's father and yet I don't seem to make such an issue of it or the beatings from my husband. One was calculated, one was an accident and my husband clearly was a violent man, and I got out of his way. But this I know, the hurt and

317

shame that comes from being dragged and treated like an animal in the bushes against my will, is never something that can be forgotten. To move forward it must be forgiven but it can never be forgotten. It is enough to make me want to abandon the one place that should be so sacred to me; my home, my roots. And if I try to seek refuge at my Church, I must contend with seeing his name engraved at the entrance because he donated a headstone. That hurts so much; it's like selecting the casket for my funeral. This is nothing to glorify. It hurts. And if I don't say the way I feel, healing will never begin. And maybe that's how you will get deliverance too by putting in black and white this has done to you as a child, a man, a father and a person. We have all been injured.

The letter is not intended to injure you, God knows you can't take one ounce more, but I find it necessary to tell you how you ended up in another persons' home and why you didn't meet me till you were about 15 years old and why things are the way they are. I have fought a battle since I was 16 years old that is not winnable. Had it not been for the Oprah Winfrey show that aired a similar story, Dawn might not have known, and I would not have had the courage to tell you. So try to imagine how you shocked the daylights out of me when I told you and you said, "Mom, this is the best day of my life; it's like a birthday present." I just didn't get it. It made me wonder if you heard that I said I was raped. You see son what was the closing chapter of a long saga for you was a resurrection of a night in my life coming home from Prayer Meeting that I wish to God I never had to remember. So you can imagine the nightmare when you told me that you shared it with the Dawson's family and Hannikim's children. And the rage I felt when you told me that you were one of five children fathered by the beast that was born the same year, my God Almighty! It hurts to know you're numbered among them. My God!

I do not expect you to fully grasp the measure of hurt that I still feel because you have borne a lot and have a lot to live with too, all I can hope for is a measure of understanding. We are both victims. And I hope you understand that I bear no responsibility for this. I was a child when something was dumped in and I didn't know what to do. And even when I tried to get an apology many years later when I was visiting with my Mother and he sent one of his sons to ask me for $20; the man didn't even dignify me with a reply when I asked him why, all he said with the same smirk on his face, "don't tell Dawson because *he could sue me," as though he and I were in any business. It was frighteningly intimidating to see him crouched over on the floor rolling on his ass from side to side and still be able to wield such power. There was not a single string of remorse in him. It was as though I meant nothing to him or what he did was "common assault" and he could still get away with anything. Either that or he still saw me as the little bare feet child that use to haul buckets of water on my head and bothered him every day for bus fare. All those things made me so much bitter for so long that all I could do was stay away from you. I wouldn't have been any use to you. Trust me. I wouldn't have. I had too much carrying.*

If I seem impossible to get along with, difficult to please, or give the appearance that I don't like you sometimes, please forgive me; it's not you. It's the shame of what was done to me and the stain that I must wear for life; the life I never had; and the belief that it all begun from the night I was assaulted. I am sorry, I am sorry, I am sorry for you but heaven knows I just didn't have the stamina to deal with things any better than the way I did. I was given more than I could bear.

At times your words sting and could ignite World War III, but I know the same could be said of me. We both struggle from time to time. It took me over 40 years to come out of the closet and nearly 4 years to pen the story. When I began I was very bitter up to about 3 years later, but I can say with surety now that I am feeling much lighter, now that I have gotten everything out. I am not saying that I can forget what happened or the shame, there may be some struggles here and there but I am nowhere close to what I was when I started writing and that has to be very good for the both of us.

Everything is now in black and white, it's clearer now, you are as much a victim as I am. I can no longer allow you to pay for another person's crime. If 2 people you weren't even biologically connected to can take you in their arms and nurture and care for you, then my conscience tells me that I should try. And even that has taken me almost 4½ decades to realize. It's the depth of my shame.

It's God's desire for you to be a part of my life, whether by test of faith, or to teach me something. I just don't know. All I know, He doesn't make a mistake. You are a child of the Universe, no less than the trees and stars . . . You have a right to be here, Oh yes you do! And I realize now that if I am going to have any joy, I must forgive myself for what I experienced. I am sick and tired of the misery. I want to live, not just exist.

While I was penning this letter, I pause nervously to flip through the channels on TV when I happened upon a CNN Chief Correspondent doing a documentary on the atrocities in Rwanda. She chronicled the story of a woman whose husband and five children were massacred by a neighbour. After spending seven years in prison for his crime, upon his release she had the gall to forgive him and even proceeded to serve him a meal. I switched channels just as they gathered at the table, my stomach couldn't take anymore, but I guess there was a message in it for me. On that day, Saturday March 6, 2010, at that moment, I knew I had to make every effort to try to move on. This letter is not intended to re-open wounds. It is to tell the story so everyone has a clear picture of what happened; and to help us all to find understanding so we can move forward. And that Rwanda story in my opinion was a clear message to me from the "Author of Forgiveness." All I could say was: "I cannot Lord thy purpose see, but all is well that's done by Thee". It was tough to swallow, but there was no one to argue with.

Use the life God has given you as a testimony to the world. He has blessed you with four lovable children; they are His gift to you. How you love and care for them is your gift to Him. In my opinion one bears a striking resemblance to actress Elisabeth Taylor, I can't wait to see what God is going to use this tragedy to accomplish, but I believe it's going to be something far greater than we could ever dream; and when it does, if I'm gone; make sure you share it with the world. They deserve to read the final chapter. In the meanwhile, rise up, unshackle yourself, you're a visionary, go out and be all you can be. There is greatness in you, unleash it and go fly like the eagle. Victory is waiting for you.

Mom

No amount of pen and paper can put into words the damage that tends to occur when promising minds destined for greatness are chopped down before they are given a chance to blossom and bloom. But I thank God for the privilege they have been given in making Canada their home where they can still dream and live their dreams. They don't need to walk with their heads hung low or be ridiculed. What happened to them is a direct result of what happened to me. For my daughter, nine to sixteen were very difficult years for her during my absence, that's why many years ago when she blurted out, "Mommy, I think you should write a book" I knew she was struggling with unanswered questions and she needed answers.

Colin and Dawn practically walked through fire with me, that is during most of my married life. They experienced the nightmare so they needed cushioning. They did not deserve to be left with a guardian. Maybe that's why I never had time to even think about Chase who I felt was lucky to have a home with two parents. I had no room in my soul to handle anymore. Dawn saw what I couldn't see, the need for me to tell them what happened to their lives. I had no idea we had been through so much, so the need for open dialogue was always shunned. And frankly, it has been so painful that my only desire was to shun the subject and pretend nothing happened.

I don't know what Dawn was thinking one day, but out of nowhere she said to me, "you make a thing happened to you one time, two times, three times?" I was so ashamed. She was referring to the three of them with three different last names. Shame almost made me want to scream out, but there again I had developed the art of looking poised and in control even when I was perishing on the inside. I credit them for getting me pumped up to share my story.

So many times I paused for weeks, sometimes months, just to ease the pain. Had it not been for the immeasurable weight my children have carried, the secrets they have lived with for so long without much clarity, and the burden that would rest on them at some point with the next generation if I chose to remain silent, I would probably be sealed for eternity. Truth is, if it is so very painful for me to recount, I cannot imagine what it does to my children who yearn to know the facts, not just bits and pieces.

The man I married was the first and only male influence in Colin's life and he inflicted such fear upon him, showed such disdain and hatred for him that I always wonder what all the rejection has done to him. But this I know, even as a grown man (in age), he's most comfortable knowing that I am living close by and that makes me wonder . . . If his classes started at 2 or 3 in the afternoon and Douglas was off duty at 7am, the poor child had to leave with me when I left for work and stayed at his classmate's home until it was time for classes. The man shred my heart to pieces. This child did not need one more ounce of pain in his life, so when the Guardian decided to seat him in her laundry room to eat while all others ate at the dining table, he gave up; couldn't take anymore. Later he would say *"Mommy when you sent Uncle to talk to me, I heard him calling. I was sitting in a tree watching him." "I knew why he came but my mind was made up to go back home to Granny."* So in spite of the guardian's "so-called well intended plans" to have him learn mechanic while attending High school he was happy to return to the loving arms of my mother and his father's mother who only lived a few doors away. Safe in the arms of the two women who loved him unconditionally, in a place where he would call home, where he could go back to playing marbles, flying his kite in peace and tranquility, swimming around in the river while Granny did her washing or just visiting with his adoring Godfather at church. It was the place where he was always known as Elisabeth's son and affectionately called "Kitty Poos." But he lost the chance to a good education and he was ripped from his sister again because I could not stretch the dollar anymore to adequately support three homes. And that was the price he paid to be treated as a child with respect and dignity, a place known as home where he was loved, appreciated and adored. It was a place where he would not have to worry anymore about mental abuse. All these things have left me frighteningly overprotective of him.

There may be times when Colin probably feels smothered, but I am stuck in a rut. My inability to protect him from the harshness he has experienced since he was 2½ has left me in fear of him snapping. And I get the impression he has no more room for losses. Whether it is the loss of a job or a girlfriend, it adds to his woes and he sees it as more rejection. That really bothers me as a mother because it's in those moments that he would complain of how tired he is and I am left with the impression that he is unable to handle any more.

Some people forget that children grow up and children don't forget. The amount of psychological damage that has been inflicted on this child is frightening. No wonder he started smoking so early; he never got the chance to develop and mature before the world came crashing down on him, punishing him from every angle. It's a guilt that has consumed me.

The few friends he has made over the years have remained the same regardless of distance. And he could be a loner too. Unlike his brother Chase who is comfortable playing a game of dominoes with the guys regularly, Colin seems most comfortable in the company of the opposite sex. It seems more like the need to always have a mother around for security. If a relationship fails, he is a total wreck and he would waste no time meeting another within a very short time. This scares me because I do not see it as love but rather the need for security, someone to always lean on. Every conversation is punctuated with the agony he bears if for any long period he is without a partner. On the other hand, he is capable of spending a whole weekend in complete silence watching television, especially if its hockey season; or exploding in laughter over a joke from his favourite Comedian, Mrs. Bucket (*pronounced Bukay*). And he could be equally contented being in a house by himself without a sound.

Even if all is well with him, I have a tendency to be always digging, maybe more than normal, in an effort to get him to open up; wanting to fix everything, just to make sure he does not experience any more hurt. It is almost as though I am protecting him from some unforeseeable danger. It's no wonder his sister and brother think I prefer him over them. The truth is, I am scared of all the sad experiences he has faced in his short life from 2½. I just want to protect him from any more pain. And because of his trusting nature, he has a tendency to take a person at face value and could easily get hurt. So much like my mother, he sees no evil, hears no evil, expects no evil, bears no grudge and he doesn't have a bone of ill will or animosity in him. I find that Dawn and Chase are much stronger than him. I still call to see if he is okay. He has no idea of the weight behind the question. Now he will.

About two years before I started penning the story he moved far away to another city to find work, but deep down inside I wondered if like me he was running scared of what his children would eventually hear, afraid to face more pain. And could it be the reason why when I told him I would be penning my story he said, "Mom, it's about time somebody does something." Only God knows! However, I am thankful for the love and support he got from his Grandmothers, Uncles, Aunts, the Godfather at church who adored him and his cousin Veronica Chamberlin who always stood up for him when students ostracized him because of a little skin rash. It is this kind of support I believe, that helps him to look back at his childhood days with some fond memories; and I suppose it was that kind of nurturing that inspired him to find his brother Chase and shared his pocket money with him long before we were reunited as a family. Recently he told me he has plans to visit the zoo to get a few rides, it caused me stop and think; I suppose the child in him that never played much, still needs to play. Even now.

Without the love and stability of a home with both parents; the chance to have had more of the growing up years with his siblings; a trade, a skill or a formal education; the legacy of tragically losing his father at 2½; the hatred meted out to him from the only father figure he ever knew, Douglas Holyday; the indignity of his guardian to seat him in the laundry room while others ate at the table and my struggle to adequately provide for him; it is fair to conclude that he has done very well. He makes an honest living working for a city in Western Canada. Hopefully, now that everything is out in the open he will find the courage to return to his family in Ontario. They need him. He needs them. And he needs to pen his story. The world needs to hear from him. And not only him, all three of them; I just hope I can withstand it.

THIRTY-TWO

Before I get to the final chapter, chapter 33, I am breaking from protocol to share with you, some very special folks along my journey who deserve to be remembered and acknowledged for the enormous role they have played in my life. It's not all about acknowledgements, for the most part it's about everyday people doing extraordinary things and making a lifetime of difference in extraordinary ways. It's worth reading and I do this with strong conviction and utmost respect, acknowledging that there are some as far back as 40 plus years who deserve this space, and others who through a book they wrote, a statement they made or a show they have done have unwittingly brought me out of the closet. It is to them and the memory of my mother that I dedicate this book. For all the grief they bore for me, the compassion they showed, the strength they gave, the sacrifices they made and the kindness they extended; I am forever grateful to everyone.

First, the crew at the Palm Spring Police Station, particularly Inspector Palms, who upon my arrival immediately phoned the station I would be transferred to. Over forty years later I can still hear his husky voice frantically hollowing to them, "Get a mattress, get a mattress, we have a little girl coming down." He was nothing less than a caring father trying desperately to get help for his child. I can never forget him; nor will I ever forget Detective Corporal Montgomery, the officer at the scene. I didn't know what to expect when he made his way through the crowd and found me standing in the middle with my cousin Rowena beside me; but when he approached and just gently rested his hand on my shoulders; that spoke louder than anything he could have said. Even when he was doing my Probationary Report he showed consideration. He was definitely one of the many angels on my shoulders.

Corporal Viscount sang his heart out whenever he transported me to and from Court in his desire to keep me cheerful and Acting Corporal Marlon in those huge goggle-looking-eye-glass always had a big grin for me. When Female Constable Kendall was at the Guard Room, I felt like Sister Love was in the house with me, and Constables Shawn, Penny and Singer always made me feel like their little sister, bringing me little goodies from time to time. Their encouragement and support, their compassion and their laughter, the dignity they afforded me were the rocks that I cleaved to when I was drowning in the tears of my soul. They were what serving, protecting, and going beyond the call of duty is all about. And not to be forgotten is the Platoon at the Rod Nellston Station who ran to my assistance when I tumbled out of the car on my way home after winning my appeal. It seemed that throughout my ordeal, God had my streets lined with an array of Angels. They too were among them . . .

As for my Lawyer: He was simply the best. His profession was truly his passion. No one could have done it better. I can never ever forget him and what he did for me.

Mr. Bartlett: The friend of the family who retained my lawyer is especially acknowledged. All through my trial and appeal he was the brain and decision maker. Without him I would have ended up with a Court Appointed Lawyer who couldn't even get me bail. And even though I have no memory of this, I am told it was him who jubilantly lifted me out of Court when bail was granted. And again he was right there when the appeal was won to take me back home to my family. I don't think my mother had another friend who she treasured as Mr. Bartlett, and rightfully so. He is equally responsible for the freedom I've been given as much as my lawyer is. The voices of a million angels could not express the amount of gratitude I owe this Good Samaritan. I hope he lives to read my real stories behind the story.

My Sisters and Brothers showed enormous strength, their support never wavered. I can't imagine what it must be like for them trying to be strong for me and for mother while they themselves were falling apart at the seams. For Sister Louise in England, with 9 mouths to feed, it must have been tough being the backbone to mother; yet through it all none of them has ever complained, they would never see me hurt anymore. I was blessed to have them to lean on. And I owe Sister Love much apology for all the pain, the suffering, the embarrassment and the memory of what she must live with for life because of all my problems. Of all my siblings I always worry about her because she's always concerned about what others may be saying. I am deeply sorry Sister, very sorry.

My Godmother's generosity every step of the way is remembered. Even though I grew up spending some time with her, I don't think I realized the significance of a Godparent until trouble showed up on my doorstep, and the enormous role my mother said she played trying *to* raise funds for my defence. She has taught me what it means to be a godparent . . . And I must never forget Miss Betty, the maid for the white people; no matter how little her wages were, my mother said Miss Betty always gave her bus fare whenever I was scheduled to be in Court. Bless her heart . . . The courage of an old Sister-in-law, Miss Inez, to step in and take a stand for my daughter when I was even afraid to ask was one of the many Angels God sent out to help me . . . My Samaritan Neighbour who was not afraid to rushed me to Emergency after a beating in my partially ripped off clothes and the blood streaming down my face, is remembered . . . My Redeemer & Friend, Pastor Shepherd, is forever inscribed on the pages of my life. I know now that it was by Divine Intervention that I had chosen him to Pastor my wedding ceremony. God knew what I was getting into and he needed someone who would not be afraid to drop everything he was doing to run to my rescue when needed. Even when I was hospitalized after a beating and was too embarrassed to call Sister Love, it seemed he was there at the very mention of his name. I don't want to ever imagine what might have happened to me without Pastor Shepherd . . . And A Very, Very Special Lady, is remembered in a Very Special Way, because after a beating once I ran away with Dawn and stayed at her home. Whether I had rented or just sought lodging I can't remember, but she must have sensed that I had nothing to cook, or I wasn't busy in the kitchen. She made sure she gave Dawn every evening. God bless her. She is my hero. May her store basket be always full and running over . . . As for David, my Deliverer, I salute him. He is the stuff Kings, Queens and Heads of States are made of—guts and determination. I'm just sorry I wasn't able to save those $20's from way back then, I'd be rich now. But more than anything else, he gave me the chance to know what it's like to be treated like a lady, and for that I am eternally grateful. I have not had such luck since then . . . Without A Very Gracious Friend, Kerona, to broker so many storms with the children and keep things running smoothly, matters would have gotten out of hand. Dawn said when Boarding Fee was late, she went straight to Kerona. And from what I understand, there was no point of Kerona telling Dawn she didn't have it, because she would never leave until she got money for school. She was truly a second mother from the day I left Jamaica until the day the children got on the plane for Canada. I am forever indebted to her . . . Thanks to Angella, she met my niece Val while visiting England and was given £300 to give to me for my winter coat. That was over 30 years ago. The loan was repaid, the coat is long gone but the friendship is still strong. And through her help, and her sister Kim, I was able to get Dawn on a vacation, and a bond signed when I left Canada undocumented and tried to return as a visitor. I am sure there were times when they thought all I did was complain, and Wade once told me I should get on a soap-opera because I always had a story; now they'll all know what was destroying me . . .

My Dear Friend Jasmine who I've known since my eyes were at my knees and who taught me that pyjamas were not for men only, deserves a medal. She was the major player in getting me out of the closet. Her persistence practically wore me out. From the day I packed a suitcase and went to see her at her London home, she saw what I could not see and got the gears in motion. And when I procrastinated she loaded me with pens, journals, and a wave of phone calls and a letter telling me that I have a flare with words and a story that needs to be told. And when I mentioned that I wish I had a home where all my grandchildren could come together and get marry at if they chose to, she said, "everything you need is in your head." Poor thing, she had no idea how the fear of anyone believing me crippled me, but she kept up the calls, the pens and the journals until . . . I am amazed that even though we were separated for over two decades, she still had the uncanny ability to pluck things out of me that I hadn't recognized. It is a testament to the bond we knitted when we were toddlers. I shudder to think what my life would be today had she not left and indebted to her for applying pressure till I picked up the pen and paper . . .

The President in a State of the Union Address who remarked, "When the gates of prison open, the path ahead should lead to a better life," is acknowledged for helping me to get out of darkness into light. Those words pierced me and got me thinking so much that they literally invigorated Jasmine's plea to put the story of my life in black and white . . . And the President in his life's story who addressed the subject on "Secrets" is acknowledged for courageously bringing me up from the bottom of the ocean though I didn't even know how to swim . . . It really takes a village.

My Precious Daughter, Dawn, deserves much more than a pat on her back. Some 24 years ago she mentioned to me that I should write a book. I never thought I would in a million years. Years later when she told me that of all the books I had read there was one that had not been written, and that was mine; I still didn't see it happening. Just how she juggled a full time job; a family of six; the gruelling task of grappling through my scribbling to draft one hundred forty two thousand words on a 420-page manuscript; brilliantly crafted the Title of the story and helped me with a Word Processing Refreshers Course that enabled me to do my never ending editing, is truly a testament of her desire to see the story told. So many times when I doubted myself if I should or not, she always said, "let it go Mom, let it go." I needed to hear that. I really, really needed to hear that. Not only did it strengthen me; it propelled me. "Let it go Mom, let it go." . . . And whatever brought out the Title of the Book in her after she typed three chapters, I will never know, all I can say, even though I had nearly 50 titles before I started writing and had narrowed it down to 3, none came close to baring my soul as this one.

The Oprah Winfrey Show is brilliantly acknowledged for a story they did in the nineties on a child borne from a rape. It was the catalyst that led me to divulge to Chase that he was the product of a rape. He had been waiting for answers for about 25 years . . .

The 3rd floor Staff and a Very Special Thursday Evenings Volunteer at Calgary Public Library in Alberta, Canada is kindly acknowledged for their generous support from my days of scribbling on paper and then repeatedly bothering them to scan and e-mail them to my daughter in Toronto so she could do all the typing for me. And Petra, at Your Print and Copy Solution in Calgary, Alberta, Canada is also remembered for everything from photocopying, scanning, emailing, or just lending a listening ear when I grew weak and overwhelmed . . . Much gratitude to my friend Elly, in West Chester, New York who I called upon a couple times to help with grammatical errors.

My Adoring Mother, who by her very example, moulded me into the person I am is remembered with deep love and affection. Without her constant intercessory prayers and fasting I probably would have perished, but they were the foundations on which I stood when all hell was breaking loose. A Legendary Gospel Singer, the late Vestal Goodman told Bill Gaither in an interview that, "God was kind when He gave her to the Goodman's. But God was even kinder, when He blessed me with such an amazing mother. Indeed He was, indeed He was. Heaven must be richer with her there. R.I.P Mother . . . R.I.P . . . And while on the subject, I dare not close without giving thanks to my unseen Guidance Counsellor who promised to Shepherd me through this project. I will never forget that morning when I was tucking away my scribbling in a folder and His voice whispered, "I will instruct thee" which led me to Psalm 32:8. I had no idea how I would start or how it would end, but He did what He said He would do and I owe it all to Him . . .

My childhood church, Mount Zion Revival, was the wind beneath my mother's wings. I was told they held prayer and fasting in the wilderness and by the ocean during my trial. Their support was crucial to my mother's well being and thank God they never failed her. The church should be proud to hear that the last words out of my mother's to me were, "Elisabeth, remember the church." They were always on her mind. And while on the subject of church, I must share a little bit about this body of people who have been mocked and ridiculed for the way they worship because some of their principles are an instrumental part of my roots. They are a band of Holy Ghost, Spirit filled people who speak in tongues. They clap their hands, play drums and tambourines; and the church has fresh flowers and candles on a table with a white tablecloth just like watching Mass on TV. They do baptism just like the way John did Jesus' at the River Jordan; immerse the candidate in water. They wash one another's feet just as Jesus taught. Their spirituality enables them to see through a person like a glass of water and pluck out demonic forces. They fast and do Communion regularly, church could be up to 6 hours on Sundays, and a day every week is set aside for Healing Services.

In my days it was where the sick went before seeing a doctor and were expected to be healed. I have witnessed a lot of healing. The laying on of hands and a little olive oil with a burning white candle under the anointing of the Holy Spirit has worked wonders for many. At our 75th anniversary in 2005, a 92 year old veteran said that if the Revival Church had their worship on the Sabbath, no other church would have been more powerful. He had seen a lot of miracles at the church in his 75 years of service. And my darling Mother must have known something when she took me from that lukewarm church. I have never regretted it. My relationship with God grew, deepened and began flourishing in the little bamboo church where we placed a pillow on the dirt floor and knelt to pray; the very place I did my first recitation:

> *Flowers on my shoulders*
> *Slippers on my feet*
> *I'm Mamma's little darling*
> *Don't you think I'm sweet?*

I have never forgotten the encore. The old fashioned hymns I sung there have been my constant companion, but two of my favourites remain "Jesus Saviour Pilot Me & I Have a Friend a Precious Friend Oh How He

Loves Me." The latter was the hymn that was sung at Prayer Meeting the night I was raped, and the first was the one I asked my mother to pen for me when I found out I was pregnant at 14.

It is my hope and prayer that during my lifetime, this body of worshippers will get the recognition they deserve and not be ridiculed by some who have never even set foot in a Spiritual Church. There's a place in Society for them and it's high time they get on TV like other denominations doing what they have been doing long before I was born. They are now being taught about in schools; now let the world see them in action.

Thank God for the power of music. Thank God for Gospel Singers. And thank God for the influence my church had on me. It was through them and a twenty four hour Gospel Station I discovered when I arrived in Canada that I was able to push aside the hell that I had lived through and withstood the loneliness for 7 years, by immersing myself in the healing powers of music. So again, please bear with me a little bit as I take a couple more minutes to acknowledge them and remind them of the therapy music provides . . .

WDCX Buffalo, aired in Ontario, was a tremendous source of spiritual help. I could count on them to be my constant companion twenty four hours a day, seven days a week. The unforgettable Doug Riley who hosted the Saturday evening program kept me firmly grounded. My little Panasonic stereo that a friend once referred to as a piece old pan gave me more than my money's worth. After 6pm I would take a nap, then be up to listen and continue recording between 11pm to 5am. It seemed like a commercial free period so I called it "My Sacred Hour". Then it was breakfast and back to sleep again to be ready for what sounded like Revival Camp Meeting in the living room with the Jimmy Swaggart Telecast. Watching him at the Piano and hearing him sing was like watching the sun bursting through the clouds. I've never had enough of him. To this day, I still emulate his then lead singer, Miss Paschal, she ministers to the audience with every song she sung from the depths of her soul. I adore that lady. Every Penny of my first Income Tax Refund was invested in vinyl records from his

Ministry and they're among my most treasured collections—Investment for my Retirement . . .

I barely had enough time after the telecast to prepare supper and hop on to the church bus from the Subway Station for Ralph's 6pm Revival Hour at Queensway Cathedral. That was "My Hour of Power". That Pastor was a chosen vessel, no other group I knew did a better rendition of "Gone the Stone Is Rolled Back the Tomb Is Empty" like Pastor Ralph and his family. And every Sunday night I left with a song in my heart; went to work singing, came home singing and went to bed singing all week till church again on Sunday. The Daily Devotional from RBC Ministries through the years has kept me focused on what matters most. The everyday stories they share bring life to the Bible Study and have enriched my knowledge of the Word. My devotion would not be complete without my Daily Devotional.

After a dose of meditation on weeknights with Dr. Gabriel Otero I was ready for a good night's sleep. But on that fateful Saturday afternoon in October 1989, when then Saturday evening host, Doug Riley, signed off from WDCX, he left a blank space in my heart. Each Saturday evening he was on the air, he took my soul to places it had never been. His Inspirational quotes and Good News Verse for the Day lifted me up. They were my strength. He even introduced me to Legendary Gospel Singers like, Rusty Goodman, Dottie Rambo, Squire Parsons, Conrad Cook & the Calvary Echoes, Henry Slaughter and so many more that I was able to put a face on years later when I started watching "The Gaither Gospel Hour." He introduced me to a whole new world and made my life far much richer. I always wished he knew.

THIRTY-THREE

At times in my solitary moments I wonder what was going on in the sixties: a Civil Rights Leader and a beloved President were assassinated in America, Nelson Mandela was fighting racial segregation in South Africa, and there I was, a teenager, in a remote part of the globe, faced with more turbulence than most people will ever face in a lifetime. Maybe those who study the stars will have the answer some day. But forty years after the storm, the shock of my son's father lying there with his eyes blinking still makes me wonder if there was something I could have done to save him or I just panicked and ran to call my brother.

The sight of Clare looking nine months pregnant, weeping mercilessly with a baby slung around her waist; my mother piercing through the crowd walking up to me as I stood in the middle; the sight of Sister Love crouched over in tears by the steps to my cell unable to climb the 3 steps to get to me; watching my innocent little baby, barely six months old, suddenly deprived of his mother's milk and taken from the home and family he knew can never be erased. The memory of my 2½ year old son waking up the following morning and realizing that he had lost his entire family will forever haunt me.

The man that raped me didn't kill me but when he treated me like an animal and left me with the evidence; it is as good as saying "you must never forget this as long as you live." That's a struggle that I have only just begun to slowly lay aside. A pain in the centre of my back and a root canal on a front tooth are constant reminders of the many merciless and senseless beatings I suffered from the hands of someone I had loved sincerely, my husband.

The very memory of someone suggesting to me years ago that I should continue using my husband's name long after we were divorced, rather than reverting to my father's name is a reminder that even though the sentence was quashed and the conviction set aside in the appeal; my name could somehow be an embarrassment. But I couldn't, I love my father's name and there's a sense of pride that comes with using my birth name; using my husband's would be like using an alias.

Even a recent trip to the dentist took my memory back to when Dawn weaned herself weeks after she was born and the financial struggle we faced trying to come up with a supplement feeding for her. It was simply the sight of a mother nursing her baby at the dentist that brought back those memories. Just little things like those, as simple as they appear, could take me straight down memory lane and way into the dark corners of a past that seems to be always in my rear view mirror.

When Colin mentioned recently of his intent to get on a few rides at the amusement park and a trip to the zoo, it reminded me of his lost childhood, and I was left to wander off again silently. Even Chase's ailment of high blood pressure reminds me of that hot nipple bottle and leaves me to wonder if something happened to him or something went undetected when he was a child. I may be feeling lighter now that I have told my story but I wonder if I'll get a chance to know what true peace is with so much on my plate, and if my family will be damaged as a result of my disclosures. Leaving my one and only daughter at 9 years old, to run away because of all the beatings, leaves a wound that no amount of time can heal. It's always very raw. Many times when I look at her I play out the scene of that day when she wrapped her arms around her guardian's knee as I walked away and leave them. It's still a nightmare. God was kind when He erased certain dates from my memory. I can only guess it was His way of helping me to preserve my sanity during crisis.

It has been a turbulent life. I wouldn't wish it on my worst enemy, but I have a lot to be thankful for. My leap of faith to Canada with a suitcase of clothes and $60 has been my single most important stride. It has changed several lives. My children and I are now naturalized Canadians. All, but one of twelve grandchildren were born in Canada. A nephew and his family of six have shared the blessings, so too has a brother and members of extended families through sponsorship by my children. Very similar to what Billy Graham refer to as the miracle of the gospel; you reach one person, then a family, then a church, then a community; just by one person stepping out in faith.

Silently though there is still some sadness for the chance I never got to be the kind of mother I could have been. I have lost the most precious years with them. Anything I do now is just make-up, and I never got to make up before they started establishing families of their own. And that's why I cringe with jealousy at their spouse with a feeling that my babies and I still belong together because of all the years we have lost. They are intruding in my space. That hurts. I will never have another chance. By the time they joined me in Canada, Dawn was in her final year in High School and the boys were adults (immature) by age only. To try to redirect adolescents who had experienced so much hurt and suffering from so early in life, and left unattended for so long, was very difficult. Too much was lost and stolen.

When I visit my daughter and see a "stranger" doing her hair I seethe with anger and bitterness. It's almost a feeling of betrayal. I didn't comb her hair enough. We didn't play enough or do enough of the little things a mother and a daughter should do together. I never had the chance to see them fill their little slates with zeros or add an ear to the zero to make an "a" or a little line beside the zero to make a "b" or "d" as mother taught me. In Sunday school at times, the class was divided and I had my own students, but when I had children of my own I never had the chance to do for them as I had done for so many. Not even the chance to walk them to Church or Sunday school as mother did with me. No mother should have to live with such pain. I am still disappointed about all those little things. I have been robbed in every way. Robbed of my childhood, robbed of my children, robbed of the joy of growing up my babies, robbed of the life I was supposed to give them, robbed of my childhood friend, robbed of the life I was supposed to have. The only thing I haven't been robbed of is my determination even now, to see that my children get the opportunity to be the best of the little they've been given to work with. When I look at my grandchildren I realize that not one of them will ever know both of their grandfathers, much less to gain from his wisdom or be taught to ride a bike by him. They too have been robbed.

Had the circumstances been different, Colin's dream of becoming a Pilot would have been realized. With Chase's aptitude for business, he would have been a runaway success; and without the shadow of a doubt Dawn would have most likely followed in her father's footsteps and become a lawyer or she'd be in Journalism; something in the corporate ladder from what I can see. The seed is definitely within her. Even within her family structure I see how she runs it like she is the Chief Executive Officer (CEO). The lack of proper guidance in the formative years compounded by all the chaos, they fell between the cracks of my misfortunes. They have paid a dear price for the life they were born into with no clear understanding until now. They never stood a chance! And even after they arrived in Canada I naively thought time would take care of everything; that I would never have to say anything so I kept searching for greener pastures in my attempt to create for them that which I was unable to give them. As it turned out, I kept hunting like a wild animal without any sense of timing instead of addressing what was really destroying me. I should have stayed with them. I shouldn't have gone to America. But it seems I couldn't cope, because I don't think my time in America was all it appeared to be; I believe that I couldn't take any more and I ran. And that's why I was furious when Jasmine suggested I address them individually because I came to realize that's what I did, but I was afraid to admit it. That's why I still dream of having a super large home where my children and their families could all live together on one huge estate, or having a stretch of homes so close we can call out to each other in our backyards. I yearn for all that I have missed from they were 9 and 13.

I hope they all find the courage to pen their story too. Until they've spoken, the story is not complete. They have been through a lot and it needs to be flushed out. If I can stand it is another question. Individually they have their pain; how they deal with it I am not sure and that's where my tendency to be overprotective kicks in. I see what they don't want me to see. They are big dreamers with rich ideas and good insights, but their dreams don't always come true because they are hunkered down under a myriad of unexplained stress. It is my prayer that some showers of blessings will rain on them; heaven knows they need a break.

I can see now how my silence must have affected everyone around me all these years, I can only assume it was my way of shielding myself from the person that I didn't recognize. My God! I was never a rude child. I wanted nothing more than to be a Healer like the Mother at my church and a Gospel Singer. There was not another child in my community or in church who was more involved than I was. A Parishioner recalled touching me on my way from Sunday school and I blurted out "Touch not the Lord's anointed nor do his Prophet no harm." "What was God thinking, where was He when I was coming from Prayer Meeting that night?" "I strongly recommend to anyone who has experienced this trauma, to resist the tendency to isolate yourself and the feeling of being scorned. You cannot and will never be able to fight that monster alone. You will succumb to it. Get help and get it fast, it is crucial. The longer you take to seek help, the deeper the wound gets and the harder it is to heal. You owe it to your well being, no one can help if you remain silent, and your silence will strangle you. I am living proof. Too much was left unsaid for too long."

There are times even now when I still feel sorry for the little girl inside of me with the big appetite for church who soaked up everything like a sponge with a feeling that she was being trained for a purpose. I can almost feel the seed of greatness struggling to burst forth. Walking around with a weight of unfulfilled dreams has been a constant struggle because the person I am and the person I see when I look in the mirror are a far cry from the person whose life story this is. And in a way, this search to fulfill this unfulfilled dream whatever it may be, has affected my motherhood because I just never feel settled. As a result I do not believe my children have had the same measure of love from me as my mother had given me, because whereas I love them dearly, and my determination to live for them fuelled me, I still feel like there's a bigger purpose to fulfil so there's still a void. I have to be constantly fuelled and replenished with Gospel Music; without it I could become restless and impatient, and memories that have been suppressed could begin to surface.

The mere fact that I have penned my story is a sign that I'm finally getting out from my shell, but look how long it has taken me, practically a lifetime. All the questions are just being answered; the weight is just being lifted; now hopefully, healing can begin. It's even beginning to feel like my brain is opening up and I want to learn new things. I am ready to live; to have a chance at life. Again.

To see everything now in black and white has left me with one conclusion, that all along I needed professional help but I didn't know. What I have carried was such a constant struggle, I battled them within while giving everyone the impression that I was in control when in fact I had spent my whole life taking care of everyone and answering every cry for help. Kindness was like a painkiller. I hid behind everything I could, but I fooled myself, they were waiting to be attended to, so they festered and in the process plunge me deeper in silence. I know now that I have existed, I have not lived. But I must admit; that of all my siblings, God chose the strongest one to carry this cross. I cannot think of a single sister or brother who could have withstood all that I have and not crumble. And even though someone told my mother that I was well made, I say thanks to the man after God's own heart who some two thousand years ago wrote, "Many are the afflictions of the righteous, but the Lord delivers him out of them all.

On the morning of February 2, 2009, at exactly 3:13am, sleep began to overpower me, so I pulled out my folder and began tucking away my manuscript. The very moment I began to draw the zipper I heard a voice said, "I will instruct thee." Instinctively, I knew who was speaking, I'd heard that still small voice within many times before, in moments of deep silence when I least expected it. In my effort to make the connection, I paused and began to recite a few of the Psalms I knew, but none of them had that line, so I went to the Bible Concordance which led me to Psalm 32:8. This is what it says, *"I will instruct thee and teach thee in the way which thou shall go, I will guide thee with mine eyes;"* . . . a clear message, that a force much bigger, more powerful and far more absolute, would divinely guide me every step of the way through the process. And He has. Apart from getting the story out in a chronological order; when I started I had no idea how I would begin or how I would end. And the only story I had ever written before, was a play in Sunday school on the resurrection of Lazarus. But every step of the way I felt like I was being led, even with words and phrases. And if some of the dreams I have had during penning, are any indication; God has big plans for this story, I don't know what it is. But it's huge.

Circumstances led me to leave home too early. Now I am eager to return to do some of the things my mother and I did together, and things I dreamed of doing, like retracing the very steps through the short-cut we took to church, do a little early morning gardening and taking a mid-morning nap on a crocus bag under the Nesberry tree. I want to hear the squashing sound of nesberries as they land on the grass and the birds chirping from limb to limb. I would like to plant a few grain of peas in the earth, water them, watch them grow, and not be worried about Douglas chopping the tree down. Pick a water coconut, chop a sugar cane, have an avocado from the tree my dad planted and wait on the fishermen to dock their boat. I want to replace the tooth that the doctor had recommended be extracted when I went for my Medical Examination Certificate for school. Just the thought of planning this 16 years after the death of my mother makes me realize how much of my lost childhood I still need to recapture. And during my lifetime I hope to get water in the home instead of hauling it in buckets from a distance, and a paved pathway so that motorists can enter without fear of getting stuck in the mud. Just the thought of it makes me feel alive.

I wonder if this was part of the vision of being the Champion of the family; only God knows, but right now, it's about doing something wonderful for the place where I was born, making life a little more decent, giving the community a lift. It is the chance to say I was here and I made a difference. My mother would have loved it; and all this can only be thought of because I am feeling much lighter now. I have told my story. The stone has been removed.

I love writing, but I love the challenge that comes with editing even more. I love the way it keeps my mind focused and allows me to create in silence. I love that. It's truly my comfort zone, except, it robs me of my personal time with the Bible. And long before I wrote the story, I entertained the idea of penning Inspirational quotes and learning to play the organ with the ambition to follow in the footsteps of Fannie Crosby, writings hymns, even one good one; or just doing something beautiful that the world could continue to use long after I am gone. But how this will all unfold I don't know, more healing needs to be done and a vacation is way overdue, but penning the story is a big help. I am no longer cooped up in the closet, I have finally spoken. My children can now have all their questions answered. Thanks to Colin, when I was afraid he said, "Mom, it's about time somebody does something." Thanks to Chase, when I sought his opinion in telling the story, he said, "Mom, nothing happens before the time."

I have emptied myself of all that had clogged my spirit, I'm ready to soar, but I'm in the hands of the Potter. I don't know what His plans are for me, but during the penning of the story, *Bishop TD Jakes in his sermon "ARISE" said,*

> *"God protects those whom He loves,*
> *The only reason you made it this far,*
> *Is because He knows He can use you."*

No doubt he was talking to me, so with all that life has thrown at me, if God can really use me, I'm curious to know for what, and I'd love it to be sooner than later. I need to write that chapter.

A Note to Readers: . . . You have journeyed with me through the valley of the shadows of death to the point where I can honestly say I am feeling a lot lighter now. As harsh as it has been, I am sure you have learnt something. I ask that you take the little you have learnt and use it to help make the world a better place, especially for victims of rape and domestic violence. Be a voice for those without one, especially, children. And with your help, I am going to do the best I can to make the second half of my life a testimony of praise. Thank you for reading and sharing, I'll be back with some Inspirational quotes after some well deserved rest. Keep watching.

Elisabeth.

Lightning Source UK Ltd.
Milton Keynes UK
UKOW052304270112

186202UK00002B/20/P